The Youth Funding Guide

Nicola Eastwood

DIRECTORY OF SOCIAL CHANGE

In association with

NATIONAL YOUTH AGENCY

Published by
The Directory of Social Change
24 Stephenson Way
London NW1 2DP
Tel: 0171 209 5151, fax: 0171 209 5049
e-mail: info@d-s-c.demon.co.uk
from whom further copies and a full publications list are available.

The Directory of Social Change is Registered Charity no. 800517
First published 1997
Copyright © The Directory of Social Change 1997

ISBN 1 900360 15 2

British Library Cataloguing in Publication Data
A catalogue record for this book is available from the British Library

Cover design by Kate Bass
Designed and typeset by Linda Parker and Kate Bass
Printed and bound by Page Bros., Norwich

Directory of Social Change London Office:
Courses and Conferences tel: 0171 209 4949
Charityfair tel: 0171 209 1015
Research tel: 0171 209 4422
Finance and Administration tel: 0171 209 0902

Directory of Social Change Northern Office:
3rd Floor, Federation House, Hope Street, Liverpool L1 9BW
Courses and Conferences tel: 0151 708 0117
Research tel: 0151 708 0136

The
Youth
Funding Guide

Contents

	Introduction	1
	How to use this guide	7
Chapter 1	Getting Started in Fundraising	9
Chapter 2	How Much do we Need? A guide to basic budgeting	19
Chapter 3	Fundraising for Projects	29
Chapter 4	Preparing and Writing a Good Fundraising Application	35
Chapter 5	Raising Money from the Public	53
Chapter 6	The National Lottery	67
Chapter 7	Raising Money from Grant-making Trusts	95
Chapter 8	Winning Company Support	115
Chapter 9	Raising Money from Local Authorities	141
Chapter 10	Raising Money from Government Sources	159
Chapter 11	Raising Money from Europe	191
Chapter 12	Youth Organisations and Charitable Status	217
Chapter 13	Tax and VAT	225
	Index of Funding Sources	239
	Useful Addresses and Contacts	241

Introduction

About this book

Raising money for young people or youth work used to be – so the legend goes – a fairly simple task. You asked your local authority grant to cover your core costs, organised a little public fundraising for the odd piece of equipment and got a salary or two from a grant-making trust to do some development work (and, of course, the local authority would take on these salary costs when the trust grant ran out). If this was ever true, it is certainly not now.

These days bids for youth funding may be made by a wide variety of people in local authorities, voluntary organisations, local, regional or national consortia, or by young people for a project they are running themselves.

Never has there been more diversity in funding for youth work. And never has it been more important to be creative in your fundraising approach. Many complain that the amount of energy and resources which now have to be diverted into fundraising could be much more profitably used on work with young people. It is fairly easy to paint a fairly bleak fundraising picture.

However, this would be wrong. There is more money than ever available to youth organisations. It may well not come through the traditional channels, nor does it necessarily come easily. But this book describes a myriad of fundraising opportunities. It covers a massive range of funding interests which collectively total millions if not billions of pounds. Hopefully, it will also enable you to get your share.

The long and the short of it

Most funding has become short-term. The whole of the voluntary sector seems to run on a three-year cycle. There is no rationale for this other than that other funders seem to adopt the same three-year period, and it becomes a self-perpetuating policy. Many of those currently scratching around for funding look back longingly to a previous golden age of long-term, open-ended grants. That approach to grant-giving has largely disappeared to be replaced by a more competitive age of contracts, short-term grants and partnership funding. One charitable foundation gives grants over three to five years. Ten years ago this was dismissed by youth organisations as not worth applying to as its funding was too short-term. It is now seen as one of the most progressive because it invests in organisations over this longer period.

The backdrop of local authority funding, which traditionally has been the mainstay of core funding for youth organisations, has now changed dramatically. Registers of nominated groups remain, as does the practice of giving sessional hours, but local authority maintained youth work has been greatly reduced. Some has been replaced by contracts or project funding may have been taken on by other bodies such as health authorities. The rest has been slimmed down or has disappeared altogether. This may change with the new government where noises about a stronger statutory base for the youth service have been made.

Many groups will point to the buildings where they meet as evidence of the lack of money in their sector. Paying the electricity bill, or redecorating the hall may be less glamorous than drug awareness projects, exchange schemes and video production workshops, but the one really cannot happen without the other.

Fitting the bill

One of the criticisms of the money available to youth organisations is that they require a certain approach that may not necessarily fit with what the organisation is trying to do. One director of a series of youth projects says that his biggest concern is that everything seems to be focused around two or three centrally determined priorities; crime, drugs and training. He observes: "You have to put your bids in on the basis of your ability to address one of these issues – irrespective of what *locally* identified priorities there may be. All this money comes with a problem attached and we're fulfilling other agendas rather than those we came into youth work for."

A common fundraising problem is when your project fits most of the funder's criteria, but not all of them. In such cases, your application may well fail. However, should you change the way you work simply to meet a funder's requirements? For example, the funder may want to see young people on your management committee. You may have good reasons for not wanting to do this – or do this yet. In such cases, it is vital that the organisation retains control of the work it is doing. Don't adopt ideas or working practices simply because a funder says so. Do it because you think it is appropriate for you – or not at all.

Having said this, there is now more interest in young people's projects than ever before. There is more money too. Organisations such as health authorities, criminal justice agencies and training bodies are often putting substantial resources into youth organisations. Furthermore, the National Lottery is a big player and made young people one of its funding themes (the impact of the National Lottery on voluntary sector funding is reflected in the length of the chapter on it). Some youth workers are now resigned to finding other sources of money for their activities; others view it positively as a real challenge and a means of injecting new life and energy into the project.

Relationships

The key to success in fundraising is the relationships you make. This involves getting to know priorities, initiatives and programmes at a local level and, wherever possible, to get to the table where policy decisions are made. Youth organisations as never before have much to offer to economic, crime, health and education strategies. They need to make their presence felt in the circles of influence that make a difference to young people's lives.

Much is said about partnership funding, and many are deeply sceptical of potential imbalances in power. However, as one practitioner suggested: "Those working with young people need to take responsibility and be involved in as much networking, partnership building, and information gathering as they can. They do however need to keep their critical stance, and work out what is genuinely for the benefit of young people, and what works against them. They have to be in there, working and debating with these people who create policy. It doesn't serve young people at all well if youth workers take their ball home and won't play."

Be creative

It is clear that some of the old ways of fundraising are still the best. For example, at a local level a good sponsored activity can raise money, increase interest and membership, generate good publicity and give participants and spectators a good time. Indeed, this kind of fundraising will remain at the heart of many youth organisations' income generation efforts.

Partnerships can also be vital. For example, to enter into bids for the Single Regeneration Budget you will almost certainly have to negotiate with the local authority, Training Enterprise Council or Regional Development Agency. Some of the schemes mentioned in the book need matching funding (e.g. some European, National Lottery and government programmes). Organisations need to show where they can raise other money from, and how they are working in partnership with other strategic bodies.

Modern fundraising effectively forces you to stop looking at your organisation as a single entity; rather you tend to view it as a series of related projects. This means you have to divide your work into different elements and look at securing funding from a variety of sources. It may mean that you have to do new things with new people in new ways. You may have to organise your work differently. All this is discussed more fully in Chapter 3.

It may be that you can no longer simply say: "This is what we do, and this is what we need"; you may have to be more subtle than that. Some of the major players want to see that you understand their priorities and what they are working to achieve, and then how you fit in with that. Some funders may need certain structures to help your work. A grant-giving trust, for example, wants to see that your work is charitable. On the other side, one church youth project split its community work into a separate entity from the church to register as charitable and to help funders to support the work.

Planning your fundraising can be an opportunity to think creatively and imaginatively about what you are doing, and the strengths you have. It can encourage you to adopt different approaches, bring in new people with new skills, contacts and energy, run high profile events, link with other countries and work with other bodies. Thinking through some of these possibilities and making them happen is the purpose of this book.

The core funding problem

Many groups complain that they can get money for glamorous projects but not for the boring, but necessary, core costs (rent, rates, heat, light, salaries etc.). As Chapter 3 explains, there is no such thing as core funding! Eliminate it from your thoughts. All your costs are, in fact, project costs and you should build them all into the relevant applications. Once groups make this leap in thinking away from the notion of core costs being separate from all their other work, fundraising becomes a whole lot easier.

The timing of the book

During the writing of the book there was a change of government (May 1997). It is too early to say what the impact of this will be, but undoubtedly some funding schemes will change and priorities will alter. Health strategies, for instance, may change to reflect an interest in the underlying causes of illness, such as unemployment, poverty, poor housing and so on, and public health programmes alter accordingly. There may also be an increased strengthening of the regions, and this will underline the importance of local and regional networks for funders and fundraisers alike. Make sure you keep in touch with developments.

Young people and their representation

Britain does not have a minister with exclusive responsibility for young people, although there is a Youth Service Unit in the Department for Education and Employment. Children and young people are also included under other government departments like Health or the Home Office. Everybody acknowledges the importance of young people and the need to help them realise their full potential. We are all aware of the consequences of exclusion and disaffection when young people are pushed to the margins. But how much space is made for the views of young people themselves to be heard?

As one grant-maker said: "Increasingly, we talk about young people. We talk around them and over their heads. In the many youth conferences I have attended on all sorts of young people's issues – education, drugs, crime, training, employment and unemployment and so on – young people themselves have been invisible and unheard. We have to start letting young people say themselves what it's like for them."

Again, maybe the renewed government priority given to young people in general – and education in particular – will allow the young people to speak for themselves (maybe through the growing number of Youth Councils at county, district, borough and parish levels). Various key funders (e.g. the National Lottery Charities Board) are banging the drum very hard on this issue.

Openness and inspiration

The Directory of Social Change has always argued that as well as describing grant schemes, funding programmes and partnerships, there should always be illustrative examples of how money is spent and who gets what from whom. This is not just about openness; it is also about inspiration. We hope that by reading about the projects that have been successful in gaining support, there will be a knock-on effect with those looking for funds. "We could do that", or, "We are doing that – and better", or, "Why aren't we doing that?" are questions that all youth organisations can ask when looking at some of the projects described in this book.

Acknowledgements and thanks

Writing this book has been a privilege. Those working with young people have been genuinely friendly and helpful in giving examples of pioneering work and good practice. They have been generous in sharing their time, expertise, insight and enthusiasm. Those funding youth work have also been helpful, constructive and generally open in how they see their role.

I am very grateful to all who have helped in any way; there are a great many and it would be impossible to name them all. Special thanks go to Lindsay Driscoll and Allan Hargreaves for their contributions. Invaluable help and support has come from the National Youth Agency, particularly Mary Durkin for agreeing to the collaboration, Keith Raynor, Terry Cane, Judy Perrett and all at the Information Centre who work to give answers to those ringing and writing in. Special thanks also go to David Ainsley, Lyn Boyd, Michael Butterfield, George Gaskell, Charlie Harris, Helen Martin, Janice Monty, Rod Moore, Alan Rogers, Robert Sampson, Lucy Swanson and Martha Wallace. I am indebted to all those who returned amended text, often at perilously short notice, and read and commented on drafts. However, the text and any errors remain mine alone.

My personal thanks go to a starry host of babysitters and helpers who took care of my own young people. Your support, encouragement and general unflappability made writing the book possible.

Conclusion

This book is the first attempt at describing what resources are available to those working with young people. The research was completed as thoroughly as possible in the time available. There may be funding sources that have been missed or information that is incomplete. Some will become out-of-date. Where this is the.

case and readers have additional information for the next edition, a telephone call to the Directory of Social Change (0151-708 0136) would be very helpful.

A final word

Fundraising may involve simple ideas, but it is never easy. There is no fundraising quick fix. This book lays out the basic rules of the fundraising game, but it still requires persistence, hard work and optimism to make it happen. Success makes it all worthwhile. There is plenty of money around and youth organisations are very well placed to get it. Good luck!

Nicola Eastwood

June 1997

The DSC is grateful to the Dulverton Trust for their support in the production of this book.

How to use this guide

....

The first four chapters of the Guide give you the basic tools to start fundraising and to increase your chances of success. The following section details the main areas of funding with information on those that support work with young people. You need to think about what you want support for in order to decide who to apply to.

The main sources of support are:

The National Lottery

This gives over £1 billion in total to good causes each year. There are currently five different 'good causes' – arts, sports, charities, heritage and the millennium – with a sixth being developed as the New Opportunities Fund. Youth organisations can in theory apply to all of them. Some of the distribution boards give mainly capital grants (building, equipment etc.); others give revenue grants as well (i.e. salaries and running costs).

For further information see Chapter 6

Local authorities

Support for project costs, programme development, equipment, salaries and so on can still be raised from your local authority. Each will be different and there are guidelines for making your approach.

For further information, see Chapter 9

Central government

Some support for youth organisations is available through the National Youth Agency and the Department for Education and Employment. Other departments and grant-giving bodies can help with project costs that meet their clearly defined priorities (e.g. crime prevention, rural development, promotion of volunteering).

For further information, see Chapter 10

European money

There are a huge variety of schemes available from Europe, and young people are often a focus area of the programmes. Programmes usually require matching funding from other sources, and many are tied to geographical areas, economic outcomes or capital projects. Some are aimed specifically at young people (e.g. Youth for Europe and YOUTHSTART).

For further information, see Chapter 11

Grant-making trusts

These are charities which exist to give money to other charities. Some are particularly interested in children and young people; others in general welfare or education; others in certain geographical areas. Most support salaries and project costs for up to three years; others give small one-off grants for equipment or individuals.

For further information, see Chapter 7

Companies

Company support is extensive and varied. It's not just about cash. Links with a company can secure donations, gifts in kind, professional advice and sponsorship.

For further information, see Chapter 8

Members, friends, the local community

Many youth organisations survive on membership subscriptions and fundraising from the general public. The public is still one of the largest funders of youth work through sponsored events, buying raffle tickets, attending events, and contributing to collections and subscriptions. It also tends to come with few strings attached. You ignore the public at your peril!

For further information, see Chapter 5

The final section of the book contains two chapters on financial and legal organisation for your group. Both are essential to efficient fundraising.

There is a list of useful addresses and contacts and an index of the funding sources.

Chapter 1

Getting started in fundraising

Raising money is a challenge. Sometimes it is frustrating, sometimes it is really enjoyable; sometimes you win, sometimes you don't. It is often rewarding; it is always hard work. Like any game, fundraising has its own rules. This section explains the basic rules and gives you strategies for success.

The fundraiser

In theory, anyone can be a fundraiser. You don't have to belong to a particular professional body; you don't have to take exams; you don't even have to have done it before. However, it is important that you get the right person to do it. The fundraiser will be saying all kinds of things about your organisation or club and making all kinds of promises on your behalf; if he or she says or does the wrong thing, it will reflect badly on you. So what do you need to be a good fundraiser?

Time
There are few quick fundraising fixes. Getting serious money takes serious time. It may be a year before you get your first big grant. It may take five years to build up a really big event. Be realistic from the start both about how much time you all have and how much time it will all take.

Commitment
This is one of the most important qualities in any fundraiser. It soon becomes clear to the outsider if people are just going through the motions. Some people can raise fortunes through sheer force of personality or their absolute conviction in what they are doing, even if they break all the fundraising rules.

Stamina and persistence
Fundraising can be a hard and dispiriting business. People who quit easily will not succeed. Those who keep their eyes on the prize are usually successful.

Truthfulness and realism
There can be a temptation to promise the earth in order to get money, or to say what you know the donor wants to hear. This is a recipe for complete disaster. Raise money for what you want and for what you know you can deliver. What's the point in having a state-of-the-art facility if you have no money to run it?

Knowledge

When talking to potential donors, you must be able to answer their questions. The fundraiser who says: "I'm never allowed to see the books so I don't know how much money we've got" is on a loser from the start.

Equipment

You will need at least a telephone (and maybe an answering machine) and a typewriter or word processor and printer. You don't necessarily have to buy them; you may well be able to borrow or scrounge them from members, supporters, local companies or whoever.

Willingness to ask

One major charity commissioned a piece of research about why people were not supporting them. Was it the charity's image? Was it the cause? Was it donor fatigue? No, it was simply that the people had never been asked. We often assume that just because people know we are there and that we need the money then they will dig into their pockets. They may well, but only if we ask them to.

Opportunism

The good fundraiser makes things happen. For example, the difference between an OK event and a really successful one could be the fact that a major celebrity turns up. This always gives an event profile and prestige. Often such people come because somebody knows somebody who knows them. The alert fundraiser breaks into these networks. If a local company is having a really good (or really bad) time, it may be ripe to sponsor an event to celebrate their success (or restore their image and profile). The opportunist gets in there, and first.

Luck

You may just happen to say the right thing at the right time, or bump into someone who could be a really useful contact. For example, a colleague was recently doing a radio interview about a new youth project. After the broadcast a major funder who happened to be listening rang the radio station to find out more and the funder and project were put into contact with each other. You cannot plan for this. However, you must be ready to make the most of any opportunities.

Say thank you

Remember, getting money is only the start of the process. Once people have given once, they are more likely to give again, but only if you treat them properly. At the very least say thank you. You should also aim to keep them informed of what is going on and turn them from a supporter into a committed supporter.

Six golden rules of fundraising

Fundraising is a people business

People do not give to organisations; they do not give to abstract concepts. They give to help people or to do something to create a better world. The fundraiser is the person who shows them how you can achieve this. Always stress the human aspect of your work – how you give people a new chance in life, or enable them to experience things they otherwise wouldn't, or whatever.

Fundraising is about the donor

Too many fundraisers concentrate on what they want to tell the donor ("we do this" or "we need that"). However, it is absolutely vital that you try and scratch each donor where he or she itches. Always ask yourself: "Why would this donor want to support us? What are their particular concerns and interests?" For example, a parent who simply wants their child to have an enjoyable evening will give on a totally different basis to a company thinking of its future workforce. Try and get into the minds of the different donors and show that you understand their interests and concerns and are doing something about them.

The more personal the better

Donors like to be treated and appreciated as individuals. So the more personal you can make your approach the better. A face to face meeting is far better than a personalised letter which is far better than a circular letter which is far better than a poster.

Fundraising is selling

Fundraising is a two-stage process. The first thing you need to do is show people there is an important need and that you can do something useful about it. If they agree that the need is important and that something should be done; and if they agree that your organisation is doing something significant to make a difference; and if you can show them how some extra support will help you do something even better – then the second stage of asking for money becomes easy. Fundraising is more about selling an idea that the donor can make a difference than it is about asking for money. Once people have been sold the idea, they will normally want to give.

Giving is a matter of trust

People give money to you on the understanding that you will do certain good things. You need to show that you are capable of doing the work, that the money will actually achieve something, that they can trust you to use their money well. This generally boils down to your credibility. In other words, can you show the donor that you have done things like this really successfully before; that you have really good people to do the work; that you are well-liked and respected throughout the community; that lots of other people trust you to do this work?

It's not all about cash now

Donors also tend to give money to organisations and causes they have heard of. This means that it is not always a case of trying to raise money now. You actually may need to spend time building your relationships, becoming better known, getting on local radio or in the press, obtaining endorsements about the quality of your work from experts or prominent people. All this will help strengthen any fundraising case that you eventually make.

Basically, in the words of the old cliché, fundraising is friend-raising. Try to build and keep your fundraising relationships with the same care as you do your friendships. Get to know your donors personally if at all possible; make them feel a valuable part of things; and try to show that you are as keen to listen to what they have to say as to tell them what you want from them.

Also, you need to think and plan ahead. If you want to approach a local company for support, can you spend time getting to know them and them getting to know you before you actually ask for money? If so, where are you going to meet them? Who is going to introduce you? What are you going to say?

The strategy

When people start talking about developing fundraising strategies, you immediately assume they are talking about a sophisticated plan that could only be drawn up by a fundraising professional. Nothing could be further from the truth. All a fundraising strategy looks to do is answer four basic questions:

- What do we want?
- Why do we want it?
- When do we need it by?
- How are we going to get it?

This section looks at how to draw up a basic plan that will make your fundraising easier.

Why do we need a strategy?

Why bother having a fundraising strategy? Why don't we just get on with the fundraising? If all you need to do is raise £250 for some equipment, you don't need a strategy other than to get 10 members of the club to do a sponsored event and raise £25 each. However, if you need £100,000 to buy and fit out a new youth centre, you will almost certainly be looking at raising large chunks of money from different sources. You need to know what to expect from each. And if you fail in one area (e.g. the National Lottery Charities Board turns your application down) the whole project may fail.

So how do you develop a basic fundraising strategy? Here's a six stage plan.

1. What do we need money for?

You are going to be asking people for money. Therefore you need to be absolutely clear what you are asking for. "Equipment" isn't much use as an answer. Exactly what equipment? You need to provide a list. If you didn't get all the money, which pieces would you buy?

2. Why is it important?

It's not enough to say to possible donors "this is what we want". You have to show them why it is important, so that they feel their money will be doing something valuable. "We need a minibus" doesn't get you very far. "We need a minibus because lots of kids hang around on street corners and get into trouble. We also live in a high crime area. Our youth club gives people something good to do with their time, but people are too scared to come. We want to be able to collect them, bring them to the club safely, enable them to have a good time and drop them off at home again." This is starting to get somewhere.

3. How much will it cost?

There are basically two kinds of costs:

- capital costs – these are the costs of physical items e.g. buildings, equipment, furniture;
- revenue costs – these are the costs of running your activity e.g. salaries, rent, rates, telephone bills.

You need to be realistic about both these costs. For example, you may want a new all-weather sports pitch (capital expenditure). Fine. The National Lottery gives capital grants. So you apply to the Lottery and get your grant. Then what? Who is there to look after it? How will you meet the higher insurance costs? Who will handle the extra membership applications as a result of the new facility? How much will the new high-tech floodlighting cost to run?

You need to think all this through before you write for money. There is no point getting your wonderful new facility only to find that you haven't got the money to run it and so the club has to close. You will also need to explain how you came up with the figures you arrived at. (See Chapter 2 on drawing up a budget for more information.)

You may need two lists:

(a) One-off capital costs

This will include all the costs associated with the building or renovation work you may be undertaking. This will look something like:

Building work	£50,000
Furniture	£10,000
Equipment	£25,000
Architect's fees	£5,000
Quantity surveyor	£2,500
Legal fees	£2,500
Non-reclaimable VAT	£2,500
Fundraising expenses	£2,500
TOTAL	**£100,000**

Or it could simply be the cost of the minibus i.e.:

Minibus (second-hand)	£10,000

(b) On-going revenue costs

These apply once the capital work is finished. So, the organisation undertaking the above building work may face itself with increased costs e.g.:

	1997 (before the building work)	**1998** (after the building work)
Rent/rates	£1,000	£3,000
Heat/light	£1,000	£3,000
Salaries	£25,000	£35,000
Insurance	£500	£1,500
Postage & telephone	£750	£1,500
Maintenance of equipment	£1,000	£3,000
Computer costs	Nil	£1,000
Events/competitions	£100	£2,000
Publicity	Nil	£500
Audit costs	£1,000	£4,000
Bank charges	£200	£750

Other (this list is not supposed to be comprehensive)

Similarly, with the minibus, you will need to cover petrol, insurance, repairs, road tax and so on.

Once you know how much you need you can then decide where the extra money is coming from.

4. How much have you got?

You need to ask yourselves:
- Can you contribute to the capital part of the project?
- Have you got enough revenue funding once it is built?

Again, you need to be honest and realistic about this. Things almost always end up costing more rather than less than you think and plan for. If you stake every penny you have on getting the thing done, you may run out of money before the project is completed. However, if you play too safe and look as if you are hoarding money, donors may think you are not committed and not give you support.

Have you got the money for all your day-to-day costs once the fundraising is over? Will you need to employ a caretaker or new youth leader? Will you need to double your membership to pay for this? Do you need an increased local authority grant? Will you get it? Will you need to get your members to run the London Marathon to raise the £10,000 extra a year? Will they do it? Will there be any loss of income while building work is being done (e.g. will you need to close the youth club for six months)? Are there any tax or VAT implications?

If you have money that you can put into the project it is an important sign of commitment and is very attractive to other funders. However, don't commit what you haven't got and make sure you allow for contingencies and overspends.

5. Where is the money coming from?

You need to know *before* you start fundraising where you expect the money to come from. Obviously this can only be an educated guess. You may well end up with something like this:

Management committee donations	£1,000
Management committee fundraising	£5,000
Members' donations	£2,500
Members' fundraising	£12,500
National Lottery	£20,000
Charitable trusts	£14,000
Company support	£1,000
City Challenge	£4,000

You now know who you expect to give what. If they don't then you need to make plans accordingly. In any case, the different funders will want to know how you expect to raise the money.

The different chapters in this Guide will help you decide where to expect to get your money from.

6. Who is going to do the fundraising?

It is all very well writing lots of plans; unfortunately this doesn't actually get the money raised! The final part of this planning stage is the hardest. This is where your arm-twisting skills will come into their own.

You may be thinking of organising the whole fundraising appeal yourself. This has the major advantage of being absolutely clear about who is doing what because you are doing everything. However, be honest!

- Do you have the time?
- Do you have the expertise?
- Do you have the contacts?
- Do you have active support from the rest of the organisation?
- Do you have the necessary financial information?
- In general, are you the best person to be doing it?

If you are convinced that you can and should organise it all, you may well still need help with administration. For example, if you are organising an event, you cannot be in more than one place at once. You will need to delegate. Equally importantly, you may well need people with contacts.

The most effective way of raising money is through personal contacts. You are much more likely to get money from a friend than from someone who hardly knows you. For example, if you were about to do a sponsored abseil, who would you ask to sponsor you? The same principles apply to other kinds of fundraising.

Therefore, if you want to get sponsorship from local companies, why not try to get a prominent local business person onto your fundraising committee? This means that any requests for their support will come from someone they know and respect (i.e. a fellow company chairman) rather from a youth club whom they have never heard of and have no incentive to support.

Ask around your club. Whose parent is famous or well-off or well-connected? Ask your staff, management committee, leaders, volunteers. Is anyone married to the president of the chamber of commerce or the president of the local Rotary club or whoever? Produce a shopping list for the ideal fundraising committee and try to recruit it. For example, you may want:

- a lawyer (to provide services free of charge)
- an accountant (ditto)
- a prominent local businessman (to raise money from colleagues in local businesses)
- a local councillor (to use influence to get money from the local authority)

- a local notable, active or retired (to make lots of fundraising speeches and appearances)
- an events organiser
- 2-3 members of the club
- a person to chair the committee

Alternatively, you could ask famous people if they want to be presidents or vice-presidents of the appeal. Presidents are usually figureheads who add credibility to the appeal and feature on the letterhead. However, they would only usually expect to make three or four appearances at key points in the appeal (e.g. to open an event, present some awards, receive a significant cheque or whatever).

The trick with getting outside people in is to make sure you get what you want from them. There is no point asking your most famous local sports personality to make six appearances in aid of the appeal only to find out that (a) she keeps letting you down at the last moment, or (b) she charges you a fortune for each appearance. The first case severely annoys your sponsors and those attending the event; the second case lands you with costs that you didn't expect, and which may even wipe out the event's surplus. When formally inviting people onto the committee, make it clear in the letter what you expect from them.

Also, avoid the temptation to go for too large a committee. It may be that the committee as a whole never or only rarely meets. If you have busy people they do not have much time; get the best from them.

Once you have done all this basic planning, you are ready to begin to raise money.

How much do we need?
A guide to basic budgeting

Success in raising money depends upon focus, planning and presentation. All of these are involved in drawing up a budget for a project. You want to be confident that what you are asking for is realistic in terms of what the funder can give, but also that you have asked for enough. Surprisingly often, funders say that projects have been under-costed and applicants should have asked for more.

A budget will help your organisation with:

- planning
- accountability
- setting objectives
- directing funders
- raising money for core costs.

Key points
- How much do we need?
- What costs do we need to cover?
- How do we draw up a budget?

Who should draw up the budget?

There is no magic formula or sorcerer's skill in formulating a budget. There are undoubtedly people who cope with figures more confidently than others and hopefully there is at least one person in your organisation who has this expertise. However, the process of budgeting should also involve those who will actually carry out the work as they are likely to have an idea of what will be involved. They will also carry the burden of an under-funded project if the costing is not realistic. Consultation also encourages accountability. Where people have been involved in drawing up targets for income and expenditure they will have more idea of what resources are really available and why they should keep to their forecasts.

What needs to be included in the budget?

How much a project really costs

Before looking at any income that will come to the project you need to look first at how much the project will cost to run. There are obvious costs and other costs that are hidden. Some items such as equipment may seem easier to fund than others. Do not leave less attractive elements out as these are part of the real cost of running a project. This is an opportunity to apportion core costs to a project and raise money for salaries, running costs, depreciation for instance. (See Chapter 3 on Fundraising for Projects.)

Some organisations are nervous about this approach, worrying that funders may be scared off by large amounts that seemed to have been "smuggled in". Do not be. Funders who have a feel for the business of sifting applications will recognise a realistic project costing when they see one. (If you are applying to funders who you suspect may not appreciate this approach you can explain your figures more fully, or simply present a shopping list of items for them to choose from.) If you ask for too little you may not be able to run the project at all, or if you do, only run it half as well as if you had allocated costs properly.

Having a realistic grasp of how much a project will cost means allowing for:

- capital costs (that is machinery, equipment, buildings etc.)
- running costs (that is salaries, rent, heating, depreciation, decoration etc.)

Whether you are budgeting for a capital item, or the running costs of the project, the processes will be the same.

> The Foundation for Sport and the Arts, the largest trust giver to sport and arts projects says:
> "Applicants sometimes seem to lack confidence to ask for the full sum that they need; this does not help their case. If your proposal is well thought out and it requires £20,000 rather than £10,000 to see it through you should apply for the full amount."

Drawing up a budget – Estimating your costs

Capital costs

If you are planning a capital project (an extension to your existing facilities, or a new building for the youth club for example) you need firstly to list all your costs. These may include all or some of the following.

Land and buildings
How much will it cost to buy the land?
How much will it cost to rent office/hall space?

Professional charges
Accountant
Architect
Feasibility studies
Quantity surveyor
Solicitor
Structural engineer etc.

Building costs
Site works before construction
Construction cost (as on contractor's estimate)
Furniture and fittings
Security system
Decoration
Equipment

You should add to this list as necessary. However, these are only the costs of *building* your extension or new hall. They do not show how you will pay for the long-term costs (such as maintenance, heating, lighting, security, insurance and so on). These on-going costs should be included in your revenue budget as below.

The above list also assumes that you will be paying for everything. In fact, a friendly architect may reduce their fees as a donation; you may be able to get your members to paint the hall with donated paint from a local factory, and your furniture may be given by a firm that has recently been refurbished. All this should be taken into account and your budget adjusted as necessary. In some cases when applying to funders it helps your case to show how much you have raised from your own resources. Gifts in kind (such as donated furniture, reduced solicitor's services etc.) should be costed and their financial value recorded.

> No budget will be 100% accurate. It is your best guess at the time you are planning the project of how much money you will need. You may wish to put in a contingency for unforeseen costs, if you feel this is a sensible precaution. And if at a later stage it appears that your figures are no longer accurate, you can always revise your budget so that it reflects the financial situation as you then know it. Remember though, that you may not be able to get any extra money from a funder to cover this.

Revenue costs

These are your main running costs and will include all or some of the following.

Premises
Rent
Rates
Maintenance of the building, inside and outside
Heating
Lighting
Health and safety measures
Security
Insurance
Depreciation of equipment

Administration
Salaries (including National Insurance)
Telephone
Postage
Stationery/printing
Cleaning/caretaking
Book-keeping, audit and bank charges
Training courses
Child care
Miscellaneous (e.g. travel, tea, coffee etc.)

Project costs

These are the costs of running individual activities or pieces of work which take place in the building or as part of your remit as a youth organisation. Where you can, split your work up into separate units that can be costed individually. You can then look at what a project costs, which includes capital items and revenue costs such as those listed above. By costing projects separately you can keep track of individual project costs; allocate some of your general running costs to projects; and prepare funding applications.

Costing a project – an example
Imagine you are running training courses in video film production (i.e. this is your project). You will have two basic categories of costs – direct and indirect.

The direct costs will include the equipment, publicity and trainer's fees – these are usually fairly easy to identify. The indirect costs (sometimes called support costs or hidden costs) can be harder to pinpoint. They generally include items such as staff time for those not involved on a day-to-day basis in the project (e.g. manager, admin worker, finance controller), depreciation, use and maintenance of the building (including rent, rates, heat and light), insurance, post, telephone, stationery and other office costs.

A difficult area is how to calculate the central or office costs. Obviously, you cannot work out in advance exactly how many telephone calls you will make, stamps you will need or paper clips you will buy. The best way to come to a reasonable estimate is to try and work out how much of your organisation's time and facilities will be taken up by the project. So if your project will be the fourth one in the organisation, it takes up the same amount of space as the others and requires the same amount of the manger's supervision time, then it would be reasonable to allocate a quarter of all your central costs to the project. However, if it is only taking up a tenth of the organisation's time and facilities, then allocate a tenth of these costs. Remember, you are not expected to predict things down to the last penny; rather, the funder simply wants to see a sensible way of calculating the full cost of doing this work.

This process may seem daunting, exacting and time-consuming in the beginning. It may also seem a little approximate, particularly where you are allocating overheads to a project. It is worth persevering so that you include a reasonable estimate of the hidden costs as well as the ones you can more easily tie down. In a climate where it is more and more difficult for groups to get funding for the less glamourous parts of their work, it is vital that applicants cost projects appropriately. They must include core costs. The process of thinking how much it actually takes to run a project can be sobering, but can also be the way to fund your running costs. Anyway, if you are successful, funders may require detailed accounts of how the money was actually spent to compare this with your initial budget.

Drawing up a budget – Estimating your income

Your budgeted costs set out what you need to spend. However, you can only spend money you have earned, raised or borrowed. The other side of a budget needs to show where you intend the money to come from.

Sample budget

Project name: Video Film Production Course

Course duration: two days a week for four weeks. Non-residential.
Number of participants: 28-30 (four groups of about seven members)
Number of tutors: two

Costs:

(a) Equipment:
Video camera hire	£
Video cassettes	£
Editing equipment hire	£

(b) Staff:
Tutors (i)	£
Project director (ii)	£

(c) Building use:
Heating	£
Electricity	£
Training room (iii)	£
Publicity	£
Office expenses	£
Caretaking/cleaning	£

(d) Overhead:
Insurance	£
Depreciation (iv)	£
Miscellaneous	£

Total costs   £_____

Notes

(i) Requires two people each working 10 hours per week for four weeks at £6.15 per hour (ie. 2 x 10 x 4 x £6.15).

(ii) A part-time post for 2 months @ £..... per month

(iii) 25% of current facilities for 8 days, so allow 25% x 8 x £X room hire per day

(iv) Equipment is usually depreciated over three years so you would need to allow 33% of the purchase price of the equipment each year – this is so that you build into the budget the cost of replacing out-of-date or broken down equipment.

Look at each source of income you can expect (e.g. local authority, subscriptions, fundraising events) and list them as you did your expenditure. You will need to look at where this year's income came from and make a reasonable guess about what will happen next year. Most of this is common sense rather than crystal ball gazing. You can look at opportunities as well as threats to your funding. Is there a new source of trust support that has opened up? Do you have more members this year than you did last year? Do you have a keen new group of parents and helpers? Has your funding been affected by local government reorganisation? Is your three-year grant from the Bootstrap Trust finishing this year?

It is much easier to predict expenditure than income. You obviously need to keep a close eye on both. There is a tendency for expenditure to be higher and income to be lower than budgeted! Monitor your income frequently and carefully. Allow for any shortfall in your expected income quickly. For example, if you had expected to raise £30,000 from the National Lottery to upgrade your premises, but your application fails, you then have to make some decisions. Have you got reserves, and do you want to use them for this? Can you borrow the money? Can you raise money through cutting expenditure in other areas? Do you have time to find another funder? Should you abandon the scheme?

It helps to list both definite and hoped for income.

Source of income	Budget	Certain	Probable	Possible
Local authority	£25,000	£25,000	-	-
Memberships subs (i)	£1,700	£1,000	£500	£250
Trusts (ii)	£5,000	-	£3,000	£2,000
Local companies (iii)	£250	£250	£250	-

Notes

(i) **Membership subs:** Imagine you have 100 members paying £10 each. You can enter £1,000 in the definite column for next year. You estimate you can accommodate more (although you will have to work out any significant increases in expenditure that this will cause). You have a waiting list of around 50, and you predict that they are all likely to join, so enter £500 in the probable column. You also hope that some publicity will bring in an extra 25, but you are not sure, so put £250 in the possible column.

(ii) **Trusts:** Your budgeted £5,000 can be entered in the probable column if you are confident of the trust (e.g. the grant is recurrent). You would put the figure in the possible column if you know less about the trust(s).

(iii) **Local companies:** Similarly with companies, if you have a warm relationship with local businesses, they are represented on your management committee, or if you play golf with the chairman of the board, the £250 can go under probable. Otherwise enter under possible.

With your income and expenditure figures you should have a budget worksheet that looks something like the example overleaf.

Income vs. expenditure

Having listed your projected spending and income you will now have an idea of where you stand. This process can give an overview for the whole organisation but can also give the picture for individual projects. You may predict that the money coming in is greater than your anticipated spending. In your understandable euphoria you should check the budget carefully. Have you been too optimistic on your sources of income, or have you missed some areas of expenditure or under costed them?

If your income is below your projected spending you will need to look carefully at the reasons for this. Is the snapshot year you are looking at exceptional in some way? Do you have a large number of one-off start-up costs related to a big project (such as building work, feasibility studies, equipment costs etc.) which will not be repeated in following years, or does the deficit come as a result of regular income failing to match routine expenditure? Wherever there is a shortfall you will have to do some planning immediately. What you should *not* do is take any of the following:

■ The Ostrich Approach: which is to panic and delay any action by putting your head in the financial sand.

■ The Lemming Technique: assume the figures must be wrong, say "We've always managed before" and carry on regardless. This is a certain recipe for disaster.

■ The Don't Worry, Be Happy Maxim: assume that you will be 100% successful in all your fundraising efforts (which is unrealistic) and that costs will also magically all go down. If you sit on your hands and think something will turn up, it almost certainly won't.

■ The Wishful Thinking Strategy : when in doubt add a nought or two to your income figures and hope that you will be more successful in fundraising than you had first foreseen. If you are going to do this you might as well have not bothered preparing a budget in the first place.

■ The Dream On Philosophy: imagine that some money spinner or fundraising event will cover the deficit, but have no idea what this will be. Another approach would be to suggest an appeal to past members when you have never done this before and have no idea what money will be raised.

Instead of being tempted by any of the above, you will need to be realistic, clear thinking and hard headed. Look carefully at the figures, again, and satisfy yourself that all are reasonable. Decide whether the shortfall is short-term or long-term. Look at what you can afford to do, and whether you can manage the deficit by some tweaking, or by more drastic surgery. You may need to scale some things down, or wait a while longer to start other things. You will need to allow for time lags if you are cutting expenditure. The effect will not necessarily be instant. You

Income/expenditure budget

Date of budget:

Expenditure ....

Item ....

Cost ....

Notes* ....

....

....

Total costs   £_____

Income:

Source   Total   ☐ Certain   ☐ Probable   ☐ Possible

Notes* ....

....

....

Total income   £_____

Projected surplus/deficit   £_____

*Notes: How reliable is this figure? What is it based on? Is it the highest, lowest or average figure?

....

....

....

....

....

may have to cut some activities altogether or use successful projects to subsidise other under funded ones. Whatever you decide make sure that it is realistic and that it is clearly understood within the organisation.

Cash flow predictions

The final phase of this part of budgeting is looking at your cash flow. This is where you try to forecast when the money will come in, and when it will go out. This is particularly important if you have a large building project where large bills have to be paid. Will you have enough money to cover them?

Take all the different areas of expenditure that you have listed. Work out in which month each will be paid. For example, salaries are paid evenly throughout the year; rent may be paid quarterly; insurance due in October; deposit for the residential activity week is to be paid in February; the printing bill for the summer arts event is due at the end of June. Once you have done this, try to then allow for the events and items of expenditure that will be extra this year. If you have some flexibility, you may want to plan them in months where other expenditure is relatively low. Once you have done this, total up each month's expenditure.

> **Budgeting – the Fat-Free Guide**
>
> Step 1   Estimate your costs (these are usually higher than you first think)
>
> Step 2   Estimate your income (this is usually lower than you first think)
>
> Step 3   Predict your cash flow
>
> Step 4   Make adjustments as necessary
>
> Step 5   Implement your budget, monitor it and make it work – it should be a standard item at management committee meetings

You should now do the same with your expected income. Again, this may be erratic and difficult to predict. If you have a local authority grant, this may be paid in April; membership subs may be collected throughout the year; Safer Cities money for your motor project may be paid in September; the grant from the Single Regeneration Budget may come in September too; and your second year's funding from the Fair Dues Trust is sent after their February trustees' meeting. These are the sources you can predict. There may be others such as the various award schemes that change each year and make planning difficult. If you have a source of money such as a grant from the European Social Fund, which is new to your organisation, you will have to spend time becoming familiar with the timing of payments.

By matching the expected monthly spending with the expected monthly income you will spot any gaps where there is little or no money to meet expected bills. You need to plan and take action for this. You may be able to re-negotiate your payment terms for some items. You may need to arrange an overdraft facility. If you are hiring equipment you will want to schedule payments in months that have less expenditure.

Forecasting becomes particularly important if you are planning a large capital project. Some funders will only pay once the work has been completed, so you will have to pay contractors before you get the grant. Some funders will not pay if work has been started already, and you may have to find money for feasibility studies and surveys before any money is awarded. You need to allow for these.

Having worked out your budget you should now have a good idea of how much you need; what you need it for, and when you need it by. You are now in a position to go to funders.

Chapter 3

Fundraising for projects

Fundraising is about getting hold of enough money to meet the day-to-day or capital costs of your organisation, plus the resources required for future development. However, it is far easier to raise money for something specific than to appeal for administrative costs or general funds. This is because donors can then match the support they give to some specific piece of work that they are really interested in. They will feel that their money is actually doing something and that they have made a real contribution.

For example, a Save the Children Fund appeal asking for money for rent and rates would not get very far; appeals asking for help with work in Somalia (or wherever) have been really successful.

The same principle applies to your fundraising. Asking for money towards the upkeep of your youth club may (just) work with your local authority; it won't get very far with BBC Children in Need Appeal. They will only want to fund a particular project or part of your work (e.g. your new work with disabled children). Your members (or their parents) will also respond much better to an appeal for one thing (e.g. a new item of play equipment) than for a generous contribution to our expenses.

Thinking of your work in project terms and designing projects which will attract support is the basis of successful fundraising.

> **Make your project sound exciting**
>
> One of the great advantages with project fundraising is that you can highlight particular areas of your work that will interest the particular person you are writing to. However, make sure you do everything that you can to show that the work is lively, worthwhile and worth funding. The donor's first response is more likely to be "Gosh, that sounds good; we ought to be backing that", rather than "I've had ten applications like that in the last month, and none of them are likely to achieve very much".

A fundable project should be:

- specific - an identifiable item of expenditure or aspect of the organisation's work;
- important - both to the organisation and to the cause or need it is meeting. If there is some long-term impact that will be an added bonus;
- effective - there should be a clear and positive outcome;
- realistic - the work proposed should be achievable;
- good value - the work should be a good use of the donor's money;
- topical - it should be looking at current issues and concerns;

- relevant - it should be relevant to the donor and the donor's particular funding concerns;
- bite-sized - it should not be too large or too small for a donor to support, although the cost might be shared through several smaller grants. If it is too large, it might be broken down further into sub-projects.

How to identify a project

Case study: Anytown Youth Centre

A range of different things go on at Anytown Youth Centre. They include general activity nights for young people of different ages, after-school clubs for primary-aged children and basic facilities for young people to practice music (used mainly by young rock bands). However, the club needs to generate another £2,000 a year to cover its costs. It also wants to re-lay its main hall floor which (a) is totally unsuitable for wheelchair users and (b) is getting unsafe anyway. This will cost £10,000. The club has £750 in the bank. What can it do?

- Put up the members' subs and hire charges to cover the £2,000 a year deficit. However, many members and groups struggle to afford the current fee and would probably leave if it went any higher. So you may end up making the problem worse.
- Have a one-off special appeal to members and users. OK, but what about next year?
- Apply to the local authority for a grant. Possible, but most local authorities are heavily strapped for cash.
- Organise an annual major rock festival. Fine, but it's a bit ambitious and who is going to organise it?
- Write round to local trusts and companies to fund the deficit. They wouldn't fund it.

Clearly there are problems with all the above strategies. Also, they don't really begin to tackle the floor problem. So, the Centre could try to divide its needs into more attractive projects.

- They could get funding to expand the after-school clubs to secondary school age. This would attract funds from various groups interested in the welfare of children. It would also be run on a fee-paying basis so would bring in extra money. They could also try to interest the members in music through the musical facilities they already have.
- They could get funding to recruit new members. For example, they could raise money for new instruments, recording equipment or whatever to get more musicians in who would then pay fees.
- They could bring in adults. For example, they could run a parenting course, sessions on drugs awareness for parents, communicating with your teenager or whatever. All these could be devised with the help of the young people and they could raise the money from a grant-making trust by showing how it's a new and exciting approach to re-building family relationships.

- They could develop specific activities for disabled children, maybe centred on music or a sports league for wheelchair users.
- They could raise money for other future income generators (e.g. social or catering facilities which They could also use to hire the premises out).

There are plenty of other options as well the above. However, the advantage of breaking things down into projects is that you can appeal to a wider range of funders. You are no longer restricted just to those concerned for young people. You can apply to people interested in music, parenting and family life, disabled people etc; having done this, the replacement of the floor is a much easier proposition because (i) the building is clearly being used for the benefit of a wide cross-section of the community; (ii) this brings in a number of potential new funders (for example, both the Arts and Sports Council Lottery Funds in the above example), and (iii) you can look at the best way of getting that particular piece of work done (in this case, for example, you may be able to bring in people under a good training scheme for young unemployed adults). Then you can hive off some of your central costs into the applications for funding (see below).

By breaking things down into projects, you can focus on activities (e.g. parenting courses, disabled children) rather than your own needs (money for bills), widen the range of possible funders (you are no longer just about your current users) and force yourselves to be a bit more creative in your fundraising.

How to cost a project

To cost a project properly, you need to include all the direct and all the indirect costs which can reasonably be said to be necessary to the running of the project. This means you should allocate a proportion of your central (or core) costs to the project. The process of costing a project has several stages.

1. Describe the project

Be clear about what the project is. By this, you should identify what the project will do for its users rather than how it will solve your funding problems. For example: "We will develop our after-schools club (as in the case study above) to include secondary school age children. This will achieve the following: …"

2. The direct costs

Write down a list of all the direct costs. For the after-school club these could include:

- leaders' costs
- extra tables and chairs (for homework)
- pens, paper and exercise books
- drinks and biscuits
- advertising and publicity.

3. The indirect costs

Write down a list of all the relevant central costs. This is where you need to be more creative in your thinking because you must include all the hidden costs. At this point you are trying to establish how much the project actually costs to run. Please note, you are not trying to fiddle any figures or pretend that you have costs that you really don't. You are simply recognising that the work you do requires a wide range of expenditure.

There's no such thing as core funding!

Groups often say they can get funding for "projects" or for capital spending but not for their administrative or core costs.

To tackle this, the first step is forget the whole notion of "core costs". They do not exist. You do not have any costs other than those which are necessary for carrying out your work or "projects".

So, you need to:
- Think of your work as a series of projects
- Build your full overhead costs into each of these activities
- Recognise that if the overhead costs have not been paid for, the project is not fully funded.

The trick is to include the relevant central costs in each project budget. You can then use the "glamour" of the project to get the "unattractive" administrative costs paid for.

So, the after-school club cannot run without a building; the building needs heat, light and insurance; the leaders of the club will need the use of a telephone and photocopier; they need supervision and support, and so on.

So your list of indirect costs will include:
- rent and rates
- heat and light
- postage and telephone
- management and supervision of the project
- book-keeping
- insurance
- cost of training courses.

4. Costing the costs

Put a figure against all the areas of expenditure. This is pretty straightforward for the direct costs, although make sure you get more than one quote on each cost. The difficulty is how to cost the indirect expenditure. You cannot put a precise figure on this; all you can do is be reasonable. You should try and work out what proportion of the central costs the project needs.

So, say the Youth Centre as a whole is currently used for 40 hours a week and you intend to run the after-school club for 10 hours a week. This means it will then be in the building 20% of the time. Say that it will occupy half the Centre's rooms. Putting these two figures together you can then say that it takes up 10% of the

Centre's building costs. So allocate 10% of all the rent, rates, heat, light, postage, telephone etc. to the after-school project.

Say you have one Youth Centre manager who has responsibility for all the activities in the building. You will need to work out how much time this person will spend supervising the after-school project and allocate the salary and national insurance costs accordingly. So, for example, if the manager works a 35-hour week and will spend on average six hours per week on the after-school project, allocate 17% of the salary and national insurance to that.

You will also need to work out an allocation for the caretaker, cleaner, administrator or any other salary costs associated with the Centre and the project.

5. Is it reasonable?

Ask yourself: "Does the total figure look reasonable?" Is it too high or too low? Does it look real value for money? Many of the costs you will put down (e.g. premises) are effectively impossible to put a precise figure on , so the budget is flexible. You may need to juggle the final total a bit. The key thing is that you can justify how you have arrived at those figures if a funder pushed you on it.

And finally ...

You now have to decide who will pay for what. Are you going to ask one funder for the whole amount for the project? Are you going to ask various funders? Are you going to allocate some of your own money to the project (e.g. 10% of your local authority grant)? Whatever you do, remember:

- apply to a funder who is interested in your kind of work;
- ask for an amount they can conveniently give;
- stress the benefits of the project and show how it is real value for money.

Chapter 4

Preparing and Writing A Good Fundraising Application

Youth Group in Funding Shock!

A youth group found some money completely by accident. The End of the Rainbow Trust left a pot of money at their door. "No-one is more surprised or pleased than us" said the group's leader "We were just about to apply for help from the trust. They must be mind readers." Eye-witnesses said they had seen little green men leaving something heavy outside the hall doors. Foul play is not suspected.

If only funders could read minds. Usually they cannot. Those giving money away have to be put in touch with those needing it and fundraising is about selling an idea to someone who has the means to make it happen. The application is the point of contact between you who needs the support and those who can give it away. The more you can help funders do a difficult job, the more they may be inclined to help you. This help may be a cash donation, sponsorship of an event, gifts for a raffle, time and expertise from a member of staff, equipment or whatever. Your task is to make them interested enough in your ideas to want to support you.

There are many ways of asking. You can ask face to face; you may make a presentation to a group or meeting of supporters; you may use the telephone. The most likely approach, however, is by writing a letter. This chapter will look at what to include in a letter, and also how to improve your presentation.

Most of the effort of application writing goes into condensing a full account of the project and organisation into a description of around 1,000 words, one to two sides of A4 or, at worst, a 3cm x 14cm box on an application form. This makes good sense from the funder's point of view. They have many applications to look through and cannot spend time reading and interpreting vast amounts of information,

> **Some cautionary words**
>
> Writing applications is not a science. You may write the clearest, brightest, most engaging application that fits all the funder's criteria, and yet still not be successful. You may not even get a photocopied rejection slip, let alone an explanation of why you did not get a grant. On the other hand you may know of people who break all the "rules" and yet their spidery illegible scrawl and rambling prose brings in thousands regularly. There is no easy explanation for this and you should not take it personally. Don't give up; keep trying.

however interesting and worth while. If looked at positively, application writing can be an opportunity to hone your strategic thinking as well as your style.

Some key points

1. You cannot tell funders everything; there is not enough time and they would not listen. Many application letters are far too long. Put yourself in your reader's place. Would you persevere through long pages of information about an organisation you knew little or nothing about? A general rule would be one and a half sides of A4 maximum for a letter to a grant-making trust, and one side maximum to a company. Proposals to local authorities and central government departments may give you more space - on the whole, officials will be more used to reading long project descriptions. This should not be an excuse for wasted waffle. You should still keep to a clear, positive and succinct style.

2. In your letter, select and concentrate on your main selling points, emphasising those which will be of most interest to the particular person/supporter you are writing to.

3. Generally, it is best if you are not asking funders to support your organisation. Instead, ask them to support the people you help, the work you do, and preferably, a specific project.

4. Believe in what you are doing. Be upbeat. Positive messages are more inviting than negative ones. Take the approach of the Tina Turner song: "We're simply the best". If you do not believe in what you are doing why should potential supporters? Too many applications strike a defensive note and end up apologising for their work. Do not focus on the gloomy consequences of not getting the money. Paint an exciting picture of all the things that will happen when you do get the money. You want to enthuse people, not resort to emotional blackmail.

Two approaches: which would excite you enough to read on?

a) The wolf from the door appeal

"The Dire Straits Youth Association desperately needs support. Any help would be gratefully received. The neighbourhood where the group meets is a very deprived area lacking most facilities. The youth group was started five years ago, and has often struggled to keep going. If it does not secure funding it will be forced to close. The association has had its core-funding reduced in successive years and now finds itself with a funding deficit. If your organisation could make some contribution to the group, however small, it would assist its continuation, and ensure that local young people at least have something to do. Without your support, the group may have to close."

b) The leading the horse to water appeal

"The Dire Straits Youth Association has met for the last five years. We run sports competitions, volunteering projects with other local charities, as well as weekly events where young people can meet regularly. Our leaders are local people who give their time freely. Some have gone on to complete youth work qualifications. Local businesses, schools, colleges, the police and the local authority all have links with us. The popularity of the group means that we now need your help with our new bus project. This will take our activities out to young people who cannot travel to us. I have included a list of equipment that we need for the bus. Is there something you would like to donate or help to fund?"

The ingredients of a good application

Before you put pen to paper, or finger to keyboard, you need first to have prepared thoroughly. Ideally, the application should be the quick part of the process; just as in Chinese cooking, more time should be spent in preparing the ingredients than in producing the final dish. These should be selected carefully for quality, consistency and their contribution to the overall presentation.

Most funders (including members of the public) receive thousands of requests each year. Although the serious business of funding important work should not be turned into a glamour contest, you do have to think carefully about how you can make your application stand out from the crowd. At very least you should be aware of the traps which could prevent your application getting the attention it deserves.

You will need to make a number of key points which will catch the readers attention, arouse interest in the work, and "sell" your proposal. Ask yourself:

- Why on earth should anyone want to support us?
- What is so important about what we are doing?

In other words what is unique about your work? What is different? Why is it necessary? What will it achieve. And why should this particular donor want to support it? You should try your answers and application out on a friend who does not work in the same field and has no knowledge of your work. Their view can tell you whether you are assuming too much of your reader, whether you need more or less information to make your case, and when you have got it about right.

Six essential elements of an application

- Who you are
- The need you meet
- The solution you offer
- Why you should do it
- The amount you need
- The future you have.

1. Who you are

The funder wants to know what kind of organisation they are dealing with. How long have you been going? What are your key activities? What have you done that has been especially brilliant? What have been some of your major successes? In other words, can you show the funder that you are reliable, respectable and someone they would want to be associated with?

2. The need you meet

All voluntary organisations exist to meet a particular need, to make society better in some way. You need a brief and clear explanation of the need or the problem that you exist to deal with. How widespread is it? Is it local or does it have regional, national or international implications? If it is local, what special features of the community make it special or interesting to support? Point to who will be helped by your work, which can be a wider group than just the young people involved in the project. Emphasise any elements that are special or unique in the need you are trying to meet. Can you explain the problem however complex, in one or two sentences?

Show how important and urgent the need is. You may want to highlight what would happen if you were not doing anything about the problem. Do not be over-emotional; give your reader assurance that something constructive can be done. However, do not undersell yourself or assume that "everybody knows this is a problem". If people do not think there is a need to meet or problem to solve, they will switch off. If they think that it is not very pressing, they will find something else that is urgent. If they do not think that you understand the problem they will assume you cannot solve it either. You need to do the following:

> Is the problem we are addressing worse than others?
>
> or,
>
> Is the solution we are offering better than others?

- describe the problem;
- support this by evidence;
- say why this is important.

3. The solution you offer

Once you have established the need and said how important it is to do something about it, you then need to show that you can offer a particular solution. For example: "We will provide peer education by visiting 15 schools, colleges and groups of young people in our area. We will speak to 700 young people and aim to recruit a further 20 counsellors from these sessions. We will produce an outreach and information pack that will be distributed to each school, college and youth group in the area."

When making your case avoid laziness in your arguments. It is a common fault of applications that they state the obvious and rely on circular reasoning. For instance, if you are asking for money to build a hall, the temptation is to argue: "The problem we have is that there is no meeting hall for the young people in our community. Building a hall would solve the problem." A funder would reasonably want to know "Why?" If you don't identify a need you cannot offer a solution.

You need to point to the actual or expected results of your work, and how these will be measured. This may be for instance, how many young people will attend; how leaders will be attracted and trained from the local community; how resources will be shared with other groups; how an information pack will be distributed to local schools.

Make sure that what you want to do is workable, that it can be done in a reasonable time, by you, and that it gives value for money. You should define clearly how you will overcome any problems that may come as a result of running the project (e.g. for a school homeworking club: safety, adult supervision, accountability, links with school etc.).

Good arguments to support your case would be to look at other communities where a similar project has led to visible benefits for young people (e.g. in the personal development of the young people, their integration into the community, enhanced opportunities for sport and art, access to courses and education, or reduced vandalism and crime). You could point to a survey that shows how young people would use your facilities, or the results of an outreach project that reflect young people's use of time and shared resources. You may also want to refer to how the facility will be used to benefit the wider community. In short, the donor should now be saying: "I can see there is a real problem and the project would certainly make things better".

4. Why you should do it

You now need to establish your credibility. Why should you be the group to run the project? Why should the funder trust you? What is different about the way that you do things?

Think about your plus points. Do you use volunteers creatively? Do your leaders come from the local community? Do they participate in leadership training qualifications? Do they have a story to tell that would interest a funder? There must be something about your group or your work that is attractive and fulfilling to those who help. By training local leaders, for example, you have given the community a vital resource, and encouraged people to discover commitment and talents they may otherwise have left unused. This builds credibility for a group by showing commitment to all in the community, not just a lucky few.

Do you have examples of media coverage that give positive images of your work? Have any of your young people achieved something as a result of your activities?

Have you helped raise money for other causes in a committed and imaginative way? Has your group or an individual gained an award or recognition for a scheme or achievement? A report in the local paper can help to support your case. Do you have a "Local Boy/Girl Makes Good" story? Has your group produced a celebrity? Do you have a famous former member who regularly supports events each year? Positive publicity can show the spectacular results of working with young people and the importance of what you do. They can also establish that you are here to stay, with a record of making things happen.

Are you successful in raising money from other sources? Do you have a mixture of supporters from a number of sectors? Do you have good working relationships with agencies, local business, schools, local authorities etc. What have these partnerships achieved? Do you have a measurable impact in the wider local community? Financial stability will impress any funder; this is one of the keys to establishing trust. The more diverse and secure your funding portfolio is, the more likely you are to be entrusted with other grants. Strong links with other groups and organisations give a good indication of how integrated you are, and further proof of how much added value your activities bring to the community. Funding your group may bring knock-on benefits to other groups you work with.

Generally, can you show that your work is good value for money, and are you more cost-effective than alternatives? What makes you the right people to be meeting this need? Is your approach an example of good practice that could be copied and applied elsewhere?

You should be able to come up with a number of good reasons why you should be supported. The more you can do this, the more credibility you have. The more credibility you have, the more likely the donor is to trust you with their money. It is also the case that success breeds success, and funders will be attracted to a confident upbeat approach. Your plus points will all help to sell your case, so make them clearly and confidently in your application.

5. The amount you need

Funders are keen to know about the project first and the value of the work being done. But you also need to tell them very clearly what it costs and how much you expect them to give. Some applications tail off when it comes to asking for money. There is no need. By now you should have made a good case for someone to support you, and proved that you can be trusted with their money. This is the point of the letter after all, and if you're too embarrassed to ask for the money, there is little point in sending it off. There are different ways to ask for what you want, and you should think about the type of funder you are applying to.

Where you are asking a funder for a small amount, or where you think they would like to see some obvious benefit from their donation, you can produce a shopping list. This can be very effective when raising money from companies.

You can suggest an item from the list that you think the supporter would like to pay for. You can give a range of items with costs starting at a level that all those you are writing to can afford (see box). However, by including more expensive items you hopefully persuade them to give more. Also, you are giving them something specific to pay for which many donors like. If you are looking for gifts in kind rather than cash this is the best way to give supporters an idea of what you want. (There is further guidance on gifts in kind in the Chapter 8, Winning Company Support.)

Young people helping 'schools at play' project	
Equipment	**Cost**
Short tennis	£60.00
Centrahoc set	£32.50
Soft polo	£75.00
Earthball	£88.50
Parachute pack	£64.00
Mini Cricket (2 sets)	£6.50 each
6 Footballs	£1.90 each
12 Cones	£4.50 (for four)

6. The future you have

Make sure that you emphasise your long-term viability. This underlines your credibility and why funders should support you. If your future is not at all sure, funders may think their money would be better used elsewhere. Show how the project will be funded once the grant has been spent. Where you are applying for money for a new facility, who will pay for its running costs once it is opened? How will you continue a project when the three-year grant has finished?

What to say in the application letter

Now that you have done your research and pulled all your selling points together you need to put them into some kind of order. There are no golden rules for

---

How to ask for money
Fraser Falconer, Regional Coordinator, Scotland BBC Children in Need Appeal

- State clearly how much the overall project will cost (e.g. "We are looking to raise a total of £30,000").

- Give the funder a clear idea of how much you expect them to contribute. You can do this in one of three ways:

   (i) Ask for a specific amount (i.e. "I am therefore writing to ask you for £2,000").

   (ii) Show how much other trusts have given (e.g. "BBC Children-in-Need have already given us £2,000"). This will indicate that you expect a similar amount from the trust you are currently writing to.

   (iii) Show how many trusts you are writing to (e.g. "I am therefore writing to you and eight other major trusts to ask for a total of £10,000"). This gives the trust a pretty good idea of how much you expect them to give (i.e. around £2,000), but gives them flexibility to give more or less than this.

- Show where the rest of the money is coming from (i.e. "The overall project will cost £30,000. We expect to raise £15,000 from our members and supporters; £5,000 from other fundraising events and £10,000 from grant-making trusts. I am therefore writing to you and eight other major trusts to ask for a total of £10,000"). This will give the trust more confidence that you know what you are doing and you can raise the necessary money.

writing proposals, no perfect letters of application. What works for the club down the road will not necessarily work for you. Inject your own personality and approach as far as possible. The following is a structure that many have found to work, and this can be a starting point for your own letter.

1. Project title

This can be really effective, especially if it is catchy and quickly describes what you want to do.

2. Summary sentence

This is the first bit of the application to be read. It may be the last! It tells the reader what the application is about and whether it is likely to be relevant to them. "I am writing to you to ask for a donation towards the cost of..." is a reasonable start. Keep it short and to the point.

3. The introduction: who you are

Many applications say little or nothing about who the organisation is; they just go on about what they want. Assume that the reader knows nothing about you. What would they need to know to trust you with their money? You need to show you are good, reliable, well-used and well-liked – in three or four sentences.

4. The problem: why something needs to be done now

Now you move onto the problem you want to solve. Remember, people are basically interested in what you do rather than who you are. Do not ask people to support you; ask them to support your work and the people you help.

5. Your proposals: what you intend to do about the problem

You now need to show what you intend to do and how you intend to do it. You should set yourself targets (e.g. how many young people will you attract to your activities? How many disabled people will become members or leaders? How many leaders will you train?) If you are having problems with this part, maybe you could try predicting what the club will be like in two years' time and how things will have changed. If there is an area of your membership you want to increase, how many will this be?

You also need to say how you intend to do something about the problem or need. It is not enough to say "Here's a real need and something must be done". The reader must gain a clear idea of how you will achieve it. Many grant-makers are moving towards 'output' funding, where they judge the success of the project on the measurable things it achieves. They will certainly want to see that you have an idea of what the money will buy and how you can keep track of the success or otherwise of your plans. Show what you will do and how this is value for money.

6. Why you should do it

By now you have stated who you are, the need you want to meet and how you are going to do it. Now you need to show why you are the best people to do it. Assume your reader is saying: "This is all very well but how can I trust this group to

The X Factor. The Plus Points That Give You An Edge

Write down as many selling points for your group as you can. Below are some possible categories which may help you to see the strengths of your group.

- People (What's different, good, or extraordinary about your members, helpers, workers etc.)

....

....

- Pounds and pennies (What's sound and bankable about your finance? What's successful about your fundraising?)

....

....

- Personal achievements (Has anyone achieved something notable through your activities? Have your members or volunteers gained experience, qualifications, employment, training etc. through being part of the group?)

....

....

- Partnerships (Who have you linked up with? What has been achieved?)

....

....

- Publicity (Have you had any coverage in the local press? Have you been successful at recruiting new members and leaders through outreach?)

....

....

- Perseverance (Do you have a good track record? How long has your group been running?)

....

....

- Performance (Has your group developed activities or projects that have been adopted and taken off elsewhere? What are you "Simply the Best" at?)

....

....

The X Factor. The Plus Points That Give You An Edge (Cont.)

You meet the following need(s) ....

The needs you meet are particularly important because ....

Your solution is new and ground-breaking because ....

You are different/unique because..

Your other strengths are.... ....

If you did not exist then.... ....

Funders are keener to support success stories rather than failures. You need to be confident of your successes to show how you stand out from the crowd. List your five greatest successes in the past five years:

1. ....

2. ....

3. ....

4. ....

5. ....

And finally, complete this tie-breaker in twenty words or fewer:
"We are the best there is in our work with young people because............

....

....

....

....

....

....

....

....

....

....

deliver on this?" This question will partly be answered by how good and clear your solutions to the problem are. However, you should also establish the credibility of your club. This can be done by showing your plus points worked out above:

- **Your ability/professionalism**: show you are a well-run outfit which helps people fulfil their potential, that you have grown over the years, that you are soundly financed and that you have a wide support base.
- **Your reputation**: show how you have support and goodwill throughout the community. Get quotes from a wide range of people, from members to parents to local councillors to business leaders to famous people to whoever makes the application sound more convincing. This shows you have across the board support. You may want to attach a quotes sheet to your application in any case.
- **Your track record**: show how you have very successfully done similar work in the past, or that you have set up other projects which have proved a success. You need to persuade people that you can turn ideas and plans into results and action.

> Remember to ask first if the funder has an application form to fill out. There is no point sweating blood to get the perfect letter of application written only to find out that you have to redo the whole thing on an application form. If you are unsure about the information required on the form, contact the funder for clarification if you can. With an application form there will be more scope for this than with a letter. Sort out all the problem areas on the form before you ring, and go through each in one phone call. This will save time for you and the funder.

7. The budget: how much you need

This is how much you intend to spend on the project. It includes direct costs and overhead costs. (See Chapter 3 on Fundraising for Projects and Chapter 2 on Drawing up a Budget for further details.)

8. Funding plan

You need to show the funder where you intend to get the money from. It may be that you are asking this funder for the whole amount, or you may be getting it from a variety of sources. Therefore, you need to say something like: "The total cost of this project is £50,000. Our local authority have agreed to give us £5,000, and this will be matched by European money of £5,000. We aim to raise £10,000

Start making sense - A guide to writing simply

- Keep sentences short and to the point. Develop a news style that cuts out long complicated sentences.
- Keep paragraphs short. Look at the layout critically. Would it entice you to read further. Are you put off by long sections of text? If you are, your reader will be as well.
- Avoid jargon. You may understand what you are talking about; outsiders generally will not.
- Be direct; do not waffle. Use as few words as possible. It adds to the "readability" of your application, and keeps the length down.
- Use personal pronouns such as "we", "our", "you" and "your" rather than "The organisation/association", "the users" etc.
- Use strong verbs and tenses, rather than weaker ones like the passive. "Our young people work closely with local schools" reads better than "Local schools have become involved with the activities organised by the young people in the club."
- Weed out waffle and waste. Say something sincerely, simply and succinctly.
- Re-read and rewrite.

from local supporters, £20,000 from the National Lottery, and £10,000 from grant-making trusts."

You also need to show how you intend to meet the longer-term costs (see Chapter 1 on Getting Started in Fundraising for more information).

9. The rationale: why the funder might be interested and what their role is

It can help to have a final rallying call before you sign off to leave the reader feeling positive and enthusiastic. There are many reasons why the donor may be interested:

- you are running a good project which is right at the heart of their stated policies and priorities;
- you have already received support from them and this further grant will allow you to build on that success;
- there is a personal contact which it will pay to highlight;
- there is a particular benefit to the donor which you want to stress. (This is particularly the case with companies who will want to see a business or public relation return on their money.)

Sometimes, people sum up on a negative note: "Wouldn't it be a tragedy if all this good work came to an end" or, "If we don't raise £30,000, the project will have to close". Avoid this kind of thing at all costs. You've made a good, convincing case with positive reasons for supporting your work. There is no reason to assume you will not get the money, so be positive.

10. The signatory: who puts their name to the application

This could be anybody e.g. the project leader, the director, the fundraiser, the chairman of the management committee, an appeal patron. Whoever signs it must:

- **Appear sufficiently senior**. This shows you are treating the application seriously.
- **Be knowledgeable**. The funder may well ask for more information. The person who signs the letter should be able to tell them what they need to know, including the overall financial position of the organisation. If the name on the letter cannot give this information it appears that the application has not been well organised, and the project not well thought through. If you have a patron who signs the letters but does not know about the day-to-day running of the project, you should include the contact details of someone who will be able to answer more detailed questions.
- **Be available**. Again, if the funder wants more information they don't want to have to leave a whole series of messages before they get the details they need to make a decision.
- **Be open**. Leave your potential supporter with plenty of opportunity to talk to you, find out more, or visit. Many will decline your invitations to come and look at the work or meet the young people, but people like to be asked.

What do you send with the application letter?

If the funder has an application form you must fill it out following its instructions. However, if you are writing an application letter, you should send the following supporting materials:

- a set of your most recent accounts, or a budget for the year if you are a new organisation;
- a budget for the particular project you are wanting support for, including estimated income and expenditure;
- an annual report (if you have one). If you have not done so before, think about your annual report as a fundraising tool. It does not have to be a dry as dust account of the last year with minimal information on what you do. It can say as much about your activities and success stories as you want it to.

You can also enclose anything else that will support the application (e.g. newsletters, press cuttings, quotes sheets, videos, photos, drawings, letters of support from famous people etc.). However, do not rely on these extra bits to get you the money. They will not compensate for a hopeless letter. Assume that the trust will only read your letter and the financial information (budget and accounts). They should be able to get the complete picture from these. If in doubt, ask yourself:

- Is this relevant to the application? Is it absolutely essential or a nice extra?
- Will it help the funder to make a decision in our favour?
- Can I afford to send all this?
- Does it present the right image? (e.g. Is the additional material so glossy that it implies you are a rich organisation? Can you get publicity material sponsored?)

Remember, everything is for a fundraising purpose. If the accompanying information does not help the application, do not include it. It is definitely not a case of never mind the quality, feel the width.

What do you do with the letter?

There are two main strategies.

1. Send it out to all relevant funders all at once. This is the most common technique. It has the advantage of getting the appeal up and running and you will know reasonably quickly where you stand.
2. It may well be better to send the application out in stages. Write to a few of your key supporters first and see if they will lead the appeal (i.e. give you a grant which then encourages others to do the same). When some of these have committed themselves to supporting you, then write to the rest saying that firstly, you have already raised £10,000 of the £20,000 needed, and secondly, that X, Y and Z funders gave it to you.

Money tends to follow money. The more you raise, the easier it is to raise more. Highlight any money that has already been raised or pledged. Sending applications

The Bare Bones Application Letter

Note, there is no such thing as a model application letter. Write your letter in the way that best suits you and the work you are doing. Be yourself and let your work be seen in its best light. However, here is one skeleton outline that will help you put fundraising muscle on in the right places.

Dear.... *(wherever possible use the name of the correspondent. If you do not know it, make every effort to find out, and get the spelling right)*

I am writing on behalf of...... seeking funding towards the cost of....

.......was set up in...... by.... to do....... Major initiatives have included....

I am writing about our....... project. The need we are meeting is particularly important because.....

We know the project will be effective because......

We know we are the best people to do this work because.....

The project will cost £.... We intend to raise the money as follows:......

As you are interested in........ (location, funding criteria etc.) I am therefore writing to you for....

At the end of the grant we expect the project will be funded by....

If you require further information, or you wish to discuss the application, or you would like to visit and see the work, please contact me on....

Yours sincerely,

This is a possible structure for a letter. Use it as a checklist to make sure everything that is relevant to the application has been included.

Don't forget: Use headed notepaper, include your charity number (if you have one) and sign the letter.

out in stages usually improves your chances because you concentrate initially on those most likely to support you. Then you widen the net to include those who don't know you as well but will take their cue from other funders' confidence in you. However this approach is more time consuming and needs more planning. Have you got the time to do this? It may not be the remedy for crisis funding where you are desperate to get money in as soon as possible.

What to do after the letters have been sent

You should keep a simple record of what you have sent where. It will help you keep track of applications and to know how supportive each funder is. Note also the supporting materials you have sent, or the events you have invited funders to.

Apart from this, mostly you can do nothing except wait for a yes or no. You can ring to check that the application has arrived, but you do not want to seem to be hassling or pressurising people. Different types of funders will have different expectations of this. Some local authority officers for instance will discuss how your application is progressing; others such as some trusts or companies will not welcome any follow-up contact at all. They will not have the time or inclination to answer your enquiries, however general.

If you get a positive response, write to say thank you immediately and put these people on your mailing list for the future. Keep them informed of your progress. Note any conditions on the grant that have to be met (e.g. sending a written report to the funder each year) and make sure you keep to them. You will want to go back to those who have supported you for help in the future. Keep them interested in your progress and how the money has been spent to help young people. If individuals have benefited, personal accounts and progress reports can be an easy and friendly way of keeping the funder interested and enthusiastic about what their money has helped to achieve.

It is perfectly possible to send those funders still considering your appeal a further letter to update them on progress. The letter can be quite short, saying: "We understand you are still considering our application about... However, you may be interested to know that we have so far raised £10,000 of the £20,000 we need. This has come from ... Please contact me if you need any further information about the project."

If at first you don't succeed...

Do not be afraid to go back to people who turned you down, unless they have said they would never support your kind of work. There are many reasons why you might not have got money: they may have funded something similar the previous week; they may have run out of money; they may have had a deluge of

---

Your application letter

Your application letter should tell any reader everything they need to know about your appeal in a short space of time. Assume they will not read anything else you send, and then answer the following:

- Will they have a clear idea of who you are, what you want, why you want it?
- Will they see what good it will do, what you expect from them, where else the money will come from, and what happens when their support has finished?

Before you send the letter, give it to a friend who knows little or nothing about your project. After reading the letter quite quickly, if your friend cannot answer the above questions, nor will your potential supporter be able to.

brilliant applications and yours was next on the list; they may have never heard of you before. Go back next year with a different proposal, and the next year and the next year.

Thinking about different supporters

In following chapters there are details on who might support you and their reasons. You will have to take into account what each funder will be looking for and why. A company for instance will be looking at the commercial possibilities of linking up with you; what is good for their business. They may look for more tangible benefits in the short term than say, a trust or local authority. Read each of the chapters that cover the funders you are hoping to approach for tips on how to apply.

And finally...

A major grant-making trust states in its guidelines: "A thoughtful and honest application always stands out in the crowd! Tell us clearly what the problem is, and how your project will do something about it. Give us relevant facts and figures, please don't use jargon, and don't be vague. You don't need to promise the moon just tell us what you can realistically achieve. Your budget should show that you've done your homework and know what things cost.

"A thoughtful and honest application isn't a hurried and last minute dash to meet our deadlines with something dreamed up overnight. It is a serious and sincere attempt by your organisation to use its experience and skill to make a positive difference where it is needed."

Applications checklist

- Does it have a personal address? (If it's the "Dear Sir/Madam" variety, don't bother until you have more information on the supporter.)
- Does the first paragraph catch the reader's attention?
- Are you clear about what you want and why you want it?
- Is your work likely to be interesting to the donor?
- Is it clear how much the donor is expected to give? Is this reasonable?
- Is the application nicely presented? Does it attract the eye with short paragraphs and no spelling mistakes?
- Does it back up what it says with good supporting evidence?
- Is it positive or upbeat? (If it's gloomy and negative; think again.)
- Does it take account of guidelines published by the donor? Does it make a connection with the supporter's interests?
- Is it written in clear, plain English, or does it use lots of long sentences full of qualifying clauses and jargon?
- How long is the application? $1\frac{1}{2}$ sides of A4 is plenty for a trust; one side for a company. Remember it does not have to say everything, but it has to say enough.
- Crucially, is the application appropriate? A brilliant letter to the wrong people will not get support.

Chapter 5

Raising money from the public

The public purse

In all fundraising the best questions to ask at the start are: "What do we want to do?" "What do we need to do it?" and "Where is the best place to get it from?" Although this book sets out the sources of money that you can apply to, by far the biggest giver is the general public. There was a time when groups raised money largely by asking those involved with the group, their nearest and dearest, and anyone else who would turn up, to support a jumble sale or car wash. Now, the emphasis is more upon honing the application letter and polishing up your presentation skills to appeal to a major funder. While you are chasing the grant, you should not forget to woo the public.

Anyone who wants to raise money should keep in mind that whilst grants are important, getting the public to support your group can be more so. It can be far more effective in terms of time and money to fundraise say £800 for video equipment from the local community rather than applying to a trust or company. This means 400 people giving £2; 300 giving around £2.70; 200 giving £4; 80 giving £30, 20 giving £50, or a combination of these amounts. It also helps to make your case to other funders if you have a well established track record of successful fundraising from the public. Fundraising can bring good publicity to raise the profile of your group locally.

This chapter will give some pointers to planning, some money-making possibilities, and some pitfalls to avoid.

There are all sorts of reasons why people give to good causes.

- *They are already involved with, and sympathetic to the cause.* Parents, helpers organisers and patrons for instance. These are usually the most dedicated fundraisers and donors. You should not have to convert them to your cause, they should already be tuned in to what you are doing and its importance.
- *They have been involved in the past.* Former members, old boys and girls networks, and people who have benefited from the club. Occasional reunions, particularly if combined with an anniversary, can be a way of focusing their financial support. Past members will still have some affection for the club, and hopefully, fond memories. They will want to support the present activities, but this is likely to be occasional rather than regular, so plan your fundraising accordingly.

- *They know some-one involved with the work.* The life-blood of sponsored events is the network of extended family and friends connected with those taking part. They will not necessarily know anything about the club, but they may want to support the individual.
- *They think the organisation is worth supporting because of the work it is doing.* This is an appeal to those in the high street, who do not have any personal contact with your organisation but value the work that you do. Your activities may tie in with their interests in some way such as health promotion, education, job prospects, social skills, crime prevention.
- *Where the organisation has had recent press coverage* and people want to help e.g. Ranulf Fiennes polar walk to help those with muscular dystrophy.
- *The heart-string factor* which is probably the most unmeasurable of all. In all fundraising this has to be handled with care, and with young people you may want to think carefully about the kind of image you want to promote.

Planning any fundraising should first take into account the support networks your group is immediately in touch with. You can then look at the wider audiences who may be attracted to the event and your cause. This planning does not have to be very scientific; a rough guide will be the best start.

Creating Support

Those at the very heart of what you are doing, such as family, friends, workers and the young people themselves are your most enthusiastic supporters. They are the people nearest the action and the foundation of any fundraising effort. Next in line will be previous members and organisations and agencies that your group has links with. These can include schools, sports clubs, arts venues which you use, as well as local dignitaries. These people do not know your group so well, but they have some affinity with it, as well as an interest in seeing it prosper.

You can also appeal to the wider community such as those you have business links with. (Is there a travel company you use regularly? Who do you bank with?) Finally, you can organise events in the high street or shopping precinct such as collections or money-spinning events such as a Christmas present-wrapping service. These will bring in people who know nothing about your group but are attracted by the activity. If you think creatively about venues, activities and audiences you can increase your chances of success.

Working with young people gives a ready and responsive group of volunteer fundraisers. Young people are often the most enthusiastic about raising money on behalf of others. They can also be energetic in taking part in imagination-grabbing fundraising events for their own group.

Making the most of the membership

Where you are a membership organisation, your members and volunteers are a vital resource. They can give:

- money
- time
- help
- advice
- contacts
- experience
- energy.

You should also remember to review membership subscriptions regularly.

> **Ten of the most popular fundraising events (although not necessarily the highest earners)**
>
> Sponsored events
> Street collections
> Jumble-sales
> Fairs
> Coffee mornings
> Discos
> Raffles
> Car washes
> Auctions
> Bring and buy sales

Fundraising events

Before organising your event you need to be sure of why you are asking people for money. It will help to decide which event and the way it will be run if you have considered why people will want to give. As mentioned above people give for a number of reasons which can be simplified to four:

- they like the **organisation**
- they like the **people**
- they like the **cause**
- they like the **event**.

You need to be sure which interest you are appealing to and plan your events and coverage in this light. If you assume too much of those who know little about what you do, you may lose the impact of the event. How do passers-by know that their money will be used well? Equally, the event itself may be a draw to watch, but may put off other supporters. Is sponsored bungee-jumping as attractive to watch for the parents and carers of the young people taking part as it is for those unconnected to the group?

Once you have decided on your event you then need to answer some key questions. A small team of people can help to think through these points and share the organising load.

- Why are you doing this? Is the event attractive in itself, or is it the cause?
- What are the risks to you in organising this event. (How easily could it go wrong? How much money do you stand to lose?)
- Who are you raising the money for, yourselves or for an outside cause?
- Who will organise the event(s)?
- Who will come to the event(s)?
- Where will it be held?

There are basically two kinds of fundraising event:

- ticket events where money is raised through ticket sales
- participation events where money is raised through sponsorship of those taking part.

- Is it safe?
- Do you need permission?
- How much money do you hope to raise?

This last question becomes increasingly important the higher your initial outlay is. It will be no good to you or your group if you organise the best screen-printing tee-shirt design competition ever if you cannot guarantee customers for the product. Young people may learn much in the process about team-work, creativity, organisation and marketing, but if your group is seriously out of pocket, or even goes bust in the end, you may wonder whether it was worth it. Remember too, that all outside events are at the mercy of the weather and you should make contingency plans.

One fundraiser has suggested that any event should have three figures for the amount of money that is to be raised, all targeted at a particular audience:

- What you think the event will raise (say (£1,500);
- What you tell your management committee it will raise (say £1,200);
- What you tell supporters you hope to raise. ("We are hoping to raise £1,000. Help us reach this total." When the total is reached early on, there should be enough momentum to raise the remaining £500.)

There is also much to be said for starting small and increasing in confidence if you are new to event fundraising. People sometimes start too ambitiously with very grand schemes. You should do what you know you and your group can achieve and build from your success. Organising a bring and buy sale may not have the appeal of a music festival in the park, but will be easier to run and have fewer risks attached. Who knows, if you really catch the fundraising bug, you could run the local answer to Live Aid next year.

Sponsored events – a guide

Getting someone to be sponsored for doing something is the most common way that groups and individuals raise money from the public. It is easy to see the advantages:

- easy and quick to organise
- easy to contact supporters
- reaches a potentially large number of different donors through personal contact
- uses participants who are members of the group and helps the group's identity
- fun – hopefully
- little initial outlay
- almost unlimited number of activities that can be sponsored
- can raise large sums of money
- can be used to focus on areas of interest: e.g. overnight lock-in in unheated church hall for the homeless; fast for famine relief; litter swoop for the environment.

With imagination and enthusiastic volunteers, you can take a sponsored event and do something different with it. People may yawn at yet another sponsored swim or walk (although they will probably support it because they know the person doing the event) but if you can give the activity a new twist you build new enthusiasm for the event itself. Sitting in a bath of jelly or baked beans (or both) will grab the attention of people who may not know the participant or the cause. They may not care about, or even like the cause but will stop to give money if they laugh in the process. Holding the event in a shopping centre or a school hall will attract maximum publicity. The humiliation or exhibitionist factor increases with the publicity, as does the number of pounds donated.

Publicity can also be increased if the event is even slightly off the wall. A group of teenagers which regularly raises money for famine relief by fasts, bike rides, car washes and the like, also looks to more alternative events to heighten their profile. They have sponsored carol singing in June, and hold marathon beach parties in December. Not only does this maintain the momentum of long-term fundraising, but also keeps their own interest from flagging. This is an important factor when young people are doing the hard work of raising money where interest and enthusiasm can seep away quickly. Youth workers will need to be quick-footed and have a few different ideas for events to keep interest high.

> The history of event fundraising is littered with grand failures where groups tried to organise too much too soon, and assumed that initial enthusiasm would become sustained commitment. Be ruthlessly realistic about the numbers involved, possible disasters and public apathy before you give something the go ahead.

Publicity

Attractive publicity materials can give any event an added boost and place it firmly within a youth context. Charity Projects which organises the Comic Relief Red Nose extravaganza is among the leaders in the field here. Even something as mundane as the humble sponsorship form is given the Red Nose treatment (see p.59).

The effect is to give sponsors a laugh, jazz up the image of the event and to encourage a certain approach to raising money. It also appeals to their vanity. Comic Relief aims to put the "fun" into fundraising, and there is no reason why your own sponsored event cannot do this as well. Remember that attractive does not necessarily mean expensive. A catchy phrase and an arresting appeal can work as well as a form printed in three colours. The sponsorship form should include all the relevant information, including your charity registration number if you have one.

Sponsorship incentives for participants

Usually, people look at the incentives to give money from the donor's point of view, but you should also consider how to encourage those participating in the event and asking for sponsorship. This is particularly important for younger children who may be easily discouraged if they only have two or three names filled in on their forms. It will not matter to them if these have given £10 each. To young children it will be the number of names on the form rather than the size of the gift that impresses.

You may want to mark in some small way the participants who raise the most money, have the most names, or even have the most imaginatively decorated sponsor form. To preserve harmony you may want to make this a team effort where older children can help the younger ones. You do not want to excite too much competition, or you will probably encourage some creative accountancy and find the whole cast of Eastenders signed up on each form. Sponsored events can become cut-throat, and Dad and Mum-upmanship is alive and well; but you do want to show participants that they will have something to see for their efforts.

Incentives for sponsors

One of the largest incentives for sponsors may be that they will not be asked for money again for some time. It will help your fundraising generally, and events involving the public specifically, if there is some sense of planning to your campaigns. "They're always asking for money" is one of the most off-putting reputations an organisation can have. Even if it is largely unfounded it can be very hard to shake off. If you draw up a calendar of events that evenly spaces those that will be specifically asking people for money it will help you and those that want to support you to concentrate their energy and money.

Many organisations use a "shopping list" of items to help people give away their money. It helps the sponsor feel their contribution is important and people generally like giving money to buy things which can be seen. Organising a fundraising event is probably not the time to raise money for core costs such as a manager's salary or the MOT for the mini-bus. There are no doubt spectacular exceptions to this rule, but by and large you will be more successful if you are raising money for equipment or a specific activity or trip that directly benefits the young people. You might try something like the following.

"Dear Beloved Sponsor, welcome to our sponsor form. *In-Tents Youth Club* is raising money to buy some camping equipment for their summer camp. We are running a sponsored sleeping bag olympics on 1st April. With the money that you generously give we aim to buy:

The Small But Perfectly Formed Red Nose Sponsorship Form

Dear Excellent Sponsor. Thank you for sponsoring this poor, tomato-crazed fool. Your cash will be the icing on Comic Relief's cake, the cream in its coffee, the cherry popped on top of its knickerbocker glory. Other sponsors may be okay: but you're the one that really matters.

We, the undersigned, pledge to sponsor.................. ....(your name)

To.. ....(your event)

Sponsor's Name And Title ....

Amount per............................	Total Received	Sponsor's Initials ....
The Divine	The Luscious	The Galactically Clever ....
The Clean Smelling	The Peachy.	The Firm but Fair ....
The Deeply Fanciable	The Youthful yet Mature	The Rippingly Torsoed ....
		Final Total _____

Please return this form and your sponsor money directly to:
Comic Relief, c/o KPMG Peat Marwick, PO Box 678, London EC4Y 8AS DO NOT send cash through the post DO NOT return this form until after your fundraising event.

Name ....
Address ....
....
.... Total Amount Enclosed..................

Signed (Parent/Guardian if under 16) ....

Comic Relief is an operating name of Charity Projects Registered Charity Number 326568

Camping equipment:
3 x tents, 1 x ground sheet, 1 x gaz stove and 1 x mallet.
All this will help 50 young children have the summer holiday of their lives!
Thanks for your help."

Or, alternatively, you may want to say what each £3 donated can buy:
Arts equipment:
Blank video tape for a video project
Entrance tickets to local festival
Face-paints for drama workshop
Sports equipment:
Table tennis balls

General equipment:
Leaflets to promote a summer activity week.

Helping people to give

The public are no different from other donors when it comes to wanting to be told how to give and even how much. Many will not have much idea when handed a sponsor form of how much they should give. The following will lead them by the hand and help to maximise their donations.

- Sponsors will usually look at the names already on the list and what they have given. Participants can ask their most generous supporter to sign the form first. This is more likely to be a mum or dad, or grandparent, rather than a younger brother or sister. Other sponsors will follow their lead. They may not pledge as much, but they will not want to be significantly lower either. They are signing their names to the form and do not want to appear too mean. If the number of sponsors is likely to be high you may want to distribute the large donors throughout the form.
- Give donors the option of sponsoring the number of units as well as a total amount. (It is always a good idea to give a total amount, rather than sting the sponsor after your group's Herculean triumphs. If the sponsor has pledged 10p a bounce, an enthusiastic claim for £25 after 250 bounces may be a bounce too far.) You should also think about the type of unit – 10p a kilometre for instance will generate more income than 10p a mile.
- As mentioned above, you might want to offer a small prize for the person who has the most names, or the biggest total. This can be an incentive for the sponsor as well as the participant but should only be token. Certificates or badges to be presented may well be enough.

Do the Right Thing – Do you need a licence?

The regulatory hurdles you will have to clear will depend upon the event you are running. Here are some you may have to consider.

- Public Entertainment Licence – Chief Executive's Department of your local authority.
- Liquor Licence – Magistrates Court.
- Lotteries – small, one-off events will not need a licence. Those brave enough to compete with the National Lottery and organise ticket sales over a longer period of time (social lotteries) should apply to the Chief Executive's Department of the local authority.
- Bye-laws – check with the Leisure and Recreation Department, or other authorities such as rivers, waterways, footpath, coastal, heritage and so on.
- Sunday Trading – check with the local authority which areas are covered.
- Health and Safety – check all aspects of your activity with the local Health and Safety Office.
- Safety Certificates – particularly if you are organising fairground rides, steam fairs, motorised tours or the like. The National Association for Leisure Industry Certificates can send an inspector to check the site.

- Public Liability Insurance.
- First Aid.

(From: *Organising Local Events* and *Tried and Tested ideas for Raising Money Locally* by Sarah Passingham)

Planning Events

Checklist – How to Organise an Event

The Community Council of Lancashire has produced a list to cover planning, preparation and running a village event.

You can adapt the following to your own activity, but remember this cannot cover all eventualities and you should use this as the start for your planning, rather than the last word.

If you are thinking of holding an event, a logical approach to the planning process will always produce a better organised, safer and more enjoyable event.

This list has been designed to be a step by step guide and checklist, taking an organising committee through all the stages necessary in planning a wide range of community events.

The list follows the logical order of event planning, starting with:

1. Feasibility

The following points should be considered to ascertain the feasibility of your event before planning starts.

- What type of event are you planning?
- Why are you holding it?
- When will you hold it? will it clash?
- Where will you stage it, safely?

2. Once you are satisfied that the event is feasible, the next stage is to PLAN IT.

3. After deciding that your idea is sound, and getting committee approval, the final task is to **appoint an overall event co-ordinator** – who has overall control – and an organising committee.

A sponsored event checklist

1. Check the event is safe and appropriate for those taking part and those who will be asked to sponsor. The event has to irresistible but not irresponsible.

2. Get parents'/guardians' permission to go ahead.

3. Get permission from any appropriate local bodies e.g. police, local authority, schools, residents.

4. Talk to the media about coverage. Look for celebrities to take part.

5. Look at possibilities for any elements of the event to be sponsored e.g. donations of prizes, sponsorship of printing, tee-shirts, drinks etc.

6. Design and print sponsor forms. Detail amounts and units, where the money is to go and what it will buy.

7. If the event is a marathon event or a 24 hour relay club activity, organise a rota and sign up participants.

8. Organise the day; first aid, stewards, refreshments, signposting, equipment and information.

9. Tidy up afterwards.

10. Thank everyone who took part. Give prizes if necessary.

11. Collect money and chase up the reluctant.

12. Publicise the amount of money collected and tell those who gave what the money has bought.

Celebrities

Working with someone famous can help to raise the profile of your event or your organisation. There are a number of advantages to attracting a 'name' to your cause:

- increased media coverage, locally and nationally;
- more people may come to an event;
- other funders may attend a celebrity event;
- morale boost for those participating and organising the event;
- positive role model for young people;
- may be able to obtain discounted rates or items from suppliers;
- may have contacts and links with other groups and 'names'.

If you do not already have a celebrity connected with your fundraising, look at whether you have a patron, notable trustees or any famous names who once had a connection with your organisation. Did the local soap star now made good once attend the youth group? Does the olympic hurdler from your patch owe her start to your group's activities or facilities? Celebrities will rally to your cause if they:

- like and trust the group and agree with what you are trying to do;
- have some connection with you;
- like the event.

As with everything else in fundraising, you need a mixture of the tried and trusted, together with the new and eye-catching. Delia Smith may be a little tired of being asked to contribute to fundraising cookbooks, but if she likes what you are trying to do she may still send a recipe for you to include.

In general, fundraising from the public is one of the most exciting ways of raising money. It can be a lot of fun. Remember, though, start small, start early, be realistic and make sure you have contingency plans for when things go wrong!

Ten tips on working with the famous

1. Think about your audience.
2. Choose someone your audience knows and likes.
3. Choose someone who is sympathetic to your cause, ideally someone with first hand knowledge, and who has a connection with your organisation.
4. Contact any celebrity well in advance of any event.
5. Be very clear about what you want their involvement to be.
6. Offer to pay expenses (mileage, materials, meals, accommodation etc.) and budget accordingly.
7. Brief them well, and advise them about any press coverage.
8. Make sure those who will be meeting and introducing them know what to do.
9. Don't overrun, unless they initiate it.
10. Say thanks, and keep them in touch with what you are doing.

Planning

Agree the date of the event, and set realistic timetables for preparation. Consider the main areas of planning. The Outline Plan for your event should cover the areas listed below:

Safety

	Assigned	Finalised
Insurance	☐	☐
Risk Assessment	☐	☐
Health & Safety	☐	☐
Safe Site	☐	☐
Occupier's Liability Act	☐	☐
Health & Safety at Work Act	☐	☐
Other...		

Budget

	Assigned	Finalised
Draft Budget & Contingency	☐	☐
Break Even Point	☐	☐
Sponsorship/Grant Aid	☐	☐
Costs/Sales	☐	☐
Trade/Concessionaires	☐	☐
Re-instatement Deposit	☐	☐
Other...		

Publicity

	Assigned	Finalised
Sponsors' Requirements	☐	☐
Trade Adverts	☐	☐
Advertising Costs	☐	☐
Publicity Material Costs	☐	☐
Other...		

Programme

	Assigned	Finalised
Time/Date – Other Local Events	☐	☐
National Events	☐	☐
Holidays	☐	☐
Legal Considerations – Food Hygiene	☐	☐
Planning Permission	☐	☐
Licences – Alcoholic Drinks	☐	☐
Music/Dance	☐	☐
Personalities/Guests	☐	☐
Other...		

Site

	Assigned	Finalised
Mains Services	☐	☐
Car Parking	☐	☐
Access To/From	☐	☐
Marquee Hire	☐	☐
Reinstatement	☐	☐
Other...		

Staffing

	Assigned	Finalised
Numbers Required	☐	☐
Paid	☐	☐
Volunteers	☐	☐
Other...		

Preparation

Having planned the event and agreed the timetable for preparation. You must assign tasks to members or sub-groups, and arrange dates for their completion. For larger events, sub-committees for each area of preparation e.g. safety or publicity, should be set up. The event committee must meet regularly to make sure everything is going to plan – or to iron out any problems. Members of the organising committee should take responsibility for individual areas. Completion dates should be set.

Safety	Assigned	Completed
Signs	☐	☐
Barrier Hire	☐	☐
First Aid Personnel	☐	☐
PA Systems/Radio	☐	☐
Public Liability	☐	☐
Other...		

Budget	Assigned	Completed
Costs – services	☐	☐
staff	☐	☐
site	☐	☐
equipment	☐	☐
supplies	☐	☐
Income – Sponsorship	☐	☐
Admission charge	☐	☐
Trade stands	☐	☐
Advertising On Site/Programme	☐	☐
Tickets/Programme Sales	☐	☐
Insurance	☐	☐
Other...		

Publicity	Assigned	Completed
Radio/TV What's On	☐	☐
Programmes	☐	☐
Press Release	☐	☐
Sponsors' Requirements	☐	☐
Handbills	☐	☐
Posters	☐	☐
Photographer	☐	☐
Other...		

Programme	Assigned	Completed
Start/Finish Times	☐	☐
Food Hygiene	☐	☐
Planning Permission	☐	☐
Insurance – High Risk Activities	☐	☐
Specific Items	☐	☐
Third Party Claims	☐	☐
Consequential Loss	☐	☐
Cancelled Event	☐	☐
Damage to Site	☐	☐
Weather Insurance	☐	☐
Catering bars	☐	☐
Other...		

Site	Assigned	Completed
Sign Posting	☐	☐
Site Plan	☐	☐
Electricity/Water	☐	☐
Toilets – Disabled Access	☐	☐
First Aid Post	☐	☐
Lost Children Area	☐	☐
Seating – Fire/Safety Regulations	☐	☐
Car Park – Disabled/Vehicle Recovery	☐	☐
Other...		

Staffing	Assigned	Completed
Recruitment – Parking, Tickets, Officials, Catering, Security	☐	☐
Uniforms/Bibs	☐	☐
Expenses/Meal Tickets	☐	☐
Troubleshooters	☐	☐
Other...		

On the Day

Arrive Early – earlier than you think you'll need. Ensure individual members know their delegated tasks. Check all tasks have been completed. Run through the event and the volunteer jobs. Event co-ordinator should not be tied to one job, but should be free to assist and troubleshoot where necessary.

Safety

	Assigned	Checked
PA/Radios & Coded Messages	☐	☐
Marshals – Bibs	☐	☐
Barriers – Secured	☐	☐
Signs – Keep Out, Exit etc.	☐	☐
First Aid Post – Signposted	☐	☐
Experienced Personnel	☐	☐
Fire Fighting Equipment	☐	☐
Police	☐	☐
Electrician	☐	☐
Other...		

Money

Float	☐	☐
Prize Money/Cheques	☐	☐
Secure Cash Boxes	☐	☐
Tickets – Start No.	☐	☐
End no.	☐	☐
Other...		

Publicity

To the Event Signs	☐	☐
Programmes on Sale	☐	☐
Radio/TV on the day	☐	☐
Banners/Flags	☐	☐
Reporters/Photographers	☐	☐
Other...		

REMEMBER – THIS LIST CANNOT COVER ALL EVENTUALITIES. SPACE HAS BEEN LEFT FOR YOU TO FILL IN THE INDIVIDUAL REQUIREMENTS SPECIFIC TO YOUR EVENT

Site

	Assigned	Checked
Car Park – Security Disclaimer	☐	☐
Toilets – Clean – Check Regularly	☐	☐
- Well Positioned – Accessible	☐	☐
Lost Children Area – Staffed	☐	☐
- Signposted	☐	☐
Seating – Set Out	☐	☐
– Checked – Anchored	☐	☐
Electrical Supply/Generator	☐	☐
Water/Drainage	☐	☐
Catering Outlets – Clean & Priced	☐	☐
Bars – Plastic Glasses – Clean & Priced	☐	☐
Other...		

Staffing

Easily Identified	☐	☐
Briefed/Specific Duties	☐	☐
Given Meal Tickets/Expenses	☐	☐
Other...		

After the Event

THANK YOUR TEAM BUT TRY TO MAINTAIN MOMENTUM TO ENSURE THAT ALL POST EVENT JOBS ARE COMPLETED. DISCUSS PROBLEMS AND HOW THE EVENT COULD BE IMPROVED NEXT YEAR. START PLANNING NOW!

Return Site to Original Condition	☐	☐
Extra Litter Collection	☐	☐
Thank You Letters	☐	☐
De-briefing	☐	☐
Press Release/Photographs	☐	☐
Bank Money - Prepare Accounts	☐	☐

Produced by: The Community Council of Lancashire, 15 Victoria Road, Fulwood, Preston PR2 8PS (01772-717461)

A–Z of fundraising ideas

A is for...   Antique Show, Auction, Anything Annual

B is for...   Birthday Cakes, Barbecues, Bingo, Buy-a-Brick, Bazaars

C is for...   Concerts, Cookies, Carol Singing, Car Washes, Car Boot Sales, Coffee Mornings, Cookbook

D is for...   Duck (plastic) Racing, Dinner Party, Dutch Auction, Discos

E is for...   Exhibitions, Eating, Everything Extreme (lowest, highest, fastest, slowest etc.)

F is for...   Fasts, Fetes, Fairs, Festivals, Face Painting, Fashion Shows, Fun Runs

G is for...   Garden Parties, Gardening, Growing (bulbs, plants, vegetables etc.), Guess the Weight, Gang Shows

H is for...   Highland Games

I is for...   It's a Knockout, Italian Evening

J is for....   Jumble Sales, Jam Making, Junk Mail/Newspaper Collection

K is for...   Knitting, Kite Making

L is for...   Lunches, Lotteries

M is for...   Marathons, Merchandise, Meals on Heels, Mammoth Markets

N is for...   Newspaper Recycling, Naming (dolls, teddies, animals etc.)

O is for...   Olympics, Open House, Old Time Music Hall, One Hundred Club

P is for...   Promise Auction, Performances

Q is for...   Quizzes, Quilts

R is for...   Raffles, Rallies, Races

S is for...   Swimathons, Show (art, craft, fashion etc.), Scavenger Hunts, Sales, Stalls, Something Sponsored

T is for...   Three Peaks, Tournaments, Tombolas, Talent Competition, Treasure Hunts

U is for...   Unusual, Unwanted Gift Sales

V is for...   Vouchers, Valeting (car)

W is for...   Wine-tasting, Welly Wanging, Walks (guided, ghostly, sponsored etc.)

X is for...   Xmas (parties, fairs, cards etc.)

Y is for...   Yodelling (sponsored, competition)

Z is for...   Zany

Chapter 6

The National Lottery

The story so far

The National Lottery started giving grants in 1995. In their first three years, the National Lottery boards distributed over £4.2 billion to good causes, in more than 18,000 grants. By 2001, when the Camelot licence is up for renewal, the distribution bodies for the five good causes will have given away around £10 billion. By the end of 1996, organisations working with young people had received over £150 million from the Charities Board alone. The Lottery Boards are not just major grant givers in their own right; they have also had a tremendous impact upon how other grant giving bodies do business with those who apply for funds.

How to use this chapter

As work with young people comes under so many headings, and as each of the eleven Lottery Boards operates independently of the others, those running youth projects have a number of options when it comes to approaching the Lottery. To make the

> **Please note**
>
> These are early days with the National Lottery and the situation is changing all the time. The information in this chapter was correct as of mid-1997, but check for the up-to-date position before you apply.

information easier to get to grips with, we have first described what each board is interested in, and given some examples of grants made to projects including young people. Read this first. Decide which broad category your project comes under. Then look at the "How to apply" section which follows. There are also hints and tips on preparing your application, supporting documentation, and a Charities Board assessor's view.

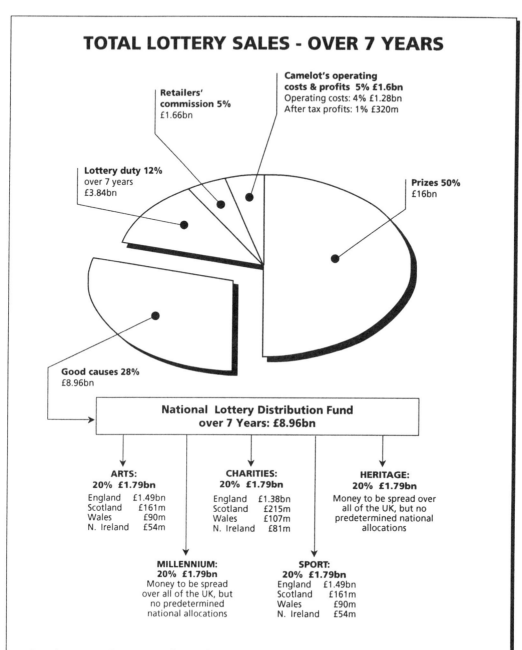

TOTAL LOTTERY SALES - OVER 7 YEARS

Camelot's operating costs & profits 5% £1.6bn
Operating costs: 4% £1.28bn
After tax profits: 1% £320m

Retailers' commission 5%
£1.66bn

Lottery duty 12%
over 7 years
£3.84bn

Prizes 50%
£16bn

Good causes 28%
£8.96bn

**National Lottery Distribution Fund
over 7 Years: £8.96bn**

**ARTS:
20% £1.79bn**

England	£1.49bn
Scotland	£161m
Wales	£90m
N. Ireland	£54m

**CHARITIES:
20% £1.79bn**

England	£1.38bn
Scotland	£215m
Wales	£107m
N. Ireland	£81m

**HERITAGE:
20% £1.79bn**
Money to be spread over all of the UK, but no predetermined national allocations

**MILLENNIUM:
20% £1.79bn**
Money to be spread over all of the UK, but no predetermined national allocations

**SPORT:
20% £1.79bn**

England	£1.49bn
Scotland	£161m
Wales	£90m
N. Ireland	£54m

Camelot's original projections for the flows of money over the full seven years of its licence are set out in the chart above. However, it is now expected that the total availablle for the Good Causes will be nearer £10 billion than £8.96 billion. In November 1997 the original distributors agreed to a reduction in their share of the take, to prepare for the 'sixth' good cause, the New Opportunities Fund being introduced by the Labour Government.

The National Lottery distribution boards

The National Lottery Distribution Fund passes lottery money to the distribution boards which allocate an equal amount of money to each of the five good causes The boards are:

- The **National Lottery Charities Board**
- The **Arts Councils** in England, Scotland, Northern Ireland and Wales
- The **Sports Councils** in the same countries
- The **Heritage Lottery Fund**
- The **Millennium Commission**.

A sixth distribution mechanism is being developed through the People's Lottery proposals of the new Labour Government. This New Opportunities Fund is of particular interest to youth groups because one of its first initiatives will be to fund after-school clubs.

The National Lottery Charities Board

- This covers any UK organisation set up for charitable, benevolent or philanthropic purposes. You do not have to be a registered charity, but you must have a constitution or a set of rules defining your aims, objectives, and procedures. Branches can only apply individually if they have sufficient independence.
- Grants can be given for both revenue and capital projects. The minimum grant is £500, and the maximum so far has been £682,000 (1995/96), although it is unlikely that anyone will receive more than £500,000 from now on.
- You do not need partnership funding for a Charities Board grant.
- Grants are awarded at present in separate grants "rounds", each with its own theme. The money is given out by five national committees (England, Wales, Scotland, Northern Ireland and the UK). Once you have received Charities Board money, you cannot apply again to that national committee until you have spent it. All applications are assessed by the Board's assessors.

> **Which board? An at a glance guide to which board does what.**
>
> **The National Lottery Distribution Boards were set up to support the following good causes:**
>
> - Arts – gives capital and revenue grants; partnership funding required
> - Charities and voluntary organisations – gives capital and revenue grants; no partnership funding required
> - Heritage – capital grants only; partnership funding required
> - The Millennium – revenue grants for individuals
> - Sport – capital grants, and revenue funding for talented sportsmen and women; partnership funding required for capital grants.
>
> Partnership funding can be raised from the local authority, central government, quangos, Europe, grant-making trusts, or in some cases, from your own income.

- A small grants programme for awards up to £500 has now been introduced in some areas for organisations with an income of under £10,000 (see p81).

This is the board that has awarded the largest number of grants to young people's projects. It designated "Youth Issues and Low Income" as one of its grant-making themes in 1996.

Examples of youth projects supported in 1996 include:

- Abeng Youth Centre Ltd, Lambeth (£172,899 for youth education and training)
- Action Group for Irish Youth (£22,500 for new edition of "Guide to London")
- All Saints Youth Centre, Langley (£7,000 to repair building)
- Azaad Asian Youth Project, Middlesbrough (£54,000 for running costs)
- Bangladesh Youth Centre, Bedfordshire (£217,000 to create a resource centre)
- Blantyre Youth Development Team (£68,358 for action on youth unemployment)
- Boredom Breakers Youth Club, Worcester (£6,750 to employ a youth worker)
- Buckland Youth Activities Centre (£65,000 to develop sports area and garden)
- Cambernauld YMCA and YCA (£382,500 to establish area foyer service)
- Carlton Youth Ministry Trust Ltd (£5,801 to install a heating system)
- Carroll Youth Centre, Stanmore (£37,500 to provide a crèche)
- Church Lads Brigade, Manchester (£2,750 for adventure weekend)
- Coalition Against Crime, Tyne and Wear (£200,000 for youth opportunities)
- Drive for Youth (£100,000 for residential training)
- Emmanuel Youth Club, Exeter (£1,116 to build new meeting room)
- Fairbridge, Teesside (£90,000 to train young people as instructors)
- Foothold Youth Agency (£137,283 for running costs)
- Hand in Hand Disabled Youth Club, Hammersmith (£3,000 for social activities)
- Homes for Homeless People (£94,979 for a help-line for young homeless)
- Hyson Green Youth Club (£135,000 for training for low income youth)
- Irchin Trust (£75,000 for advocacy for young people)
- Island Youth Activities Centre, Isle of Wight (£35,908 to buy water sports equipment)
- Kids Clubs Network (£60,157 to develop after school clubs project)
- Kings Langley Youth Club (£10,383 to increase access for disabled)
- Leicester Mission for the Deaf (£93,760 for staff to help young deaf get work)
- Lincoln YMCA (£120,000 for housing for young people)
- Manchester Young People's Theatre (£15,000 for drama project for homeless)
- Young Builders' Trust (£90,000 young people building their own homes)
- Young Homelessness Forum (£69,234 to help young and single homeless)
- Youth Clubs Scotland (£36,785 to involve youth in the community)
- Youth Works (£185,500 for two estate environment projects)
- Youthaid (£89,800 for help for unemployed young people)
- Zone Youth Project, Nottingham (£250,000 to set up youth project)
- 1st S. Normanton Scouts and Guides (£59,300 to replace scout hut)
- 1st Wood End Guides (£3,600 for camping equipment)
- 6th Carshalton Scouts (£1,000 for free places for low income scouts)
- 6th Dagenham Scouts (£20,000 for minibus)

The Arts Councils

- Criteria for grants varies between the four national arts councils (addresses are given at the end of this chapter). All require some partnership funding, generally at least 25% (although can be less for some smaller grants).
- Capital projects over £2,000 will be looked at by the Arts Councils of Wales and Northern Ireland, whilst the English and Scottish Arts Councils will consider capital projects over £5,000.
- Revenue grants, for new projects only, are available in England under the Arts 4 Everyone scheme. Scotland, Wales and Northern Ireland have similar schemes.
- Applications are accepted all the time and decisions generally take up to six months.

Projects are assessed for how wide the benefit is (is it for a wide audience or just a privileged few?). Is it open and accessible to everyone, including people with disabilities? Is the organisation financially secure? Can it handle a large grant? How well has the project been designed? How will artists contribute to the project? Is it of a high artistic quality? Does it offer something different which is not currently available? How will the activity be promoted? Does it have an educational value? Does it fit in with any existing plans for the arts in the area or region?

The Lottery White Paper

In 1997 the government published a White Paper entitled *The People's Lottery*. It made four key proposals.

1. To create a sixth good cause for health, education and the environment. Entitled the New Opportunities Fund it will initially concentrate on:
- information and communications technology training for teachers and library staff
- out of school activities attached to primary and secondary schools (homework clubs etc.)
- a network of healthy living centres.

2. To improve the mechanisms for distributing lottery funds ensuring that all sections of the community benefit.

3. To establish NESTA (the National Endowment for Science, Technology and the Arts) to foster British creative talent and innovation, and allow it to flourish.

4. To improve the arrangements for the selection and regulation of the lottery operator.

Any changes are likely to take effect in 1998.

Young people's arts activities that were successful in the first year of the Lottery include:

- Abertillery Youth Band (£27,000 for instruments)
- Brent Association for Jewish Youth (£16,000 for mini van)
- Burnley Youth Theatre (£20,000 for improvement feasibility study)
- Cwmbran Young People's Centre (£37,913 for a studio)
- Lewes All Saints Arts and Youth Centre (£96,330 for roof and heating)
- Liverpool Jewish Youth Centre (£36,957 for staging and lighting equipment)
- Patrician Youth Centre, Down (£14,848 for instruments).
- Quicksilver Theatre for Children (£48,379 for a van)
- St Theresa Youth Centre, Belfast (£20,680 for improvements to dance/drama space)
- Saxilby Youth Band (£28,000 for instruments)
- Seaham Youth Theatre Group (£31,000 for equipment)
- Southend Jewish Youth Centre (£7,917 for a darkroom).

The Sports Councils

- Grants are distributed by the four national Sports Councils (addresses given at the end of this chapter), and eligibility criteria for schemes vary between them.
- Organisations *must* have the playing of sport as part of their constitution and you can only get a grant if the sport you are playing or promoting is recognised by the Sports Council (a list of recognised sports is available from the Sports Council).
- Grants are given for capital projects costing over £5,000 (over £10,000 in Scotland), and funds from other sources are needed to match the grant.
- Revenue grants are also available to help talented individuals and teams, develop coaching programmes, identify new talent and to stage international events.
- Applications can be accepted at any time.
- In England, there is an excellent Priority Area Scheme. For these areas, only 10% partnership funding is required.

Some sports projects receive support on the strength of their youth policies, and these are not easily identifiable from the grants list.

The Heritage Lottery Fund

- Grants are given for capital projects which preserve and improve specific areas of land, buildings, objects and collections of local, regional or national heritage importance (listed buildings, sites of special scientific interest, conservation areas etc.).

Examples of youth projects which have received sports grants include:

- Aberporth Youth Club (£45,000 for sports facilities)
- Batheaston Youth Club (£61,408 for extension)
- Battersea Youth Centre (£200,000 for refurbishment)
- Broadwell Youth Centre (£40,911 to convert building)
- Hayden Youth FC (£73,961 for changing rooms)
- Hinckley Boys' Club (£32,859 for women's toilets and improvements)
- Holwell Boys' Club, North Hertfordshire (£35,438 to extend clubhouse)
- Hull Young People's Institute (£143,970 for table tennis centre)
- Latika Junior Tennis Club (£16,690 for courts)
- Ledley Hall Boys' Club Trust, Belfast (£4,200 for boxing ring)
- London Borough of Southwark (£350,000 to renew Warwick Park Youth Centre)
- Milton Rovers Youth FC (£48,450 for clubhouse)
- Saints Youth Club, Lisburn (£49,077 for boxing facilities)
- Sherborne Youth Centre (£2,709 for climbing wall)
- Tiffin Boys' Club (£39,189 for a sports room)
- YMCA Southampton (£209,555 towards basketball hall)
- Youth Clubs, North Yorkshire (£84,050 for sports hall)

- These schemes will usually be for at least £10,000. Partnership funding will be required.

This board will apply to youth groups or activities where a building or piece of land of historical interest is involved, but it is an unlikely source of Lottery money for most youth groups.

The Millennium Commission

Grants were distributed by the Millennium Commission. How a project was eligible for support was undefined, but the scheme needed to be one that will enjoy public support, be a lasting monument, have partnership funding of at least 50%, and would not be able to go ahead without Lottery funding. Large capital landmark projects have been supported with up to £50 million. However, the third (and probably final) round of applications under this programme closed at the end of 1996, and it is unlikely that further capital grants will be made by the Millennium Commission.

£200 million is also being made available under the **Millennium Award Scheme**. The purpose of the scheme is to provide bursaries to enable individuals to "achieve their potential, enriching their lives and their communities in the new millennium" and, for the first few years of the scheme, will focus on the theme "You and Your Community". The Awards will enable individuals, on their own or with others, to undertake activities for which they would otherwise not have been properly resourced. An example in the youth field is the £2 million to the British Council, announced in November 1997, to offer young adults the opportunity to undertake an international experience that will benefit their local communities.

Applying to the National Lottery

When you have decided which board is most appropriate for your project, you need to get full details and an application pack. Each board has a different application procedure. However, they all welcome enquiries and questions. At each point, even at the earliest stage when you are telephoning to make enquiries about applications, list all the questions you want to ask. This will save you time and money and will ease the process for you and the board. You will also need to do some preliminary work before you apply, particularly if partnership funding is needed or you need to show how you work together with other bodies.

The Charities Board

This is the most common way for youth projects to apply for Lottery funds. Grants range from £500 to £500,000 and are available for capital and revenue purposes. You do not need matched funding.

By the end of 1996, the following Millennium Award schemes had been approved:

British Trust for Conservation Volunteers Millennium Awards
£3 million for 1,000 awards for training/experience in environmental and conservation activities.
Contact: 01491-839766

Help the Aged Millennium Awards
£2.5 million for 1,250 awards for helping people over 60 in rural areas to share their experience with local communities.
Contact: 0171-253 0253

The Prince's Trust Millennium Awards
£2.7m for 2,500 awards for disadvantaged young people aged 14-25 on projects to benefit local communities.
Contact: 0171-543 1243

Birmingham Partnership for Change Millennium Awards
£1.4m for 450 awards for skill building activities for people of African and Caribbean origin.
Contact: 0121-236 4010

MIND Millennium Awards
£1m for 500 awards to help people with emotional distress develop their potential.
Contact: 0181-519 2122

Arthritis Care Millennium Awards
£1m for 300 awards to train people with arthritis help others in a similar position.
Contact: 0171-916 1500

CSV Scotland Millennium Awards
£600,000 for 160 awards for mentoring and training for Glasgow people who are disadvantaged socially or economically.
Contact: 0141-204 1681

Tyne and Wear Foundation Millennium Awards
£600,000 for 120 awards for formal and informal training for community leaders.
Contact: 0191-222 0945

Raleigh International Millennium Awards
£1.9m for 360 awards for 10 week overseas projects for young people from Leeds and two other cities.
Contact: 0171-371 8585

Royal Society/BAAS Millennium Awards
£1.7m for 500 awards for scientists and engineers to stimulate public awareness of their fields.
Contact: 0171-973 3500

Earthwatch Europe Millennium Awards
£1.4m for 550 awards for teachers and educators to join in international environmental projects.
Contact: 01865-516366

Farmington Institute Millennium Awards
£700,000 for 75 awards for sabbatical terms for teachers involved in religious education.
Contact: 01865-271965

Techniquest Millennium Awards
£300,000 for 30 awards for science popularisers in Wales.
Contact: 01222-475475

Grants are given out in separate rounds, each with its own theme. They fit within the board's general aim of helping "those at most disadvantage in society, and to improve the quality of life in the community". Since 1995, three rounds have been completed. The themes of the grants so far have been:

- improving the quality of life for people and communities in the UK who are disadvantaged by poverty (summer/autumn 1995)
- youth issues and help for those on low incomes (winter 1995/spring 1996)
- health, disability and care issues (summer/autumn 1996)
- providing people with new opportunities and choices (spring1996/ summer1997)
- improving people's living environment (summer 1997/winter 1998)
- promotion of community involvement (summer 1998/winter 1998).

It is intended that from 1998, the Charities Board will move away from its present cycle of grants rounds to a system of continuously open applications for the central themes of poverty and disadvantage, but supplemented by additional rounds for specific topics such as overseas grants, medical research and the like.

A small grants scheme for grants between £500 and £5,000 has been launched on a pilot basis in a few areas only, and is directed at smaller groups and organisations which have an income of less than £10,000 each year (see p77).

Who can apply?

To apply for money from the Charities Board, you have to be a charitable, benevolent or philanthropic organisation. You do not have to be a registered charity, but you must have a written constitution and your organisation should not be about self-interest, private benefit or personal profit. You should also not be party political.

When applying, you will need your constitution to hand as well as your latest annual accounts. If you do not have annual accounts, you should have evidence of some other system of financial reporting, such as an income and expenditure account, or recent bank statements. If you are very new, you should give estimates of income and expenditure for the first year.

There are five different committees giving out Charities Board money, namely the England, Scotland, Wales, Northern Ireland and UK boards. (England is sub-divided into regions for assessment purposes.) You can make separate applications to each of the committees and, in theory, can have five Charities Board projects running at once. It depends on where the beneficiaries of the project live, not where you are based. However, once you are in receipt of money from that particular board (say the Scotland board) you cannot get any more until you have spent it. However, you can still get money from the other four committees (i.e. England, Wales, Northern Ireland and UK) if you also have projects in those countries.

Types of grant

There are a number of restrictions relating to the size and types of grants you can get. You can apply for:

- one, two or three year funding
- some or all of the project's costs
- revenue costs (including core costs, as long as they are not being paid for by anyone else)
- capital costs
- matching funds for European Union funds.

You cannot normally apply for:

- endowments
- loans or loan payments
- retrospective funding
- making up deficits
- promoting particular religious beliefs
- sports, art or heritage projects (as these are the responsibility of other Lottery boards).

No grants will be awarded which replace (or may replace) lost statutory funding, nor where the money will subsidise statutory provision, nor where it will make up a deficit on a service otherwise funded by the state. This provision is rigorously enforced and may be a problem for many youth organisations.

How much to apply for

The amount you ask for should be:

- realistic for the size of your organisation
- reflect the actual cost of the project.

The minimum grant is £500; you are unlikely to get more than £500,000. If the project cost is more than £200,000 (even if you ask the Charities Board for less than £200,000), you must supply a business plan for the project (rather than the organisation as a whole). The Charities Board can ask you for a business plan for the project even if the project totals less than £200,000.

If you apply for two or three year grants, you will need income and expenditure projections for each year, clear targets, monitoring arrangements and a description of how the project will be financed after the Charities Board funding runs out (if you want it to carry on, that is).

If you apply for a capital grant, you should usually base them on quotes or estimates. These should also include associated costs such as maintenance, running costs and insurance.

What the Board wants to see in an application

The Charities Board assesses all applications on the same set of criteria.

- Is the organisation financially sound and well managed? For example, does it produce annual accounts which show a reasonable surplus? Do you pay your bills on time? Do you have a reasonable amount of money in the bank? Does the management committee meet regularly and review what is going on? Does the organisation have a good track record in delivering the kinds of services it is wanting funding for?
- Is the project properly planned and organised, and staffed appropriately? Is there a project plan? Does it seem sensible? Has it got measurable targets? Are they realistic? Are the management structures clear?
- Is the budget accurate and does it offer value for money? Are all costs covered, including overheads? Do they seem appropriate for the work that is being done? Can you show that this is money being very well spent?
- Will the project be monitored and evaluated in a meaningful way? Are there clear targets for the project? Will there be regular progress reviews? What will happen if they are not met?
- What will happen when the Charities Board money runs out? Will the project simply stop? If you want it to continue, how is it going to be funded (not by the Charities Board)?
- Show that you are committed to equal opportunities. A statement on a piece of paper is not enough. You have to show that you are genuinely representative of your community at management committee level, among the project leaders, volunteers and users. If you are not, what are you doing about it? (The argument that "I don't think we have those kinds of people here" does not carry much weight.) How many people with disabilities are involved in your activities? What access do you offer to people with special needs?
- How does the project encourage the people who benefit to be involved in the planning and running of the project. The Charities Board is very serious about self-help and user involvement. You need to show that you have actively consulted young people in the planning of the project and how they will be part of the management, monitoring and evaluation of what is happening (e.g. by setting up a project steering committee which will include users).

The Board also takes very careful note of how the project fits into their programme for that particular round. For example, in round four (New Opportunities & Choices), there were six programme criteria to choose from, one of which was: To what extent will your project extend opportunities to individuals and groups which currently do not have access to mainstream education, training, or education opportunities?

There are two ways in which you show how you fulfil all the above:
- By filling out the application form. Many of the questions are very clearly aimed to answer one or more of the above questions.

What does the application form ask for?

The application form is lengthy. It is divided into a number of sections. Broadly these cover:

1. Information about your *organisation*, its legal and financial status, its aims and objectives, its size and the number of employees.

2. Details about the specific *project* you are applying for. This will include a short description, the benefits the project will bring, which users were involved in its creation, and how it fits in with the Board's current grants theme.

3. Details about the *beneficiaries* of the project, who and where they are, how they will be involved in the planning and running of the project and how they will have access to what is going on.

4. Information about the *financial* implications of the proposal. This will be items such as the amount you are asking for from the Board, the total project costs (broken down over a three-year period if appropriate), as well as any money you have already raised and where else (if anywhere) you are going to apply to for more.

5. Details of whether you have previously applied to the Charities Board or other Lottery boards, the name and signature of an independent referee, a standard declaration to be signed by a member of your organisation, and a checklist of what documentation must be returned for your application to be assessed.

■ By giving additional information to the assessor either by telephone or face to face (see below).

It is essential to bear the above criteria in mind when filling out the application form. Try to ask yourself: "Which of the criteria is this question getting at and how do I show that we can meet it?"

How to apply

Obtain an application form. You will need to ring the National Lottery Charities Board's application line (0345-919191 for English speakers and 0345-273273 for Welsh speakers). You will be asked a few simple questions to check your organisation's eligibility before a pack is sent out. *You cannot obtain an application pack by writing to any of the Charities Board's offices or by calling any other number.*

Application packs will be specific to the grants programme that is the current focus for the Charities Board, and will therefore only be available for a limited time. Application forms that apply to previous grants themes will not be eligible for subsequent grants rounds. When you are sent an application pack, it will have your organisation's name and address and unique reference number. This application form can *only* be used for your organisation, and you cannot use a copy of another organisation's form to apply. If you use the wrong form to apply, you will automatically not be eligible for a grant.

You need to complete the form and get it back before the deadline for that particular programme. You must send the form back to the Admail address using the pre-addressed envelope provided (do not send it to your regional or national office).

The application pack has a helpful Guide to Applicants which includes a large section on How to Complete the Application Form. Make sure you read this carefully before filling out the form.

How will the application be assessed?

Your application should be acknowledged within 14 days of the Charities Board receiving it and checking it for eligibility and completeness. They may also request further information at this stage to help assess your application.

The application form is then passed to the most relevant country office – England, Scotland, Wales or Northern Ireland. (The country office will be decided on where most of your proposed beneficiaries live, rather than where your organisation is located.)

Once the grants officer has made sure that your form and supporting documentation is complete, the application is passed to one of the Charities Board's assessors to evaluate the application. These assessors will look at your application and may need to seek out further information, usually directly from you.

The assessor may contact you either to arrange a visit or to discuss your application over the telephone. Either way they will want to gain a complete understanding of what you are hoping to do and your organisation's ability to do it. You may also be asked to provide up-to-date financial information, and to explain your plans more fully.

> ### What if we have problems with the assessment criteria?
>
> The essential point to get over to the assessor is that you are taking active steps to resolve the difficulties. For example, if you have lost money for each of the last three years and it would appear that your finances are not sound, you will need to draw up a business plan which shows how you are going to stop the rot. Or if you live in a multi-ethnic area but have no leaders from different ethnic groups, show what steps you are now taking (e.g. working with appropriate agencies, discussing the situation with relevant community leaders, leafleting and advertising in different places) to achieve a better balance.

Remember, you are still being assessed on the criteria described above, so try to make sure your answers show how well planned the project is, how soundly financed you are, how users will be involved in running the project or whatever.

Assessors can ask you for a lot of information. A three hour telephone call is not uncommon (do not worry, it's their bill!). Do not assume that if you are visited rather than telephoned by an assessor, you are more likely to get a grant. Remember too, that assessors do not have powers to decide who receives grants and who does not – only committees of the Charities Board have this authority. Assessors only prepare numerically based reports on the application.

Whilst you cannot ring the assessor to get information about how to complete your application, your local council for voluntary service (CVS) may have advice on how to fill in the form. Ring them if you need more help. Alternatively, the Directory of Social Change runs training courses on how to apply (ring 0171-209 4949).

In the case of UK, Scotland, Northern Ireland or Wales a decision will be made the country office. In England, one of the nine Regional Advisory Panels will look at the application and assessor's report and then make recommendations to the England Committee of the National Lottery Charities Board.

Trouble-shooting your own Charities Board application

- Is the proposal clear and realistic? Bigger sums of money will be harder to get approval for and will need more supporting documentation. If the project totals over £200,000 you will need a business plan. If the proposal is too ambitious, can you scale it down e.g. convert one floor of a building rather than refurbish the whole structure?
- Are the organisational details correct? Check carefully.
- Are your costings as accurate and precise as you can make them?
- If you applying for a building grant, what are your plans for disabled access?
- How precise is the proposal? If it is too vague an idea, think again.
- Have you included copies of all relevant information? Incomplete information will delay the whole process.
- Make sure all the relevant questions have been answered. Make a copy of everything you send off to the Charities Board.

These decisions are final. If you are successful and your application is to be funded, a letter will be sent stating the amount of the grant, how it will paid, over what period it will be available, and the terms and conditions which apply. If you are unsuccessful, you will receive a letter of rejection, but this will not include any explanation of why you have been turned down. The Charities Board are determined not to get into discussions about why applications fail. If you are unsuccessful, you can apply in a subsequent grants round if you have a project that fits that theme.

You will be expected to show that your organisation can cope with the additional work and responsibility that a Lottery grant will bring. You should be confident in your ability to do this, whatever the size of grant you are applying for.

The Small Grants Scheme

The Charities Board has developed a grants scheme specifically for small organisations. At the end of 1997 it is operating only in Scotland, Wales and the NE and SW regions of England.

Please note the following:

- If you are a small organisation you do not have to apply just to the Small Grants scheme. You can apply to the main programme.
- However, the rule about not having money from more than one Charities Board grants committee at once still applies (see above). Therefore, if your project is in Wales, for example, you cannot get money from the Charities Board main programme in Wales and a Small Grant in Wales. You could, though, receive money from the Wales Board and a small grant from England if you had separate projects, one benefiting people in Wales and one for people in England.

Who can apply?

Any organisation which is eligible for a Charities Board grant (see above) and:

- You need a grant of between £500 and £5,000
- Your income last year was under £10,000.

When can you apply?

At any time. The small grants scheme is open all the time. There are no grants rounds or grant themes.

What can you apply for?

The Charities Board gives the following examples of grants:
- equipment and computers
- training courses
- publicity materials
- fees
- feasibility studies
- start-up costs
- events
- volunteer expenses
- conference and seminar costs
- repairs
- travel and outings
- other items to help you run your group and provide services.

You can apply for things other than those listed above. But you have to buy the equipment or complete the activity within three months of the grant being paid.

You *cannot* apply for the following:
- rent
- community charges and utilities
- endowments
- loan payments
- activities promoting religious beliefs
- uniforms or outfits
- second-hand vehicles
- costs which have already been incurred.

How to apply

You need an application form from the Charities Board (ring 0345-919191). It is simpler and shorter than the form for the main programme, so you may be telephoned for more information. They will be looking at:
- how well the grant will meet the needs of disadvantaged people;
- how effectively the grant will be used;
- how realistic and appropriate the costs are.

How to get the most from a National Lottery Charities Board assessor's visit or call

1. Remember that not all assessors have a youth work background. Do not assume too much knowledge of what you are trying to do and how you do it.

2. Have all your documentation to hand. If an assessor rings and you do not feel prepared with the necessary information, ask for another more convenient time when you will be organised. Ask what information they will be looking for so that you can everything ready. An assessment phone call is lengthy, between one and three hours. It will save you time and stress, and make the assessor's job easier, if you are organised and prepared.

3. Remember that assessors are human. There is no need to go over board but make sure they feel welcome. Cocktails and canapés are too much, but coffee and biscuits will probably be welcome.

4. If you are having an assessment visit, make sure that the person conducting the tour and answering the questions knows the details of the application.

5. Be open and honest. Do not be over the top or try to cover the cracks. If your organisation is perfect, why do you need the money anyway?

6. See the assessment as a discussion not an interrogation.

7. Use friendly, jargon-free language. Be straightforward in your answers.

8. If your proposal is for a mini-bus or a building or a salary, you may need to supply copies of your supporting documentation to the assessor if they do not have them.

9. Keep a record of what you have been asked for. This will help you after the assessment to make sure you have fulfilled your side of things. At key points in the conversation, ask the assessor to reflect back his or her understanding of what has been said. This will avoid misunderstandings.

10. At the end of the assessment, do not be afraid to ask questions about anything you are unsure of. It should be a two-way process, and this is your chance to get some first-hand knowledge of when you can expect to hear, what happens next, or anything else that is needed.

The Arts Councils

The Arts Councils have exactly the same amount of Lottery money as the Charities Board to distribute. Obviously it is all tied to the arts and most of it is given in capital grants (buildings and equipment), although some new – and important – revenue programmes have been set up. However, you will need to show that your project meets clear artistic needs.

The minimum grant for capital projects is £5,000 in England and Scotland (£2,000 in Wales and Northern Ireland) and you need to show where partnership funding (usually at least 25%) is being raised from.

Revenue grants range from £500 to £500,000. At least 10% (15% if the project is over £100,000) must be in partnership funding.

It is wise to work out your application with the help either of your local regional arts board, or your local authority arts officer, or the association for the particular kind of art concerned.

Who can apply?

A wide range of organisations including registered charities, non-profit distributing bodies, local authorities, schools, colleges, universities, amateur or voluntary arts groups, and public sector agencies.

Individuals cannot apply on their own behalf for Lottery funds from any of the Arts Councils.

What will be funded?

All forms of the arts are eligible including:

- architecture
- circus
- crafts
- dance
- drama
- film
- the moving image
- literature
- mime

Arts Council of England tips for applicants

- Seek the advice and help of the lottery officer at your regional arts board when you are preparing your application. Many of the regional arts boards run workshops and advice surgeries.

- Be ambitious. Arts organisations are used to a "funding drought" and often have had to cut corners. Lottery funding is different as higher quality bids have the greatest chances of success, especially if these result in lower running costs in the long term.

- Think creatively about your capital needs. Do not automatically assume that you have no current requirements for capital support.

- Organisations which are not specifically "arts" based, should consider applying for Lottery money to fund eligible areas of their work. (This should include youth organisations running arts activities or facilities.)

- Above all, make sure that you fulfil the eight criteria (capital projects; public access; long-term financial viability; quality of design; quality of artistic activity; relevance to other areas of the arts; demand not currently met; education and marketing plans) that the Arts Council for England uses to assess applications. **The present situation is that if your organisation is eligible and your project meets the criteria, a grant will almost certainly be awarded.**

- music
- photography
- video
- the visual arts
- any combination of these (such as arts centres and festivals).

Capital projects

Grants for capital projects include the construction of new buildings, purchase or extensions of buildings, improvement or refurbishment of old buildings, architectural design competitions and feasibility studies, purchase of equipment, instruments or vehicles, production of a film, and commissioning works of public art. The minimum grant is £5,000 (in England and Scotland) and £2,000 (in Wales and Northern Ireland).

> **The situation with Arts Lottery funding is changing all the time. This section is simply a general guide. It does not take account of all the differences between the various Arts Councils. Ring to check the latest position before thinking seriously about applying.**

Assessment criteria

The project will be assessed on the following basis:

- The benefit to the public (including maximum access for disabled people).
- The long-term effect on the organisation's financial stability. You need to show that you are viable in the long term and have a clear and comprehensive management plan (which includes budgets and timetables) controlled by a named manager.
- The amount of partnership funding (generally at least 25% for projects over £100,000 and 10% for projects under £100,000).
- The quality of design and construction.
- The quality of artistic activities planned.
- The relevance of projects to local, regional and national arts plans.
- The contribution of artists, crafts people and film and video makers – they should be consulted about planning and design, employed as part of the design and construction team, and be consulted about purchases of equipment.
- The quality of the organisation's plans for education and marketing.

How to apply for capital projects

1. Obtain an application pack

From the Arts Council in the country where your project is based.

2. Submit Advance Notice Form

This gives basic details about the project (including a brief project description, total project cost and amount requested from the Arts Council). This must be done at least four weeks before submitting a full application.

3. Receive acknowledgement of Advance Notice

You will be sent an acknowledgement of receipt of the Advance Notice and this will include your application number for the full proposal.

4. Return application form

This is highly detailed and includes information on:

- The organisation.
- The project (timetables, cash flows, art forms, preparations undertaken etc.).
- Benefits of the project (including how you will reach the widest possible audience, how it fits with local authority plans to develop the arts, how the needs of disabled people will be addressed).
- If the project includes a building, who will manage the project and their level of experience, how design/architecture agencies have been chosen, what planning permissions have been obtained.
- Supporting documents such as constitutions, accounts, detailed and comprehensive project description, financial projections, equal opportunities policy, strategic monitoring form (provided with the application pack), access checklist (provided with applications pack), at least three competitive quotations for equipment, vehicles and so on.
- Additional documentation if required such as relevant market research, education and audience development plan, marketing strategy, recent promotional materials, architectural plans, photographs and so on.

5. Receive acknowledgement

Once you have applied you will receive an acknowledgement of your application.

6. Consultation process

Your application will be processed by a named Lottery Officer, who will consult with other relevant bodies (e.g. Arts Council departments, Regional Arts Board, British Film Institute, Crafts Council). The Lottery Officer may contact you for more information.

7. Decision

A decision is then made by the Arts Council National Lottery Panel. The Lottery Officer will then present your application to the Arts Council National Lottery Panel (Lottery Committee in Scotland; Lottery Advisory Board in Wales; Lottery Committee in Northern Ireland). This body will then make a recommendation to the national arts council which will say whether the application should be accepted or rejected. You will be informed "as soon as possible". Applications generally take three to six months to assess.

Revenue project grants

In 1996, the government allowed a range of non-capital arts programmes to be set up. These were to create new artistic opportunities and provide individuals from every cultural, financial and geographical background with new opportunities to enjoy cultural activities as creators, participants and audiences. It is intended to support a much broader range of activity than either the Lottery capital grants or the mainstream Arts Council revenue grants.

The new programmes are called *Arts 4 Everyone* and *Arts 4 Everyone Express* (in England) and *New Directions* and the *Advancement Programme* (Scotland). There are similar programmes in Wales.

Whatever the names, the schemes will offer funding for:

- Non-capital projects
- The creation of new work
- Opportunities to reach new or develop existing audiences
- Encouraging new audiences to experience high quality arts activity
- Training and professional development.

The schemes are particularly concerned to give people from all walks of life a chance to participate in arts and cultural activities, and to give young people a chance to realise creative potential.

They will not fund
- Individuals
- Training and educational institutions for services that are part of their statutory job
- Organisations who have received an Arts 4 Everyone grant within the last two years, or whose previously funded project is still unfinished.

Arts 4 Everyone

This is a new Lottery scheme in England which aims to reach new audiences and to involve new groups in the arts. The two parts of the scheme are *Arts 4 Everyone* and *Arts 4 Everyone Express* and both look to encourage more young people to become involved in the arts. This scheme is particularly good for groups which may not have any experience of raising money for arts activities. However, the *Arts 4 Everyone Express* programme was launched on a pilot basis and may not be repeated.

Like other Lottery arts awards, you will have to find some partnership funding of at least 10% of the total cost of the project. At least 5% must be cash, and the rest can be in kind such as buildings, volunteer work or materials.

Your project will qualify if it meets at least one of the following:

- Encouraging and developing participation in arts activity – helping people take part in the arts through voluntary and non-professional organisations;

- Getting more young people actively involved in arts and cultural activities – the intention is to support and develop the talents and skills of those under the age of 30;
- Supporting new work and helping it develop its audience – the funds are intended to stimulate new work which is then promoted and presented in a way that builds an audience for it;
- Building people's creative potential through training or professional development – including work experience, training, study or international exchange;
- Encouraging new audiences to experience high-quality arts activity.

> **Examples of Arts 4 Everyone Express youth grants given in Berkshire**
>
> - Newbury Young Stars, Young Stars Showcase (£3,975)
> - Newbury Youth Theatre, Junior section and outreach initiative (£5,000)
> - Alfred Sutton Playground Group, Gateways (£3,300)
> - Creative Kids After School Arts Club (£4,000)
> - Noise Cage Youth Culture Magazine (£5,000)
> - Woodley Airfield Intermediate Youth Club (£900)
> - Earley Youth Arts Project (£3,330)
> - Youthreach (Wokingham district) Artsreach (£4,000)

How to apply

The application and selection procedure has been made as simple as possible.

- Firstly, contact your regional arts board for information on applying. Your local authority may also have advice on how your project fits in with local plans.
- You will need two referees to confirm that the project is viable, and that it should be funded. One should be from a formally constituted organisation (e.g. local authority, theatre, TEC etc.) and the other can be someone who knows your group, but will not benefit directly form the grant (e.g. councillor, youth officer etc.).
- Complete the form. The Arts Council have kept this as simple and straightforward as possible. Regional arts boards will be able to help if you need it.
- Wait for the decision. During the trial period, decisions were to be made within eight weeks of receiving the application.

The Scottish Dimensions and Advancement programmes are similar but by no means identical. Ring the Scottish Arts Council Lottery Unit on 0131-243 2443/4 for further information.

The Sports Councils

Any youth club or group can apply for Sports Lottery funds as long as it has all the following:

- a constitution
- promotion of a recognised sport as part of the constitution
- membership is open to all parts of the community
- wide public access will be provided to the facility.

Therefore, you will need to check your constitution. If you do not have the playing of sport as a recognised part of your constitution you cannot receive money from the Sports Council. Children's play activities are not eligible either, although "mini" versions of recognised sports (e.g. mini rugby) are eligible.

The minimum capital grant is £5,000 (£10,000 if you are in Scotland).

So, if you need a new table tennis table for your youth club you may well be ineligible before you start because of the following:

- Your constitution does not allow you to apply because you do not have the playing of sport as an objective.
- The minimum grant is £5,000, much more than the kind of £350 table tennis table you are likely to be after!

Grants are also only available to organisations involved with sports which are recognised by the Sports Council (a full list is available from the Sports Council). You may need to be affiliated to the sport's national governing body for safety reasons. Again, the Sports Council will tell you if there is this additional requirement for your application.

Revenue grants

There are various new revenue grants programmes. These are:

- The World Class Performance Programme – to help national sports governing bodies develop structures to enable individuals and teams compete at the highest level
- Subsistence awards – to help elite individuals compete at the highest level
- Major international events – to help bid for Olympic or Paralympic Games or other prestigious events (none of which are in the scope of the average youth group!)
- Coaching, leadership and talent identification programmes – details will be available at the end of 1997.

None of the above are likely to come within the orbit of most youth groups. However, youth groups have had success with the capital grants programme (discussed below). Further information on any of the above revenue programmes is available from the Sports Council.

Capital facilities funding

Despite the introduction of the above revenue programmes, most of the Sports Council grants will be used for capital projects. Eligible schemes include the following:

- New, upgraded or extended playing facilities
- Buying major, permanently-based equipment
- Essential support facilities
- Refurbishment schemes
- Purchase of land/water/facilities.

Preference is given to projects that cater for the widest possible cross-section of people, and especially when they encourage people who do not usually have much opportunity for sport and recreation.

No grants will be given for:

- Renewals, repairs and maintenance
- Transport (team buses, vans etc.)
- Support facilities
- Personal equipment.

This is a list of some of the low priority projects:

- Spectator stands or other provision for non-participants
- Artificial surfaces without floodlighting
- Outdoor swimming pools
- Floodlighting for grass match pitches simply to meet league requirements
- Automatic watering systems for bowling greens/golf tees
- Car parks
- Perimeter fencing (unless for security reasons)
- Informal recreation projects (e.g. footpaths, cycle tracks) unless they can clearly demonstrate improved access/participation
- Stand alone social facilities (or projects only concerned with social facilities)
- Kitchens and bars (unless an integral part of a large scheme)
- Finishing off projects which have already started
- Maintenance projects
- Office administrative equipment or accommodation
- Second hand equipment (unless reconditioned and providing value for money).

Applicants are expected to find a contribution of at least 35% and ideally 50% (unless it is part of the School Community Support Initiative or Priority Areas Initiative – see below).

Criteria for applications

Applications are considered under the following general headings:

Strategic:

- Do you conform with the strategies of the Sports Council, relevant sports governing body and local authority?
- How do you fit in with other similar facilities?
- What evidence is there for unsatisfied demand?

Management and usage:

- Have you got clear aims and objectives?
- Is there a good balance between use by the community and elite performers?
- Does it have the capacity to be worthwhile (e.g. numbers of users and hours of use)?
- Does it have the commitment to use by all sectors of the community regardless of sex, race, religion or disability?

Technical:
- Does it conform with the appropriate technical specifications in the technical guidance notes?
- Will the facilities be of high quality and stand up to sustained use?

General:
- Does the proposal represent value for money?
- Can you get partnership funding?
- Can you meet the running costs?
- Can you show community support?
- What do the local authorities, sports governing bodies and other key agencies say about it?

Applications procedure

You will have to apply to your country's Sports Council. Before contacting the Sports Council you must have a reasonably well though-out project. You will be asked about it when ringing up for the applications pack. Then:

1. Ring the Sports Council Lottery Line for your application pack and your personal reference number.
2. Read the pack carefully to see if you are eligible and can meet the technical requirements.
3. Send off the consultation forms in the pack (e.g. to the local authority, local sports advisory body or other appropriate agency).
4. Complete the application and return it to the Sports Council alongside the relevant supporting materials (this does not include videos or other expensive presentations).
5. You will receive confirmation that you application has been received.
6. The Sports Council will then evaluate the project thoroughly, including consultations. This takes time.
7. The Lottery Awards Panel will then consider the application.
8. You will be told of the outcome – award, provisional award, qualified rejection or outright rejection.

The School Community Sport Initiative

This has been set up to support the establishment of successful school community facilities. Lottery funds cannot be used to fund facilities solely for curricular activities as this would not benefit the community generally. There has to be a genuine school-community partnership (including at least 40 hours a week of community use) and there must be well thought-out sports development plans. The school can get up to 80% of the funding required from the Sports Council.

For further information contact the Sports Council.

The Priority Areas Initiative

The Sports Council for England has identified 99 areas of sporting and social need where the amount of required matched funding has been reduced from 35% to 10%. (In exceptional cases it may ask for even lower amounts.) These areas are mainly in towns and cities, although rural areas may be included in any revised list. You should contact the Sports Council for a list of identified areas.

As with the other boards the Sports Council will assess the organisation's long-term financial viability and the quality of the project. There should also be clear evidence of the breadth of appeal and support and how the project will increase access to and participation in sport. As with the funding for the arts under the Lottery you should also demonstrate how your project fits in with existing plans in the sector drawn up by appropriate bodies. If, for instance, there has been a regional initiative on increasing healthy lifestyle and participation in sport for young people, the proposal should show how your plans will take this aim further.

In addition to the above criteria, the Sports Councils for Wales and Northern Ireland will look at how young people and schoolchildren are included in the proposal; how links are encouraged between schools and sports and the greater use of schools' sports facilities by the wider community; provision of multi-purpose or multi-sport facilities, and access to coaching and specialist training/playing facilities.

And finally...

To get your share of the Lottery windfall should not be a lottery in itself. We have concentrated on the National Lottery Charities Board in this chapter as this will be the Lottery distributor that attracts most applications from youth organisations. This does not mean you will not have something that fits with the other distribution boards. However, the Sports and Arts Councils have clear plans and priorities which you will have to comply with.

Also, the indications are that decisions on Lottery grants are based as much upon the record of the organisation as the strength of the project. The emphasis may increasingly be upon a "safe pair of hands" and you will need to look as carefully at how your organisation presents itself, as the quality of the activity you are proposing.

At the end of 1997 the Arts and Sports Councils, in England at least, are coming under increasing financial pressure, partly because of the reduction in their income to pay for the proposed New Opportunities Fund. In addition, the Arts Council of England has already committed much of its future income, and the English Sports Council is facing an upsurge of top quality applications, not all of which it can fund. It expects to fund fewer very large projects in the future.

Assessment Criteria – Test Your Project

Write down three things under each of the following:

1. We know we are well managed because…

....

....

....

2. We know our organisation is financially sound because…

....

....

....

3. The project will achieve the following…

....

....

....

4. We will know the project has been successful when…

....

....

....

5. The project is excellent value for money because…

....

....

....

6. We are the best people to undertake this work because…

....

....

....

7. The project is clearly sustainable because…

....

....

....

8. In three years' time, the project will be achieving…

....

....

....

9. We will finance the project in the future by…

....

....

....

Useful Addresses

Charities

UK
National Lottery Charities Board
St Vincent House
30 Orange Street
London WC2H 7HH
0171-747 5299

England
Readson House
96-98 Regent Road
Leicester LE1 7DZ
0116-258 7000

Northern Ireland
2nd Floor
Hildon House
30-34 Hill Street
Belfast BT1 2LB
01232-551455

Scotland
Norloch House
36 Kings Stables Road
Edinburgh EH1 2EJ
0131-221 7100

Wales
Ladywell House
Newtown
Powys SY16 1JB
01686-621644
Welsh speakers wanting an applications pack: 0345 273273

Arts

Arts Council of England
14 Great Peter Street
London S1P 3NQ
0171-312 0123

Arts Council of Northern Ireland
Lottery Unit
185 Stranmillis Road
Belfast BT9 5DU
01232-667000

Scottish Arts Council
12 Manor Place
Edinburgh EH3 7DD
0131-226 6051

Arts Council of Wales
Lottery Unit
Museum Place
Cardiff CF1 3NX
01222-388288

Sport

English Sports Council
16 Upper Woburn Place
London WC1H 0QP
Lottery Line 0345-649649

Sports Council for Northern Ireland
House of Sport
Upper Malone Street
Belfast BT9 ALA
01232-382222

Scottish Sports Council
Lottery Sport Fund
Caledonia House
South Gyle
Edinburgh EH12 9D
0131-339 9000

Sports Council for Wales
The Welsh Institute of Sport
Sophia Gardens
Cardiff CF1 9SW
01222-397571

Heritage

The Heritage Lottry Fund
7 Holbein Place
London SW1W 8NR
0171-591 6000

Millennium

The Millennium Commission
2 Little Smith Street
London S1P 3DH
0171-340 2030

Chapter 7

Raising money from grant-making trusts

One of the main sources of support for work with young people is that given by grant-making trusts. Not so long ago trust money would be a fairly exotic flower in the youth funding greenhouse. Now it is a central source of income, looked at and tapped into by the majority of those working with young people. To get the most from your links with trusts and to improve your applications you need to know how the trust world works and what trusts are looking to give money for.

This chapter does not give a definitive listing of trusts interested in supporting young people. The good news is that there are too many to write about in this book. There are also a number of listings and directories available which will give you detailed information on who to apply to (see box.) This chapter will set out instead some directions to consider, how you can improve your approach and some examples of how trusts fund youth work.

How are trusts run?

- **Trustees.** The key players in the trust game are the trustees. They are responsible for running the trust and, crucially, making the grant decisions. They meet every month, every three months, once a year or whenever there are enough applications to make it worthwhile – it depends on the trust.

- **Staff.** Most of the larger trusts have paid staff to administer the trust. They may have a full or part-time Secretary, Clerk or Director (the name varies). These people are not trustees, so they do not make grant decisions. However, they receive all correspondence, may visit applicants or request more information and make recommendations to trustees about whether a project is good or

---

Directories of grant-making trusts

There are a number of directories on grant-making trusts and foundations which all offer slightly different things. Ideally, you would have access to all of these:

A Guide to the Major Trusts Vol 1 and 2 1997/98 – Details of the top 1,000 trusts. Available from: The Directory of Social Change, 24 Stephenson Way, London NW1 2DP (0171-209 5151) £18.95 for each volume.

Grants for Youth Groups (B4) – The National Youth Agency information bulletin with details on around 50 trusts together with some companies and award schemes. Available from: The National Youth Agency, 17-23 Albion Street, Leicester LE1 6GD (0116-285 6789).

Focus Series: Children and Youth – one of The Charities Aid Foundation's offspring of the Directory of Grant-Making Trusts. Indexes trusts by field of interest and beneficial area. Available from: the Charities Aid Foundation, Kings Hill, West Malling, Kent ME19 4TA (01732-520 000) £19.95.

not. However, the trustees always have the final say on what is and is not supported.

- **Policies**. Most larger trusts will have grant-making policies. These will say what kinds of activity they support (e.g. environmental charities, projects for ethnic minorities), where they support them (e.g. throughout the UK, only on Merseyside, or wherever), what kinds of grants they like to give (capital or revenue) and what they will definitely not support. Trusts with such policies almost never give grants outside their stated policy. If you do not fit the criteria, do not apply.

- **Written applications**. Most trusts receive written applications. On the basis of these applications they decide who they will give a grant to and for how much. Some trusts, however, do not consider any applications at all, rather they go out and find the projects they want to support. There is nothing wrong with this. However, when a trust states that it does not respond to applications or that it only supports projects known to the trustees, unless you have a personal contact with one of the trustees, leave the trust alone.

Most grant-making trusts are swamped with applications. They could easily give their money four or five times over on the basis of applications they already receive. This does not mean that you should not apply, but rather that you will have to put time and effort into making a good application to an appropriate trust. So how do you decide who to apply to and how do you go about it?

What kind of grants do trusts give?

- **Cash.** Most trusts simply make cash donations. These vary in size depending on the annual income of the trust. However, most grants from national trusts will be in the £500 to £5,000 range, although some give up to £1 million. In the list below grants range from £500,000 to the headquarters of a mainstream youth organisation down to £150 for equipment for a very local group. Small local trusts may give as little as £10, especially where there may be a concern to give a little to a lot of applicants, rather than large grants to a few.

- **Short-term/pump priming.** Most grants are given for one to three years. Trusts do not see their role as paying for core services for a long period of time; rather, they like to kick start new and exciting projects into life and then expect someone else to take on the long-term funding. Once you have come to the end of your trust grant, it will rarely give more money for the same thing. However, you can go back for funding for a different project. Therefore, unless you are new or very small, do not ask trusts to support your organisation as a whole, rather ask them to support a particular piece of work or meet a specific need.

- **Revenue and capital.** Trusts will give grants both for revenue (salaries, rent, rates etc.) and for capital (e.g. building and equipment costs). If you are applying for revenue costs, try to show how the project will be self-funding once the trust money runs out. If it is for a capital project, show how the facility will be used and how the running costs will be met.

- **Innovation/difference.** One of the most important parts of any application to a grant-making trust is where you show what is new about your project. What makes it stand out from the crowd? Is it a brand new project? Are you moving into a new area? Do you have a new approach to a problem? Are you reaching a new group (e.g. homeless young people at risk, or those truanting from school)? Are you using new ways to solve old problems (e.g. using sport or the arts to empower young people with few skills, or using peer group education to teach about health)? Are you giving disadvantaged people new skills (e.g. encouraging local people from deprived communities to take part in youth leader training)? Do your activities break down barriers in communities in new ways (e.g. organising sports events to bring divided communities together)?

- **Not statutory.** Grant-making trusts will not fund things that they see as the responsibility of the state (i.e. that central or local government should be funding). Just because the state is cutting back on its commitments, it does not mean that trusts will automatically step in. Trust funding is certainly not a substitute for lost local authority funding.

Which trusts give money to work with young people?

A large number. Trusts may respond to your application if your activities are educational, have social welfare objectives, or just because you work with children and young people and they want to support that. It might also be that you are within a geographical area of interest, such as a town, county, region or even parish. Even if they do not have a stated priority to give to young people's activities, your work may still be eligible. A number of trusts have "General charitable purposes" as a broad description of their grant-giving. Your project will fit here as well as any other, unless they have drawn up a list of beneficiaries which remains unchanged from one year to the next. Where a trust gives to support education, you may be eligible if you work with schools or TECs or have an innovative

The Foundation for Sport and the Arts

This is one of the largest givers to sport and the arts. It gives around £2 million a month, although income fluctuates as it is funded by the football pools. Capital costs such as equipment, transport and buildings are looked at very favourably, although the foundation is now considering revenue support as well. Typical grants include: funding a sporting educational trip for a youth club; buying instruments and supporting tour costs for a youth jazz orchestra; buying video, television, OHP etc. for a regional association of youth clubs; basketball equipment for a youth and community centre; climbing wall for a district scout council; and camping and canoeing equipment for a boys' club.

An information pack and clear guidance notes are available from: The Foundation for Sport and the Arts, PO Box 20, Liverpool L13 1HB (0151-259 5505).

approach to vocational training for example. Similarly, where a trust is concerned with the environment, your young people's project to create urban green areas may fit snugly with their stated interests.

It stands to reason that the best known trusts will be the ones that receive the most applications. It is also the case that the large national trusts have the most money, unless you are very fortunate to live and work in the area where a very large local trust operates. Generally, it pays to find local trusts first to apply to, as these will have geographical limitations on the number of organisations that they can help.

Much local giving is done on a friendship basis where trustees give to projects they know and like. Sometimes they give to the same organisations year in year out. If so, try to work your way onto their list. You should make a real effort to get to know local trustees personally. At least you can send them regular information.

You can find out about local trusts by:
- word of mouth. Ask around your management committee, leaders, parents or neighbouring groups. Where someone has been successful with a local trust, build on their experience.
- your local or regional association headquarters if you have one may have details of trusts in the area.
- a local Council for Voluntary Service. The address of the nearest will be in the telephone book.
- local directories of trusts. These are produced locally by Councils for Voluntary Service and nationally by the Directory of Social Change.
- the local press. Some trusts advertise their applications procedures and closing dates through local papers or community networks. Donations to local organisations may be covered in news stories.

In recent years some areas have started large local trusts from scratch. These community trusts/foundations raise money from industry and other grant-giving bodies to then distribute in the local area. Children and young people will be a natural area of interest, and you should let them know what you are doing, and find out how they can support you.

National trusts

Where there is no local trust that works in your area you will have to throw your funding net wider to include national trusts. These usually have more money but are the most heavily applied to. They also tend to be narrower in their focus. Circular letters to them almost always fail; carefully targeted applications to relevant trusts have a much greater chance of success.

The Ten Largest Trust Givers to Young People's Work

The following trusts and foundations have stated an interest in supporting work with children and young people. Their priorities differ greatly within this field.

	Grant total	Grants to children & youth	Year
1. Children in Need	£15,326,000	£15,326,000	1995/96
2. Garfield Weston Foundation	£19,082,000	£2,396,000	1995/96
3. Rank Foundation	£6,758,000	£2,054,000	1995/96
4. Bridge House Estates	£7,130,000	£1,908,000	1995/96
5. Prince's Trust	£1,500,000	£1,500,000	
6. Tudor Trust	£16,879,000	£1,355,000	1995/96
7. Henry Smith's Charity	£12,145,000	£1,350,000	1995
8. John Lyon's Charity	£901,000	£901,000	1995/96
9. Help a London Child	£733,000	£733,000	1995/96
10. Dulverton Trust	£2,416,000	£700,000	(under "Youth and Education") 1995/96

The following are recent examples of projects and activities funded by grants from trusts. They are divided into general cost areas.

Activities

£51,000 to the Rona Trust to run sailing activities for young people (Viscount Amory's Charitable Trust)

£150 to The Chain and Sprocket Youth Motorcycle Club (Carnegie United Kingdom Trust)

£2,000 to the Boys' Brigade for sports education (Sir John Cass's Foundation)

£20,000 to the Toffee Park Youth Club for outreach work and summer trips (Cripplegate Foundation)

£25,000 to 1st Farnfield Scouts, Nottinghamshire (Sir John Eastwood Foundation)

£500 to Neighbours in Poplar for summer activities (Grocers' Charity)

£30,000 to North Bedfordshire's Scouts and Guides to improve outdoor camping facilities (Harpur Trust)

Around £17,000 to Youth for Christ (Jerusalem Trust)

£500 each to Birkenhead, Bromley and Downham, Catford and Billingam, and Worthing Boys' Clubs (Joseph Levy Charitable Foundation)

£30,000 to Brent Youth and Community Development Service for child care for a summer scheme (John Lyon's Charity)

£1,000 to St John's Youth and Community Centre, Liverpool (Moores Family Charity Foundation)

£1,000 to Youth Music Centre Education Trust (Radcliffe Trust)

£5,000 to New Horizons Youth Centre (Rowan Trust)

£1,300 to Southmead Youth Centre to stage an exhibition in Bristol City Museum (Foundation for Sport and the Arts)

£1,000 to Youthwise (Douglas Turner Trust)

£10,000 to Sutton Coldfield YMCA (29th May 1961 Charitable Trust)

£34,000 to Chester Boys' Club (Westminster Foundation)

£5,000 to Church Lads' and Church Girls' Brigade, Rotherham (Wolfson Foundation)

£5,200 to Crown and Manor Boys' Club (Geoffrey Woods Charitable Foundation)

Headquarters

£32,000 to the National Association of Boys' Clubs (Beaverbrook Foundation)

£20,000 to the Association of Combined Youth Clubs to run a training programme for youth workers (Sir John Cass's Foundation)

£10,000 to the Northamptonshire Association of Youth Clubs (Clothworkers' Foundation and Trusts)

£30,000 to Prince's Youth Business Trust for a youth development scheme in Northumberland (Dulverton Trust)

£30,000 to St John Ambulance Association for youth training (Dulverton Trust)

£6,000 to West Yorkshire Youth Association towards training for youth workers in creative activities (Gulbenkian Foundation)

£20,000 to the Methodist Association of Youth Clubs (Maurice Laing Foundation)

£21,000 to Youth Clubs UK to set up a bursary fund for youth leaders (Lloyds TSB Foundation for England and Wales)

£50,000 to National Council for YMCAs (Peacock Charitable Trust)

£100,000 to London Federation of Clubs for Young People (29th May 1961 Charitable Trust)

£500,000 to the Scout Association (Garfield Weston Foundation)

Equipment

Up to £500 each for non-alcoholic bar, VHF radio set, rope swing, disco equipment for local organisations (Percy Bilton Charity Ltd)

£2,500 to the Rubery Youth Marching Band (Edward Cadbury Charitable Trust)

Social welfare

£3,000 to the Action Group for Irish Youth for health promotion among young Irish people (Bridge House Estates Trust Fund)

£70,000 to the Capital Housing Project for resettlement of ex-homeless young people (Bridge House Estates Trust Fund)

£10,000 to Crime Concern's Dalston Youth Project (Carlton Television Trust)

£10,000 to Cities in Schools, Knowsley for work with truanting teenagers (Ernest Cook Trust)

£15,500 to Prevention of Addiction for drugs work with young people in Islington (Cripplegate Foundation)

£20,000 to the Cedarwood Trust, Tyne and Wear for educational support for truants and young people dropping out of school (Equitable Charitable Trust)

£50,000 to the Industrial Society for the 2020 Vision Programme to improve educational opportunities for disadvantaged young people (Equitable Charitable Trust)

£31,600 to the Who Cares? Trust for a telephone and correspondence helpline for young people leaving local authority care (Esmée Fairbairn Charitable Trust)

£3,000 to Albert Kennedy Trust towards finding supportive homes for lesbian and gay teenagers (Hilden Charitable Trust)

£15,000 to Soho Housing Association towards a foyer project for young people looking for work (Pilgrim Trust)

£50,000 to Young Gloucestershire for a mobile drugs information unit (Henry Smith's (Kensington Estate) Charity)

£25,104 to Youth Clubs UK to train young English speaking radio journalists in the Ukraine (Westminster Foundation for Democracy)

Buildings

£75,000 to Young People's Hostel, Kettering (Horne Foundation)

£2,000 to Brunswick Boys' Club Trust to refurbish gym floor (John Lyon's Charity)

£5,000 to Ilkley Youth and Community Centre for essential equipment to re-open (Sir George Martin Trust)

£10,000 to Cleaton Moor Boys' Club Building Fund (Francis C Scott Charitable Trust)

£50,000 to Congleton Youth Projects (Henry Smith 's (Kensington Estate)Charity)

£30,000 to Barry YMCA to upgrade a gymnasium (Foundation for Sport and the Arts)

General costs

£45,000 over three years to LEAP Confronting Conflict, Islington (Llankelly Foundation)

£4,000 to A Voice for the Child in Care (John Lyon's Charity)

£40,000 to Somers Town Youth Service as second grant towards its youth programme (John Lyon's Charity)

£24,000 to Consett Youth Project over three years (Tudor Trust)

£30,000 to Roden Street Youth Action Group (Tudor Trust)

Employment training

£19,000 to the Unemployment Unit for training unemployed young people (Sir John Cass's Foundation)

£27,000 to Homeskills Limited, Barrow in Furness for employment training for young people (Church Urban Fund)

£10,000 to the Young Builders' Trust to train unemployed and homeless young people to build their own homes (Gulbenkian Foundation)

Salaries

Wiltshire Youth Action on Drugs (Chippenham Borough Lands Charity)

Parish youth worker, Kings Norton (Church Urban Fund)

Friends United Network (FUN) for a befriending scheme running over three years (Cripplegate Foundation)

Co-ordinator, Youth Action, Bedford (Harpur Trust)

Youth and disability officer over three years, West Midlands Rural Media Company Ltd. (Llankelly Foundation)

Administrator, YMCA, Ealing to work with homeless young people (Rank Foundation)

Training officer, Foyer Federation for Youth, to work with homeless young people (Rank Foundation)

Drugs Outreach Worker, Council for Voluntary Youth Organisations (Richmond Parish Lands Charity)

Research

£9,873 to the Trust for the Study of Adolescence for a national survey of projects involving young people with disabilities in voluntary and community work (Gulbenkian Foundation)

Note: the above examples were all taken from the most recent Guide to the Major Trusts Volume 1 listing the top 300 trusts and foundations. It should not be used as the basis for a mailing list. You should read up on the policies of all the trusts mentioned above, as well as those which have not been included and which may be interested in your work. The list is an indication of how wide the variety of work that can be supported is, and also, how many foundations can support young people.

Who to apply to and how to do it?

The crucial question in deciding whether or not to apply to a trust is: "What do we and the trust have in common?" What you want to do must meet with what the trust is seeking to fund. This may be in terms of geography, where you and a local trust operate in the same area. There may be a particular target group (e.g. young people, older people, those with disabilities, or disadvantaged people) who you want to involve in your activity and the trust wants to help. The activity itself may be an area where the foundation has a long-standing interest (e.g. diversionary activities for young people). As in most fundraising, the motto with charitable trusts might be: "Only connect".

With this is mind, you should do the following:

- Read Chapter 4 on Writing a Good Fundraising Application. The six key elements of an application are all highly relevant to trusts. It helps to be clear about all the information you need to put in before you start your serious planning.

- Devise one or a series of projects that you need money for. Unless you are very new or very small, it is unlikely that a trust will support your entire organisation. Rather they will want to support a particular piece of work that fits in with their specific interest. Hence the emphasis on projects. Also, make sure you can show them how your project fits into their grant-making policies.

- Work out what is new about this work. Trusts are not interested in picking up the tab to meet existing costs; they want to see something new about a project. Does it give new opportunities to needy young people? Does it try to solve a long-standing problem in a new and exciting way? Is it developing a new service in that town, village etc? If there's nothing new about the project, your chances of raising significant trust monies are remote.

- Decide how the project can be funded in the long term. Trusts generally only give grants for up to three years, but they like to see long-term benefits. You will need to persuade them that you can pay for the work once their funding has run out.

A NATIONAL TRUST AND ITS GIVING TO YOUNG PEOPLE

This trust which has asked to be unnamed in this guide is a national trust with local interests. Its income was around £166,800 in 1995/96, and grants totalled £100,600, of which £95,500 was to new beneficiaries. Although the trust operates nationally, over half (56%) its grants are given in the north-west. Furthermore, it has links with a particular company, and gives in areas where there is a company presence.

The trust has a number of priorities for its giving which are ranked in the following order: medical; welfare; education; humanities; religion and environmental. Young people come under the welfare heading, and were given £14,000 in total in 1995/96, or about 14% of the trust's total income.

The trust is typical of a number of local trusts in that whilst it has defined general areas it wants to support, its grant-giving is largely reactive and in response to unsolicited appeals.

In 1995/96, 135 grants were given. All but 18 were for less than £1,000, and most were between £100 and £500. The trust does not see its role as a strategic giver, able to support projects with large sums. Rather it is there to give small grants to a large number of beneficiaries and to therefore spread the benefit as widely as possible. Those working with young people have to see their application in this overall context and consider what they are asking for and what they expect from the trust. Among the beneficiaries were: a local scout group (£300), a local guide headquarters (£400), a local youth club (£500), a national youth association (£500), the national youth brass band (£400), a number of national children's charities (£300-£500 each), an organisation working with disadvantaged young people (£1,500) and an after-school club (£500).

These organisations were supported alongside a wide variety of other causes. The trust has no specialist knowledge of youth work and reads all applications with the same level of open-mindedness. In 1995/96, for instance, beneficiaries included the Prison Reform Trust, Tree Aid, the Mayor's Toy Appeal, Primary Immunodeficiency Association, the Disabled Angling Federation, the Dian Fossey Gorilla Fund, Leprosy Mission, and a number of local churches, community associations, and schools.

The trust is open with financial information, although its correspondent is very keen to avoid a large flood of speculative applications that cannot be supported by the trust. He urges applicants to read very carefully what trusts can and cannot support, and then to act upon it. Wherever possible applicants should build up a picture of how any trust operates and what its particular interests are.

Go with the grain rather than against it. In this case youth organisations are only a small part of the overall picture. Grants are relatively small and one-off. Support is likely to be given for costs such as: equipment, grants for individuals to participate in an activity, help towards a specific project where the trust is not the major funder, or an event.

- Maximise the impact of your personal contacts. Ask around your organisation, your management committee, staff, members, members' families, supporters, anyone! Does anyone know any charity trustee or trust administrator personally? If so, get them to make contact with the trust and see how the land lies. Personal applications are always the best!

- Look through the guide books. There are various trust guide books (see box on p.95) and see who you can apply to.

- Get hold of guidelines published by the trusts themselves. Read them carefully and address the points they raise in your application. For example, if the guidelines ask how the project will be evaluated, you need to give them a clear idea.

- Where the trust has paid administrators, you can ring them to discuss your application (e.g. would it be eligible, do you have to be a registered charity, when would it be considered, do you need to fill out an application form?). Most of the larger trusts are prepared to have a preliminary chat over the phone. However, if you get the impression that they don't want to talk, don't push it.

- Write to the trusts you have identified. The letter should be not more than two sides of A4. In this letter you should state clearly:
  Who you are
  What you do
  Why it is important
  What you need
  What it will achieve
  Where you will get the money from.
  You should also send a budget for the particular project, a set of accounts for the organisation as a whole, an annual report and maybe one or two other documents to support your application.
  The above is the most basic strategy. The following should help you stand out from the crowd.

> ### The Prince's Trust
>
> The Prince's Trust is an important funder of work with disadvantaged young people. It also fundraises itself to promote its own programmes of work. It has a number of interest areas to support both groups and individuals who are contending with social and economic disadvantage or who "have had it tougher than most". Around £1.5 million is given each year to organisations of disadvantaged young people or to those helping them, often where Prince's Trust volunteers are involved. It does not give grants centrally, but through local committees which can award grants of up to £2,500.
>
> General information is available from: The Prince's Trust, 18 Park Square East, London NW1 4LH (0171-543 1234; Fax: 0171-543 1200). You can find out about your local committee by ringing 0800-842842.

- Build contacts. You will probably be able to identify 10 or 15 key trusts who you have a good chance of getting support from, maybe now or maybe in the future. If you can, warm them up by sending some information before you

---

The Irish Youth Foundation gives the following tips to those applying for its funds:

"In making your application it is important to realise that yours is one of many competing for limited resources. It is helpful to us if your application is:

- Clear, concise and to the point – say what you do or propose to do, how much it will cost and how it will impact on your clients.

- Be transparent, open, direct. Do not try to hide what you want funds for in the guise of something else.

- Be realistic – don't just pick a figure out of the air and work your project/programme around it.

- Start with need, justify the need and outline a tangible response to meeting the need that makes sense.

- We have found that projects are very strong in telling us about their aims and objectives, but weak in telling us what they do and how it impacts on young people and children."

---

actually write to them for money. This could be your annual report, some press coverage or a newsletter. The main purposes are: (a) to show yourselves in a positive light; (b) to try and get your name known before you write for money, and (c) to show that you are committed to a longer-term relationship with the trust. Many trusts complain that the only time they hear from people is when they want money. They actually like to know how things are going.

It does not need to be fat and glossy. Most trusts are run by busy people with little time to wade through long project descriptions. A letter saying: "In May, 1994, you supported us with..., and we are now able to report that..." is all you need. Remember, this is not an appeal letter; you are not asking for money. Be brief, upbeat and informative. Practice writing your update on a postcard to keep the length down. Send the trust this kind of information once or twice a year. If you don't know trust people personally, this is the next best thing.

- If the project is new or unknown to the trust, get well-known sponsors or supporters to say how well-run the project is and how much needed it is. This helps create a bridge between you and the trust.

- Offer to visit the trust to explain your work, or better still try to get them to come and see you. Put them on your VIP list for events you may be running. They probably will not come, but they might. If they do, you will be half way to getting a grant so long as you take time to show them round, introduce the kind of people they want to meet and generally get them enthusiastic about what you are doing.

- When you do get a grant, remember this is the beginning of the relationship not the end. Keep them informed of how things are going (they will probably ask for information anyway). Always try to be positive and upbeat. If you get one grant and spend it well, you have got a good chance of getting another grant for something different later on.

A closer look at a major trust working with young people

The Rank Foundation

The Rank Foundation is one of the most established and best thought out funders of youth work. It is also one of the largest. Therefore, we thought it would be interesting to look at one major foundation in more depth to give an idea of how it goes about its work.

In 1995, the Foundation gave £6,758,000 in total to voluntary organisations, and around £2,054,000 in 178 grants to youth projects. Although it supports other areas including promoting the Christian religion and education it places great emphasis on its work with young people, as "the seed corn for the future well-being of our society".

As one of the top 300 grant-making trusts its grant-giving policies are detailed in *A Guide to the Major Trusts Volume 1*. The Foundation produces extensive guidelines for applicants, as well as a series of publications that relate directly to work with young people. It also employs a number of staff to assess applications and visit projects. What makes it different as a grant-giving trust to youth projects is its on-going commitment to the work that it supports together with a strategic approach to investing in youth work.

It has four major strands of investing in youth projects which are detailed below. As well as these, the Foundation also receives around 600 general appeals to be decided on at each quarterly meeting. Grants can be for £250 to £1,000 for equipment to local youth groups and branches of the Scouts, Guides, Boys' Brigade and Sea Cadets, or can be for up to £25,000 to support the salary costs of an outreach worker with homeless young people. For many youth organisations this may be the first point of contact with the Foundation.

The Foundation has defined a number of areas for strategic investment. Although fewer projects are supported than under the general appeals, there is a greater financial commitment to each, and the emphasis is upon focused development of the project. The four main strands are:

- **Youth or Adult?** Priority is given to training local youth leaders to become qualified and then continue to work in their communities. In this way local leaders who might otherwise be unqualified can discover and use their skills within their own areas. There are currently around 50 people supported by the Rank charities involved in the training at YMCA George Williams College. (The Joseph Rank Trust is also a substantial funder of youth work and works closely with the Foundation.) In 1995 £161,300 was given to the college. Other groups supported under Youth or Adult? were All Saints Church Youth Project (Brixton) £28,800; Challenge for Youth, Belfast (£22,900); Fort William Youth Cafe (£25,700); Paddington Arts (£25,700); Skylight Circus in Education (£26,500); and Villages Youth Project, Driffield (£22,700). Youth or Adult? grants totalled £1,352,700 and all but one were for amounts over £20,000.

- **Key Worker posts.** The Rank Foundation stresses that its role is not just about giving money away. Rather it sees itself as a partner, investing in a project and allowing work to continue and develop. Key Worker posts may be funded by the trust where projects are known by recommendation or have received previous support. Where a specialist qualified worker is needed to extend a project, perhaps in housing, business, outdoors, arts or urban adventure for example, the Foundation will look to support the costs. Often this is building upon initial support for a project under another strand, and would be largely pro-active following discussions and debate between the trust and the project.

- **Investing in Success Initiative.** This is again pro-active where the Foundation has a significant partnership with an established agency, built over a number of years. The focus is on training and qualifying young local apprentices, volunteers and peer leaders. The Foundation looks to give significant support to a small number of key youth organisations, and grants range between £162,000 and £650,000. This has increased from recent years and is an indication of how the Foundation invests strategically in organisations which can influence and help others in the field. In 1995, five organisations were supported (with grants of between £41,000-£59,000): Manchester Youth Community Service; the Centre 63 Church of England Youth Centre, Liverpool; Cheshire & Wirral Federation of Youth Clubs; Devon Youth Association and the West Yorkshire Youth Association. There are now a further six projects that are being supported in Wales and Scotland as well as England. There is a firm intention to support projects in Northern Ireland in the future.

- **Young Volunteer Scheme – GAP.** There are currently 35 young volunteers (rising to 40 next year) aged between 17 and 24 years who show potential as leaders in their communities. These young volunteers come from an impressively wide range of social backgrounds and experiences to spend six to nine months with a host agency where Rank is already involved. The period is seen as an apprenticeship in youth work which may be a start for the young person to continue in this direction, although volunteers acquire skills that can be, and are, transferred to a number of other fields. Training is integral to the time spent as a volunteer, and the emphasis is upon growing people who can continue as leaders in their communities. The Young Volunteer Scheme illustrates how young people have a voice in the Rank Foundation. Their experiences and ideas on how the training should develop have contributed substantially to the GAP scheme's current form. In 1995 Rank funded 25 volunteers with a total of £141,000. Each volunteer placement costs around £5,500 to support.

The first three of the above are largely pro-active and build upon existing relationships between the Foundation and known organisations. Rank has two youth projects directors who research applications, make recommendations to the trustees, visit projects, and monitor, encourage and support the main beneficiaries. The grants that are given are only the start of a relationship that is intended to grow and mature. In discussion with Charlie Harris, Director of Youth Projects for the Rank Foundation in England and Wales, some key points emerged about applications and how they are assessed by the trust. Whether the application is relatively small or for a grander scheme there are some key principles that applicants should bear in mind. Many of these apply throughout when you are approaching any charitable trust.

Rank has so far remained free of application forms. You should be able to present your case in one to two sides of A4. Charlie Harris stresses that many applicants do not realise how important the application letter is. "With unsolicited appeals, in many cases this is all we have to go on. A letter telling us what you are going to do, how you are going to do it; who's going to do it and what difference it will make is vital for us to understand what you're about. The letter can be hand-written. *[This is unusual for a charitable trust.]* That doesn't matter, so much as what's in it. We need to see what we're being asked to invest in." Documents such as annual reports, a recent set of audited accounts, and details of other funding that has been raised should be attached, but this is supporting material. Do not rely on it. The star of the show needs to be the case you make in the letter.

Organisations already supported by the Foundation and looking for help with further projects present a summary of around one side of A4. Like the application letter for the general appeals described above, the case in the summary needs to be made clearly, concisely and compellingly.

Like many of the large grant-giving trusts, Rank invests time and effort in assessing applications. The two directors of youth projects spend a great deal of time on the road researching and visiting new projects as well as keeping up with existing ones. Charlie Harris is emphatic: "Where a project is new and we don't know it, the first visit is vital. Applicants should realise how important these are to us. We look for a personal contact, to build relationships. From Rank's point of view once we have decided to support something we act from a total position of trust. When we're assessing a project we need to see if the people there are likely to deliver what they say they can. We want to work with people we can get to know and like, and who like us! Our support is often over a long time, three to five years perhaps. The partnership has to be able to endure and to grow over that time."

Evaluating an application involves looking at four areas:

- What is the work about? Does it fit within Rank's priority areas and current concerns? How are young people involved?
- Who will do the work? Is it the right worker? Can they do what they say they can?
- Who has responsibility for the work? Is the management right? Are the finances sound? How will the project continue in the future? How will the worker be supported?
- Where does the work fit in with the organisation? Is the project integral to the life of the organisation? Does it grow out of previous experience and learning within the agency? Rank argues "The project must be integral to the agency's long-term policy." The Foundation is looking for forward-looking projects, for new ideas, energy and vision, rather than funding on-going expenses.

The directors of youth projects who visit to research and assess projects report to the trustees who make all the grant decisions. This is an important point for applicants to grasp about foundations, particularly those which employ staff to look at projects. Trustees have the final say on applications and are accountable about how a charity distributes its income. In Rank's case the trustees decide on policy, strategy and priorities. Grant decisions are made in the light of these. Charlie Harris underlines their importance: "I could not do my job of visiting projects if the trustees did not take the final decisions on who receives a grant. I do not go with a cheque book. All I can do is look at the evidence and the case presented by the project and make any recommendations on the strength of what I pick up. It's then up to the trustees to say yes or no."

Where applications are weak they usually fall down on one or more of the above. Although Charlie Harris is keen to point out that applications have generally improved, the following are the areas where applications fail:

- Lack of focus. What is the project trying to do, and how will it be achieved? Is the project so general that is says it will do everything, and will end up doing nothing?
- Concerns about the management of the organisation and the project. How integrated is the work with the organisation? Does it have the backing and support of the whole organisation? What about the future?

Some dos and don'ts when writing to trusts

Do

- Plan a strategy
- Plan ahead
- Select a good project
- Believe in what you are doing
- Select a target
- Write an application tailored to the needs of the trust you are approaching
- Use personal contact
- Prepare a realistic and accurate budget for the project
- Be concise
- Be specific
- Establish your credibility
- Keep records of everything you do
- Send reports to keep trusts informed
- Try to develop a partnership or long-term relationship
- Say thank you

Don't

- Send a duplicated mail shot
- Ask for unrealistic amounts
- Assume trusts will immediately understand the need you are meeting
- Make general appeals for running costs
- Use jargon
- Beg

- Impression that the organisation has applied for the sake of it. Is the project part of a strategy, or has it been conjured up to fit within the guidelines? Does it spring from genuine roots within the agency or has it been hastily grafted on?

Rank values personal contacts, and stresses that professional fundraisers working on behalf of an organisation do not have the same appeal. Charlie Harris is clear: "The people who can best speak about an organisation and what it's doing are those who work for the organisation themselves. They have the enthusiasm, knowledge and commitment that no professional fundraiser can match."

Rank is different from other funders in its commitment to long-term funding. As recently as ten years ago potential applicants would have applied to other trusts rather than Rank because their funding was only for three years. Now Rank with its commitment to long-term funding is seen as one of the most understanding funders of youth work. Alongside this comes a commitment to follow-up and making the investment work. This policy goes hand in glove with Rank's concern to build a partnership between the organisation and the Foundation, rather than be seen as a benefactor with supplicant organisations. Monitoring takes five forms:

- Rank's involvement in project staff selection
- Membership of project management or support groups (although this is not seen as a priority)
- Reasonable regular access to, and participation in, the project (i.e. regular visits)
- Regular written progress reports and an annual report and financial summary
- Attendance by the project at the Foundation's regular evaluation conference.

Rank like many other trusts is also conscious of the impact of the National Lottery. The Rank Foundation gives around £6 million, compared to around £250 million from the Lottery. Funding may have to change and may have to become more specialised. At the time of writing there was also a new government and the Foundation was taking a wait and see approach as it was unclear what budgetary changes would mean for investment income and therefore the level of grant-giving in the future. The challenge for Rank will be to remain committed to youth work that takes risks, and to continue to invest in people over time rather than to seek a quick return on its investment.

Contacts for youth projects:

Charlie Harris, Director of Youth Projects (England and Wales), 28 Bridgegate, Hebden Bridge, West Yorkshire HX7 8EX;

Chris Dunning, Director of Youth Projects (Scotland, Northern Ireland, Cumbria, North East), Sunnyside, Great Strickland Penrith, Cumbria CA10 3DF;

General applications should be addressed to: 4/5 North Bar, Banbury, Oxfordshire OX16 (01295-272337; Fax: 01295-272336).

Preliminary enquiries about applications are welcomed.

Young at heart – The trusts that give to children and young people

The following list of trusts is taken from *A Guide to the Major Trusts Volumes 1 and 2*. All have some interest in supporting young people, although their priorities and patterns of giving (amount, regularity, average grant) will differ greatly. They are ranked in order of their annual overall grant total to all organisations, not just youth.

Large trusts (annual grant total over £1,000,000)

Gatsby Charitable Foundation
Garfield Weston Foundation
Tudor Trust
Charity Projects
BBC Children in Need Appeal
Henry Smith's (Kensington Estate) Charity
Bridge House Estates Fund Charity
Esmée Fairbairn Charitable Trust
Rank Foundation
Nuffield Foundation
Variety Club Children's Charity Limited
Linbury Trust
City Parochial Foundation
Clothworkers' Foundation
Church Urban Fund
Joseph Rank Benevolent Trust
Bernard Sunley Charitable Foundation
29th May 1961 Charitable Trust
Lankelly Foundation
Balcraig Foundation
Dulverton Trust
Lord Ashdown Charitable Trust
Gulbenkian Foundation
Headley Trust
Children Nationwide Medical Research Fund
Equitable Charitable Trust
Eveson Charitable Trust
Northern Ireland Voluntary Trust
Wates Foundation
Kirby Laing Foundation
Prince's Trust
Lloyds TSB Foundation for Scotland
Alchemy Foundation
Mary Kinross Charitable Trust
J Paul Getty Trust

Clore Foundation
Hampton Fuel Allotment Charity
Peacock Charitable Trust
Mackintosh Foundation
Save & Prosper Educational Trust
Rufford Foundation
Ernest Kleinwort Charitable Trust
Maurice Laing Foundation
Westminster Foundation

Medium-sized trusts (annual grant total £125,000-£1,000,000)

Sir James Knott 1990 Trust
Artemis Charitable Trust
John & Lucille van Geest Foundation
John Lyon's Charity
Carnegie United Kingdom Trust
Mental Health Foundation
Tyne & Wear Foundation
Sir John Cass's Foundation
Hedley Foundation Ltd
Joseph Levy Charitable Foundation
Francis C Scott Charitable Trust
Jones 1986 Charitable Trust
Cripplegate Foundation
P F Charitable Trust
John Moores Foundation
Baron Davenport's Charity Trust
Vivien Duffield Foundation
Capital Radio – Help A London Child
Trust for London
Percy Bilton Charity Ltd
Laing's Charitable Trust
MacRobert Trusts
Andrew Balint Charitable Trust
W O Street Charitable Foundation
Oxfam
Beatrice Laing Trust

Milly Apthorp Charitable Trust
Charles Hayward Trust
Spitalfields Market Community Trust
John Beckwith Charitable Trust
Irish Youth Foundation (UK) Ltd
H B Allen Charitable Trust
Sobell Foundation
Radio Clyde – Cash for Kids at Christmas
Harpur Trust
Tompkins Foundation
Hobson Charity Ltd
Carlton Television Trust
Talbot Village Trust
George A Moore Foundation
Sir James Reckitt Charity
Rose Foundation
Herbert & Peter Blagrave Charitable Trust
Alan Edward Higgs Charity
Great Britain Sasakawa Foundation
Allen Lane Foundation
Adint Charitable Trust
Blatchington Court Trust
Chippenham Borough Lands Charity
Mr & Mrs J A Pye's Charitable Settlement
Dellal Foundation
Horne Foundation
Harry Crook Foundation
Weinstock Fund
Charles & Elsie Sykes Trust
Enid Linder Foundation
Geoffrey Woods Charitable Foundation
Douglas Turner Trust
Bernard Van Leer Foundation
Beaverbrook Foundation
Jill Kreitman Foundation
Dibden Allotments Charity
Mid Glamorgan Welsh Church Fund
Greggs Charitable Trust
Summerfield Charitable Trust
Southover Manor General Education Trust
Robert Gavron Charitable Trust
Joseph Strong Frazer Trust
W A Handley Charity Trust
Duchy of Lancaster Benevolent Fund
Chase Charity

Viscount Amory's Charitable Trust
Privy Purse Charitable Trust
Lillie Johnson Charitable Trust
Sheffield Town Trust
Clover Trust
Hull & East Riding Charitable Trust
Ward Blenkinsop Trust
Emmandjay Charitable Trust
Alfred Haines Charitable Trust
Sir John Priestman Charity Trust
Handicapped Children's Aid Committee
Black Charitable Trusts
Isabel Blackman Foundation
Nancie Massey Charitable Trust
Sheepdrove Trust
Peter Minet Trust
Herbert Baron Austin Will Trust
Walter Guinness Charitable Trust
C A Redfern Charitable Foundation
Weavers' Company Benevolent Fund
Charles S French Charitable Trust
Patrick Charitable Trust
Edward Cecil Jones Settlement
Prince of Wales' Charities Trust
Yapp Welfare Trust
Homelands Charitable Trust
Benham Charitable Settlement
Grange Farm Centre Trust
Kathleen Hannay Memorial Charity
M A Hawe Settlement
Gordon Fraser Charitable Trust
Oakdale Trust
Vaux Group Foundation

Small trusts (annual grant total under £125,000)

Sheldon Trust
Wall Charitable Trust
Dinam Charity
Princess Anne's Charities
R J Larg Family Trust
I A Ziff Charitable Foundation
Dorothy Gertrude Allen Memorial Fund
Norman Collinson Charitable Trust
Salters' Charities
Paget Charitable Trust

Noel Buxton Trust
Gay & Peter Hartley's Hillards Charitable Trust
Bill Butlin Charity Trust
Yorkshire Bank Charitable Trust
Kulika Charitable Trust
Dorus Trust
Late Barbara May Paul Charitable Trust
Priory Foundation
Christopher H R Reeves Charitable Trust
Ripple Effect Foundation
Dumbreck Charity
Forte Charitable Trust
Pennycress Trust
Northmoor Trust
Harold Bridges' Charitable Foundation
Thomas Sivewright Catto Charitable Settlement
Fairway Trust
A M McGreevy No 5 Charitable Settlement
Charles Brotherton Trust
London Law Trust
Bill Brown's Charitable Settlement
Women Caring Trust
Augustine Courtauld Trust
Richard Desmond Charitable Trust
Northumberland Village Homes Trust
Emerging Markets Charity for Children
J P Jacobs Charitable Trust
Stanley Smith General Charitable Trust
Matthews Wrightson Charity Trust
Cattanach Charitable Trust
Gilbert & Eileen Edgar Foundation
Friarsgate Trust
Access 4 Trust
Besom Foundation
Wilfred & Elsie Elkes Charity Fund
Leslie Sell Charitable Trust
Stella Symons Charitable Trust
David Brooke Charity
GNC Trust
Reginald Graham Charitable Trust
Arthur James & Constance Paterson Charitable Trust
Haymills Charitable Trust
Emerton-Christie Charity
Shipwrights Charitable Fund
Worshipful Company of Shipwrights

Pilkington General Charity Fund
Woodlands Trust
Gibbins Trust
Vernon N Ely Charitable Trust
Lanvern Foundation
Divert Trust
Leslie Smith Foundation
De Haan Charitable Trust
JMK Charitable Trust
Ellis Campbell Charitable Foundation
Felicity Wilde Charitable Trust
Norton Foundation
Ravensdale Trust

Chapter 8

Winning company support

●●●

Why apply to companies?

Giving to good causes by companies has been seen as a source of great untapped income for the voluntary sector. Many groups looking for support assume that because some companies make large profits they must have similarly large pots of money just waiting to be dipped into by deserving organisations. Some fundraisers assume that companies have an unwritten obligation to give to voluntary activity in the community. They do not.

Before applying to companies you must understand why and how they give. Their support will be different from that of other funders. They will not be motivated primarily by philanthropy or by a desire to see new and pioneering voluntary activity. Rather, they will be looking to improve their economic position in relation to their competitors, whether at a local, regional or national level. Any charitable support that they give will be in the light of their profitability and how this decision will be seen vis-a-vis other companies. They have to answer to their share-holders as to how they spend any surplus.

Companies only rarely pay for salaries and almost never for core costs. You should aim to give the company a particular item or project to support. Also, company giving only amounts to about 3% of voluntary sector income so you should look at company support as a bonus rather than core income to be relied on year in, year out.

What charities say about company support

"It takes too much time. The support you get does not measure up to the time you put in." Maybe.

"I don't play golf or know anyone in the Rotary Club. How can I get a foot in the company giving door?" There are other ways to build contacts.

"Companies? They're only interested in what's in it for them. Photo opportunities, celebrity gala nights, press coverage. We're too small time for them." No you're not!

"You never get to speak to the person who makes the decisions. It's a wild goose chase around departments, until they find someone who can say no." If this is the case, you've gone about it the wrong way.

"You have to start small and then go back for more later. Local shops often help with prizes for raffles, but aren't interested in giving large cash gifts." But they can be used as levers to get at people who are.

Reasons to be cheerful

10 good reasons to apply to companies

- Their employees are connected with your organisation
- They need good publicity
- They're interested in young people
- Your event will be good for staff to take part in
- You know the chief executive or personnel officer, or someone in the marketing department helps out in your club
- Young people buy their product
- You're asking for something that's easy for them to give
- They've given to you before
- Your activities help their business
- They like you

Reasons to be doubtful

10 good reasons to think again about applying

- You know nothing about the company
- It's about to go bust
- They are not located in your area
- Their business is not connected in any way with young people
- They have a stated policy of never giving to unsolicited appeals
- You have received well-publicised sponsorship from a rival firm
- You are asking for £10,000; their total budget is £500
- Their policies, product, image etc. is not compatible with your work with young people
- Your supporters would be against having their support
- Their charitable giving is already fully committed for the next two years

Applying for support from companies is time-consuming and can be frustrating. More groups than ever before are chasing very limited company resources. Well-known high street companies such as Boots receive over 100 applications a *day*. Many companies end up supporting, at best, one in ten of the applications they receive and most grants are for £250 or less. It follows then, that the large majority of charitable applications for company support are unsuccessful, and the large majority of successful applications are for small amounts of money. Company giving can seem small in relation to the amount you are looking to raise.

On the upside, when you are successful, you can have a new source of support that has lots of spin-offs: important contacts; work experience opportunities; management committee members; use of company facilities; in-house expertise provided free or at low cost; staff time and so on.

A common mistake when thinking about company giving is to see it as only about raising money. Whilst some companies can and do give large sums of money to voluntary organisations, the majority will not. You have to think clearly about why you are approaching them, what benefits they will receive from being linked with your group, and whether you can ask for something other than financial help.

Why companies give

Companies give because it is in their interests to do so. The more they see the donation as a business opportunity, the more likely they are to work with you. The onus is on you to give them good reasons to support your organisation. Some companies give because they see the benefit that will come to the company from being seen to be a good corporate citizen. This **enlightened self-interest** can be motivated by the following:

- To **create goodwill** within their community. Companies may want to be seen as good citizens and good neighbours, so they support local charities. A quick look through *A Guide to Company Giving* published by the Directory of Social Change will show that most company donations are to local organisations, although in money terms this will be under half of the total value of community contributions made by companies.
- To **be associated with certain causes**. This can help a company's image and provide public relations opportunities. This is one reason why there is strong company support for children and youth charities.
- To **create good relations with employees**. This can be through supporting charities where a member of staff is raising money, or where staff volunteer in their spare time. Some companies have schemes where they match any money raised by an employee; others may give some preference (though not necessarily an automatic donation) to charitable appeals proposed by them.

There can be other reasons why companies give support and these can be broadly categorised as follows:

- **They are expected to**. Companies receive appeals and know that other companies give their support. They will probably support trade charities or benevolent funds connected with their industry; beyond that they will try to pitch the level of their giving more or less at that of their competitors.
- They have been asked by an **informal network**. A large part of company giving can be through donations that have been solicited by company directors on behalf of their favourite charities (or those of their partners). They will pass the hat to directors in other firms through informal networks (i.e. by telephone or over dinner), and if their charity receives support they will be obliged to return the favour when they receive similar requests for those charities favoured by other directors.
- Giving is **decided by the chairman or managing director**. Those causes that they are personally interested in stand more chance of support than others. Even with some large companies that have well-established policies and criteria for their giving, you are more likely to be successful if you can persuade a friend of the managing director to ask on your behalf, even if it does not exactly fit into the company's criteria. Often, you do not need to do the asking yourself; the trick is to find the right person to do it on your behalf. Recruiting an eminent local businessperson onto your fundraising committee and persuading them to approach their colleagues on your behalf saves you time and raises more support.
- The **director's special interest**, where the managing director, chairman or any director uses the company's charitable budget as an extension of a personal account to support their own charitable commitments.

- Because they have **always given**. Some companies will never review their policies. If you are on their list, all well and good; if you are not, it may be almost impossible to join the favoured few.
- Because the **charity persists** in their approach to the company, and the company does not want to keep refusing a worthwhile cause. Persistence can pay, although if you are turned down you should consider whether you can improve your application, or ask for something else.

How much do companies give?

Company giving is not easy to quantify. Companies can help in a number of ways, including products and services for free, staff time, secondments, advertising, low-cost or free use of facilities, expertise, free equipment, as well as money. In 1995/96, the top 400 corporate donors gave almost £182 million in cash and a further £70 million in other forms of community (and non-cash) support. This total support accounts for 0.29% of these companies' pre-tax profits and accounts for over 90% of all company giving in the UK. Indeed, the top 25 companies listed to the left give around 40% of the total corporate support available.

The Top Twenty-Five Corporate Givers By Community Contributions

		1995/96 (£ million)
1.	British Telecommunications plc	£14.9
2.	GlaxoWellcome plc	£10.7
3.	National Westminster Bank plc	£10.6
4.	Marks and Spencer plc	£8.5
5.	Barclays plc	£8.4
6.	British Petroleum Company plc	£6.1
7.	Midland Bank plc	£5.5
8.	British Gas plc	£5.0
9.	Grand Metropolitan plc	£5.0
10.	Shell UK Limited	£4.8
11.	Lloyds TSB Group plc	£4.6
12.	Seagram Distillers plc	£4.3
13.	Guinness plc	£4.2
14.	Boots Company plc	£4.1
15.	Unilever	£4.0
16.	BAT Industries plc	£3.0
17.	Halifax Building Society	£3.0
18.	Esso UK plc	£2.9
19.	Royal Bank of Scotland plc	£2.8
20.	Ecclesiastical Insurance Group plc	£2.5
21.	Mercury Communications Ltd	£2.2
22.	Sainsbury plc	£2.0
23.	Allied Dunbar Assurance plc	£2.0
24.	Whitbread plc	£1.8
25.	The RTZ-CRA Group	£1.7

Building your confidence

A large part of raising support from companies is about confidence. Those who are successful at company fundraising will probably tell you that they started small and worked upwards. Most local groups will have some experience of trawling the local high street for gifts for their annual raffle. To a small organisation, a £20 meat voucher from the local butcher or a discount at the hairdresser's can make a big difference to the amount of money raised from a raffle. Even at this level, use the contacts you have locally to improve your chances of success. Ask the hairdresser or butcher that you use to help out. The local branch where you bank regularly may be prepared to match any money you raise in a sponsored event. Local businesses may think twice about jeopardising your regular custom. Make sure that you give them plenty of notice of the date. Do not leave asking for gifts and contributions until the eve of the event.

Do not ask too often. A good fundraising plan, even for modest amounts, will ensure that you ask people once in a year rather than every three months. Think carefully about what they can afford, and even here, sell your event as something that will give their enterprise good coverage locally. Word-of-mouth custom is the lifeblood of local shops and businesses. If you live in a very local community such as a village where everyone knows each other, a skill auction with local people and local businesses donating lessons, services or time can be very effective.

If you have been reasonably successful at this level you will want to build upon your success and start to make contacts in larger businesses. Whilst you may have a regular conversation in your corner shop, you will not necessarily know people in the larger stores and factories in town. This will be a case of building relationships over time and getting to know the business of business.

Start by asking around your organisation – parents, helpers, staff, committee members, the young people themselves, to see if anyone knows any local business people. Build on any links that already exist. A good way to build a relationship may be to have a presentation evening where the manager of a local business is invited to attend and perhaps present an appropriate award. You may have asked them to donate the award, or it may be just a simple way to introduce them to your organisation. If there is coverage in the local press (including the free press) so much the better.

Once you have contacted and met the local manager or departmental head, you now have a real link with a company. Use your contact to increase the profile of your organisation in the business. They may be able to advertise your activities on the staff notice-board. You could invite a staff team to take part in a fun-day, sponsored event, or a sports contest. There may eventually be an opportunity to have a collecting tin in the staff canteen. You may have opportunities for staff to volunteer and work with your organisation. You need to work out imaginative ways of linking your organisation to the business and keeping them informed

---

The most common mistake when applying to companies

Most organisations write to companies for support in the same way that they write to grant-making trusts. That is, they write along the lines: "This is what we do; this is why we are important; and this is what we want." This is fine for a trust, but will not work well with a company. You must say: "This is what we do; this is why we are important; this is what we want and these are the benefits the company will see from supporting us." If you cannot find anything to say about the last part, if you cannot give the company some obvious benefit from its contribution, do not bother writing to the company at all.

Read companies' policies if they exist and find out about the company's interests and charitable priorities. Where you know these, abide by them. Dealing with a mass of clearly inappropriate applications is the single biggest headache in corporate giving and has even led some to consider winding up their charitable support programmes altogether.

of what you are doing. Do not just keep to selling raffle tickets to the staff, or asking them for cash donations. It will become harder to engage the firm's support if you allow news to go stale, or if the contact you have fades through lack of interest on your part. You do need to put time into nurturing the link you have made, and keep the company updated on what you are doing.

Remember that businesses thrive on personal contacts, and also that telephone conversations are a key part of how business works. You cannot avoid using the telephone to make things happen. If this is daunting, either delegate the contact work to someone else (perhaps someone on your management committee who already has links with business people) or try to increase your confidence in some way.

Local giving – Ainsley Gommon Wood Architects

This is a medium-sized practice specialising in community architecture. The two partners have their own particular interests in the non-profit sector; the arts, and education. This does not preclude them from supporting other causes, but it emphasises that corporate givers have their personal enthusiasms like the rest of the general public, and charities need to remember this.

Ainsley Gommon Wood reviewed their charitable giving in the light of the recession. "Quite simply, there wasn't enough money." They used to make annual donations; now the giving has been scaled down to gifts of generally between £10-£25 to appeals which attract their interest. Staff time is also at a premium as numbers are small and people are usually stretched with their workload. Staff volunteering schemes are therefore unlikely to be entered into.

The partners value personal contact. Where a member of staff is already involved with a charitable cause there is an immediate connection with what they are doing. Continued feedback from any organisation that has been supported is warmly welcomed. The practice helped with a holiday for young people with learning difficulties and greatly appreciated the regular letters and scrapbook sent by the participants.

Decisions are made immediately on speculative letters asking for support. There is not time to go through lots of information. "We have a bundle of post to look through. Decisions have to be made quickly." One of the partners suggested the following points to think about when writing to a business:

■ Match your request to what the business can afford. If a project is too large and the business can only give a small donation, "we would see our contribution as being swallowed up and not making any difference at all. It's not worth us bothering".

■ False praise in a letter rings hollow and starts off on the wrong note.

■ Lengthy letters "drive us mad. It's much better if they're simple, succinct and concise".

■ Letters should be typed rather than hand-written.

■ A professionally written introduction to a letter would be looked at straight away. A good track record gives the appeal credence.

■ Corporate giving is not just about money. "As partners, we tend to give of our time and skills through involvement, more so than cash."

Ainsley Gommon Wood, Architects

The kind of help companies give

Giving cash is usually the most expensive way for companies to give to charity. There are plenty of other options which are just as valuable to you but cost the company a lot less to give. Here are some of them:

- Gifts in kind
- Advertising
- Sponsorship
- Staff.

Gifts in kind

If you need general equipment or goods, a company may be able to provide these free. This can be in the form of outdated stock that would otherwise be destroyed (e.g. food at its sell-by date, letterheads that have recently been changed, old lines of fabric, wallpaper, paint etc.); or equipment and furnishings that have recently been updated (e.g. telephone systems, desks, chairs, filing cabinets, fax etc.). When companies have a regular refurbishment, replaced furniture may be kept in store for a while. Banks or building societies for example may have a regional headquarters where discarded equipment is stored. You will have to arrange transport to collect the furniture. Some companies have supplies of waste paper which may be useful for a play scheme or art project.

It's not all about cast offs. Companies can give you their existing products (e.g. soft drinks for your fun run) or you may be able to help them launch new ones. Alternatively, some may be able to give limited printing or photocopying facilities. You may be able to borrow a room for a function, seminar or training course.

> ### Free Dulux Paint
>
> Dulux makes 180,000 litres of paint available free to voluntary organisations in their annual Community Projects Scheme. There are also five special Colour in the Community Awards for projects using paint in a particularly bold and imaginative way. The work must be completed by volunteers. For further details and an application form, send an A4 49p SAE to: Dulux Community Projects Office, PO Box 343, London WC2E 8RJ. When you return the completed form you should include photographs of the project.

Companies can give expertise, services or time. This can be worth more than a cash grant if the help is given free or at cost. Some architects and solicitors for example may be able to offer a reduced fee for legal or building consultation. (Others may not as they will not want to muddy the waters at the beginning of a business relationship. You will not find this out unless you ask.) Designers may be able to give you an hour for free, or may be able to give a small project to a junior member of staff as a training exercise. You should not have to compromise on the standard of the work and advice that you need. It does mean however that you have to stick to your guns, and that you are well prepared to take advantage of the limited time that will be available. Make sure you have your outlines and questions well thought out before any meeting to

What kind of gift is a gift in kind?

Gifts in kind are donations of items or services, rather than the money to buy them. The only limit to gifts in kind that can be given by companies is your imagination. Here are some examples of products that have been given by companies:

Paper	Tee-shirts	Brochure design
Furniture	Hampers	Air-time
Telephones	Car	Catering
Photocopier	Tools	Transport
Computer	Maintenance	Two hours book-keeping a week
Carpeting	Accounts	
Paint	audit	Office space
Soft drinks	Film	Etc.

make the most of the time and to ensure that you get what you want from the donation.

Advertising

Voluntary organisations sometimes ask companies to take up advertising space in their publications such as yearbooks, calendars, or diaries. This is still a way of generating income but more and more companies explicitly state that they are not interested in this form of help (see *A Guide to Company Giving*).

There are two kinds of charity advertising:

- a glorified donation as a goodwill gesture;
- a commercial exercise where returns are expected for the investment.

With the former, the process is very similar to securing donations from companies where you use personal persuasion, either face to face or over the telephone with a follow-up letter. With the latter, it is a case of selling your charity and using your publication as an advertising opportunity for the company. You will have to calculate the reach and audience for the publicity you are producing. Will this increase the company profile in a way that other advertising does not? Will the company's image be sharpened by the coverage? Will your members, supporters, parents, staff and helpers be translated into customers?

When the advertising is a genuinely commercial exercise you should make sure your rates are realistic. If you expect good coverage with your publication then make sure your advertising rates reflect this and sell the idea to the company accordingly. You will also have to approach marketing and publicity departments rather than those that deal with charities. However, companies are increasingly sceptical about the value of charity advertising and see it as little more than a glorified donation. So you will need to show them that this is a genuinely commercial proposition. The fact that you are a voluntary organisation is irrelevant – you are offering a genuine advertising opportunity.

Sponsorship

Sponsorship arrangements between a charity and a company are where the largest sums of corporate money are to be found. Some companies will be keen on a commercial partnership with a voluntary organisation which goes beyond the advertising opportunities outlined above. Sponsorship can work at a national, regional or local level. A company may be prepared to underwrite the costs of an event, provide money for catering for a presentation, pay for a brochure or sponsor an individual on a training course for example. You will have to be very clear about what you are asking for, and what the company can expect to see as their return. Obviously, the more they sponsor an activity, the higher their investment, and the more benefits they will expect to see.

Firstly, you need to decide what connection you have with the company. Do they already know you and your work? If they do not, you are probably approaching them too soon. Build the relationship between your organisation and their business first. The next question is, are they interested in young people? Do they have a product or service which readily links into the audience of young people? Do they have a record of sponsorship or will this come as a new idea? What sort of budget are they likely to have? (Remember, your proposal must be commercial in its appeal. Again, this is not about you being a charity – it is about you providing a commercial opportunity.)

> **A successful sponsorship has three essential elements:**
>
> 1. It matches the **image** of the company and the **work** of the charity.
> 2. It has the **correct target audience** for the company.
> 3. It **sells the benefits** of sponsorship to the company (including how the sponsorship would meet the company's commercial objectives).

Secondly, you need to tie your proposal into reaching the company's target audience. Sponsorship is about the company selling a product, enhancing its image, gaining access to opinion formers, persuading new audiences and consolidating old ones. You need to show how your sponsorship proposal will help the company to achieve this. If all you can offer are some vague promises or an introduction to the wrong audience, you should forget sponsorship; the company will not be interested.

Sponsorship negotiation can take up a lot of time. Bear in mind the following:

- You should allow plenty of lead-in time (at least nine months before the event, preferably more) to prepare the ground and to make sure that your proposal is sound.
- Precise costings are vital; they should take into account both what the sponsorship will cost, and what the return is likely to be.
- How many people will come to the event, see the product or read the brochure?
- What is their age, sex, income profile, etc?
- Will there be any press coverage and what will this mean?
- Will celebrities be involved?
- How prominent will the company's name be?
- Are there any other companies involved and could these be potential or actual commercial rivals?
- Are there long-term benefits from the arrangement?

You will need to draw up a sponsorship agreement. This is essential if the sponsorship involves large amounts of money. Even if it is a relatively small amount you should draw up a list (or sponsorship audit) of the benefits the sponsorship will bring to your organisation and what return the company can expect to see from their involvement. (See Your Sponsorship Package overleaf.)

The key to successful corporate sponsorship is to start small and build up. Make sure that the person responsible for negotiating on your behalf with the company is well briefed and gives regular feedback to others in the organisation. Guidelines on which companies are acceptable to work with, and which are not need to be agreed within the organisation beforehand. This differs from group to group and over time. Recently, some youth organisations steered clear of Shell and their environment initiatives for example.

Never promise more than you can deliver. In fact, try to deliver more than you promise, which will lead to an even more satisfied company. Remember too, that sponsorships have their own shelf-life. After two or three years, the company may wish to pull out of the arrangement, not because the sponsorship is not working, but simply that they have got as much from it as they are going to. Prepare yourself in advance and plan how you will continue the activity. You will need to give yourself time to find another sponsor or to prepare an alternative sponsorship package.

Staff
The people working in a company are a vital resource for both a voluntary organisation and a business. The best way into company giving is knowing someone in the company and asking them to put the case for the organisation within their business. So ask around your leaders, parents, management committee to see who works where. Those working in companies will be your best advocate in the workplace.

You can also try to get companies to encourage their staff to volunteer with your organisation. Employee volunteering is a newish concept but one which many companies are keen to push. You may well be able to find a use for new volunteers. The greatest advantage in fundraising terms, however, is that these volunteers can then approach the company for money when you need it. Through them you have a really strong link.

You may need some expertise that otherwise you would have to pay for. For example, do you need help with management training, marketing, finance, strategic planning or design? If so, why not ask a company to "lend" someone for two hours a fortnight to help with this. It gives you the help you need and the person giving the help a fresh impetus and challenge in their career. If this is done formally, it is called a "secondment" and would need clear agreements on both sides. However, you may well be able to get the help you need without the formality of a secondment agreement. Both parties must be realistic about the time, expectations and commitment involved.

When you need help and advice in getting a secondment organised, contact Action: Employees in the Community at 44 Baker Street, London W1M 1DH (0171-224 1260).

Cash donations

At the end of the day, money is what most organisations want from companies. Whilst companies are not cash cows to be milked, they do give grants. Again, this will vary from company to company. Some will have well-defined policies which work in a similar way to grant-making trusts. They know what they want to give to, and what they do not. Guidelines are publicised regularly and applications may be handled by staff with job titles such as "Charitable Appeals Manager" or "Head of Corporate Support".

However, the large majority of companies – especially the smaller ones – will have a "make it up as we go along" approach. Here, any applications will be looked at by anyone from the personnel officer to the chairman. Unlike their charitable appeals colleagues in other companies they will not necessarily have any special insight into the voluntary sector. Furthermore, they will be deciding charitable giving on top of their "proper" job, and so may have to fit it into the odd Friday afternoon a month. They do not have the time to work through piles of paper or attend lengthy meetings.

Most companies will have some ceiling for how much they give in a year and once this is reached the cupboard is bare until next year. A good number of companies will operate on the basis of the chairman's six favourite charities. If you are on the list, all well and good. If you are not, you will have to find a way on, as the company giving policy is otherwise set in tablets of stone. Inevitably, if you are successful with this sort of company, you will be successful with others, as part of company giving works on spreading the word and passing the hat on the charity's behalf. It's not what you know …

You may stand more chance of success if you can tie your application in with an event or celebration. Anniversaries are useful; your 50th year or your 1,000th member. You may be able to find a company to tie in with this. It will be particularly attractive if you have a time limit to your fundraising – say a year. This gives those working in the supporting company a definite target to work for.

The Scout Association - The business of badges

The Scout Association took the plunge in 1989 to sponsor some of its 80 proficiency badges. The attractions to sponsors are obvious:

- a large national membership (total membership of 631,400 including both young people and leaders);
- a direct link with the company and its product (see below);
- high profile organisation with a presence throughout the country and links with the

great and good (The Queen is the patron, and 60% of all adults have been involved in either scouts or guides);

- links with parents and helpers (25% of adults have at least one child involved in beavers, cubs, scouts or ventures);
- good press coverage;
- attractive product with the company name on the proficiency badge;
- finite and manageable sponsorship;
- events at local, regional and national level;
- add-ons such as related competitions and materials;
- contribution to young people's education and development.

The value of the sponsorship varies a great deal according to the badge, numbers awarded and any added value from media coverage, personalities, and branded resources that tie in with the badge. Sponsorships can range between £10,000 and £50,000 each year (over three years). Some badges will inevitably be more popular with the members; the Cub Scout Swimmer badge for example is awarded to 120,000 young people a year, whilst in contrast, the Scout Paraglider badge has fewer than 1,000 takers. Sponsorship agreements would take this into account.

The following badges are currently sponsored:
- *Scout Administrator* sponsored by *ADECCO*
- *Scout Athlete* sponsored by *BUPA*
- *Scout Camp Cook* sponsored by *Walls'*
- *Scout and Cub Scout Community* sponsored by *Woolworth*
- *Scout DIY and Cub Scout Handyman* sponsored by *B & Q*
- *Scout Electronics* sponsored by *Comet*
- *Scout Emergency Aid and Cub Scout First Aider* sponsored by *Superdrug*
- *Scout Fire Safety* sponsored by *Kidde*
- *Scout I.T and Cub Scout Computer* sponsored by *Compaq Computers*
- *Scout Lifesaver* sponsored by *Associated British Ports*
- *Scout Mechanic* sponsored by *Automobile Association*
- *Scout Orienteering* sponsored by *INA*
- *Scout and Cub Scout Photographer* sponsored by *Dixons*
- *Scout Public Relations* sponsored by *British Energy*
- *Cub Scout Cook* sponsored by *Asda*
- *Cub Scout Camper* sponsored by *Marmite*
- *Cub Scout Health & Fitness* sponsored by *Weetabix*
- *Cub Scout Home Safety* sponsored by *Guardian Direct*
- *Cub Scout Map Reader* sponsored by *Ordnance Survey*
- *Cub Scout Road Safety* sponsored by *Vauxhall Motors* (and winner of the Prince Michael Road Safety Award)
- *Sportsman Badge* sponsored by *Hasbro*

Each sponsorship is managed differently, depending upon the joint resources which are available. This is decided and agreed beforehand, then written into a contract to be signed before the sponsorship is launched. The sponsorship department emphasises: "There are many dos and don'ts associated with sponsorship and in our case, these reflect the aims of The Association and the resources available. It is important to remember that sponsorship involves a mutually beneficial relationship and that relationship must be nurtured and developed from day one."

Competition for corporate sponsors is intense. The Scout Association uses direct mail shots to companies and their sales promotion agencies; advertising in the marketing press; and personal contacts and contacts developed by members to make links with potential sponsors. There are strict guidelines when signing up any sponsor, and the Association is very aware of its image. Sponsorship from alcohol or tobacco industries, for example, would not be acceptable.

Who to approach

The company

You need to decide on a company and then on who you should contact within the company. The choice of company will depend upon what connection you have with them.

- Have they supported you before?
- Are they local to your community?
- Are you consumers of their service or product?
- Do they need better publicity in the community and could you offer that with a link?
- Do your activities contribute to improving the business environment?
- Do they have a stated interest in young people or a project such as the environment that you are organising?
- Is the company a large employer in the area with an interest in the current and future workforce?

The person

Once you have decided on the company, you will need to find out how it is organised and who makes any decisions about charitable giving. Where a company has a number of branches or operating units throughout the country these may have some autonomy in grant decisions. There is usually a maximum amount that they can decide, over which the application will be passed to the next level, regional or national. If you can find this out beforehand it will save time in the long run.

Once you have established the level, you will then need to find the right person to talk and write to. Many organisations find this the frustrating part. There is no short cut if you have no inside knowledge of the company. Be prepared to spend time on the telephone, particularly if the company has no decided policy on giving. If there is no policy, there is not likely to be a name at the switchboard either. You may have

> ### Which companies give to youth organisations?
>
> There is no ready-made list of companies you can approach. In *A Guide to Company Giving (DSC)*, a great number of companies indicated their interest in supporting children and youth. Potentially any company can give to your organisation so long as you:
> (a) Make a connection between you and them
> (b) Show them the good commercial reasons why they should support you.

Your Sponsorship Package

It is not enough to offer 1,000 contacts to a company if they sponsor your event. Most of them may be irrelevant to the company. You need to say which 1,000 people will be involved and how.

Think of each group that you reach in one way or another. Estimate an annual number for each. The following are general groups of people to get the process started but there may be more specialised areas that you are in contact with. Some groups will overlap. The more you can define your different groups of contacts, and the more information you can give about them, the more help it will be to you and potential sponsors.

Group	Number	Group	Number
Adults	_____	Clubs	_____
Men	_____	Employed	_____
Women	_____	Unemployed	_____
Young adults	_____	Trainees	_____
Teenagers	_____	Agencies	_____
Children	_____	Local authority	_____
Consumers _____ (what, how and where people buy – drinks, clothes, transport, which shops, areas etc.)		Central government departments	_____
		Quangos	_____
Businesses _____ (who do you use for products, services etc.)		Health authority	_____
		TEC	_____
Schools	_____	Other.	_____

Sponsorship benefits that you might offer.

Tick all that apply and try to note numbers where you can.

	Yes	No	how much/how many
Goodwill in the local community	☐	☐	_____
Contact with local authority	☐	☐	_____
Contact with health authority	☐	☐	_____
Contact with government departments	☐	☐	_____
Training	☐	☐	_____
Specifically targeted groups (which ones?)	☐	☐	_____
Visits to projects	☐	☐	_____
Contact with celebrities	☐	☐	_____
Events	☐	☐	_____
Opportunities for staff volunteering	☐	☐	_____
Work experience	☐	☐	_____
Other	☐	☐	_____

Publicity material

This covers all the items that you have printed, and perhaps some that you may like to have printed but are unable to do so without funds. Estimate the number to be printed/produced.

	Number
Letter heading	_____
Envelopes	_____
Press releases	_____
Information leaflets	_____
Catalogues	_____
Annual reports	_____
Project reports & brochures	_____
Programmes	_____
Newsletters	_____
Event materials	_____
Mailings	_____
Educational materials	_____
(manuals, work packs, games etc.)	
Posters	_____
Directories	_____
Books	_____
Guides/maps	_____
Project video/film	_____
Slide	_____
Exhibitions	_____
Other............................	_____

Advertising

Advertising space
Look at all the spaces and places where there is room for advertising signs and sponsors' names to be placed and estimate how many people will see it:

	Number
At the entrance to your site or project	_____
Over the door of your building	_____
On a major wall or roof of a building	_____
Inside your building	_____
On the sides of organisational transport	_____
On staff overalls or uniforms	_____
Your own media advertising	_____
Team strips	_____
Achievement awards/badges	_____
Other.	_____

Media

Say how much coverage you already receive:

	Frequent	Occasional	Possible
National television	☐	☐	☐
Regional television	☐	☐	☐
National radio	☐	☐	☐
Local radio	☐	☐	☐
National press	☐	☐	☐
Local press	☐	☐	☐
Free press	☐	☐	☐
Specialist press	☐	☐	☐
Magazines/journals etc (circulation?)	☐	☐	☐
Your national organisation's publications (circulation?)	☐	☐	☐
Your own publications (circulation?)	☐	☐	☐
Web-site links (how many visit?)	☐	☐	☐
Other...	☐	☐	☐

to go through a number of different departments and repeat your request a number of times before you find someone who knows what the company can help with. At this point, do not give up. You should eventually get through to someone who knows and can give you a name to write to.

You must be clear which budget the money is coming from. For example, a youth orchestra in the North East secured a sponsorship agreement with a major oil manufacturer located in the area. The orchestra's selling point to the company was: "You want to recruit your future workforce from the cream of the local population. We have the cream of the local population in our orchestra. Therefore, publicise your company here first with these young people by supporting our orchestra and giving us some money." Crucially, the payment came not from the company's charitable donations budget, nor from its marketing budget. It came from the personnel budget. It was also much more cost-effective than running adverts in local papers and saved the company time visiting lots of local schools and giving careers talks.

> **A company giving cast list**
>
> The following is a selection of some of the different job titles and positions where charity applications end up. The following are some of the titles listed in *A Guide to Company Giving*:
>
> - Company Secretary
> - Managing Director
> - Personal Assistant to the Chairman
> - Group Secretary
> - Finance Director
> - Personnel Director
> - Head of Accounts
> - Administration Director
> - Public Relations Executive
> - Chairman
> - Marketing Manager
> - Public Affairs Manager
> - Charitable Committee Secretary
> - Corporate Communications Director
> - Chief Executive
> - Community Affairs Manager

The name

When you have tracked your man or woman to their corporate lair have your questions prepared. Even with an initial enquiry, you will need to be concise and to the point in your explanation. You may be asking for general information about how you should apply, but you should also use the opportunity to talk briefly but enthusiastically about your organisation, your proposed project and the way in which the company stands to benefit.

If your letter outlining your proposal follows swiftly on from your telephone call you may stand more chance of being remembered and rising – if only slightly – above the pile of competing applications. Always check on the name and spelling of the individual and the company you are applying to (even to the point of whether they spell it PLC, Plc, plc or whatever). Individuals move on and you may have out of date information. Companies like to see that their name is recognisable rather than prone to misspelling.

How a large national business gives - The NatWest Group

NatWest has a well thought out and structured approach to giving to voluntary organisations. Reading between the lines below you can see how important it is to make personal contacts at every level to win friends and gain support.

"Like most of the UK's leading companies, NatWest Group invests significant resources in local communities. We aim to meet social needs and recognise the potential benefits for the Group and its employees. In 1996 this investment totalled more than £15 million in cash and kind.

"We aim to make a measurable difference in areas of social need relevant to our business. In partnership with not-for-profit organisations we are improving financial and enterprise skills across the country in schools, the voluntary sector and independent money advice agencies.

"Staff involvement and interest drives much of our support for local communities. More than 6,000 employees make monthly donations to charities; we match their giving £ for £. And if a NatWest employee is a regular volunteer or board member with an organisation, we can support their efforts by making a cash donation of up to £250 to the charity under the Community Action Awards scheme. Some 4,000 organisations benefited in this way last year (1996).

"Outside our major partnerships, we have limited funds available for grants to charities and community organisations, managed according to the priorities of the NatWest Group Charitable Trust. The trust recognises the role of locally based community groups in finding responses to major social problems, and typically funds projects for up to three years. We recognise that complex social issues call for sustained and focused investment. Many of the projects supported with a cash grant are also helped by our staff as advisers, trustees, trainers, volunteers or secondees. Over 10,000 staff volunteered in 1996 to help community groups, schools and charities.

"In 1996, our central objective was helping disadvantaged young people respond to the changing world of work. We invested more than £1 million in 30 leading projects equipping young people to take advantage of new opportunities in the arts, care and leisure industries; supporting them in delivering valuable local services (and gaining the skill and confidence to prepare for independent living); and helping them set up new businesses.

"Applications for major grants, averaging £50,000 a year, are considered against set criteria in specific funding rounds. If you want to apply, are a registered charity, and have a particular project which you think would be interesting to us, telephone NatWest Group Community Relations (0171-726 1720) to check the criteria and opening times for applications. We will tell you whether we are likely to help and if not we'll try to suggest alternative routes."

Some recent major grants from the Charitable Trust given over three years include:

- Bolton Lads' and Girls' Club – £50,000 (1996-98) for a co-ordinator and secretarial help to recruit and support mentors helping 60 young people a year who are excluded from school or employment.
- Bristol Cyrenians – £225,000 (1996-98) for a learning facilitator and mentoring co-ordinator to train, support and mentor 50 young homeless people.

- Bromley by Bow Centre – £223,500 (1996-98) to develop local services and set up a training scheme for 12 young social entrepreneurs.
- Foothold – £79,205 (1995-98) to support one of the few enterprise agencies focusing on young people.
- Matson Neighbourhood Project – £135,000 (1996-98) for two members of staff to help young people on a depressed housing estate to gain employment.
- South Shropshire Youth Initiative – £140,000 (1996-98) for a youth led initiative to develop work opportunities in a rural area in decline.
- West Devon Environment Network – £180,000 (1996-98) to encourage young volunteers to undertake physical environmental improvement work.
- Yeovil Foyer – £180,000 (1996-98) for two project workers to support the community enterprise element of the training and accommodation scheme for homeless young people.

" In addition to major grants, we support local issues with smaller donations. NatWest staff at a regional level make decisions on priorities and criteria and award grants in line with these.

"NatWest is also promoting new services for community organisations. As the major business partner in the Local Investment Fund (run by BiTC), we encourage loans for projects which benefit communities while earning income, which traditional banking has not been able to back. We helped CAF set up Investors in Society, which will also provide loans to smaller community organisations. And if your charity wants free independent advice on financial management, you can telephone the NCVO/NatWest helpline (0171-713 6161)." - Lucy Swanson, NatWest Group Community Relations Manager

The letter

The content of your letter will reflect any relationship that already exists between your organisation and the company. You may need to remind them of past support and how this has helped you achieve something definite. Start with a brief outline of your project and activity. You need to be brief and snappy; the letter may not be read beyond this point if you do not get the reader's attention.

Make the link between the company and what you are doing as early as you can. The

Five dos when asking for money

1. Ask for a small amount first. You can build up the amount with each subsequent approach, having successfully spent the previous money well.

2. Ask for something specific. Do not imply that the company contribution will just be one of a number and will therefore be almost anonymous.

3. Explain what the PR benefits to the company will be and show how its support will be acknowledged.

4. Use the personal contacts you have to ask for the money (or at least create a link between you and the company).

5. Say thank you for any money you receive, spend it well, achieve publicity for the company, tell them you have done all of this and go back for more.

reader will ask themselves at the outset: "Why should we support this? What's it to do with us?"

Point to results and successes, and name drop. Companies will want to be linked with positive images and will want to see what their support will achieve.

Stress what you have in common; locality; commitment to the community; staff volunteers; historical link with founders; shared anniversary – anything that suggests you know the company and have thought about the mutual benefit that would follow their support.

Make sure you have factual information that is accurate. Do not for instance ask for a Nissan mini-bus if you are writing to Toyota.

At the end, invite a company representative to an event or to visit, and sign the letter appropriately. Your patron or committee chair may have more clout than a fundraising officer, although the fundraiser may be the best person for the company to contact for further information.

What you should avoid at all costs is the assumption that the company will know your organisation and the importance of the work that you do. They probably will not. It is largely up to you to do the persuading. Do not overload your letter with jargon, technical explanations and long paragraphs. They will probably not be read, and if they are, would they be understood by an outsider? Do not include too much supporting material; it will probably not be read, and you should assume that all the relevant information is in the letter. (For further tips, see Chapter 4 on Preparing and Writing a Good Fundraising Application.)

Making your case

- Think in terms of a project or specific items to ask for.
- Find the right name in the company to approach.
- Research the company's budget and ask for a realistic amount.
- Make a connection between your activities and those of the company: geography, people, director's interest, customer relations, employee concerns, community profile.
- Find out if they have a defined giving policy – and keep to it.
- Keep your letter short. Aim for one side of A4 at the most – less if possible.
- Don't send circular letters – make sure you have addressed it properly.
- Do persist – unless it is clear that you should not.
- Keep records of companies you have approached, when and what for.

Think...

- Sponsorship is a business expenditure, not a donation. You have to go about it in a business-like way.
- When costing a sponsorship package the issue is what is the value of the sponsorship to the company, not how much will it cost you to provide it.
- Evaluate what the sponsor will get from the sponsorship that they cannot get in any other way for the same or less money.
- Evaluate what your organisation can offer that could not be achieved in any other way for the same or less money.
- Why are you offering the sponsorship to that particular company (as opposed to the one down the road)?
- Which budget is the money coming from? If it is the marketing budget, contact the head of marketing.
- How do you get over their prejudice about you being a voluntary youth group and that it's too risky being associated with you?
- How do you show that you are really well run and that you understand their needs and aspirations?

Top 300 UK Company Givers 1995/96

Here is a list of the top 300 UK company givers in 1995/96. The figure we give is for their cash donations only. Many give much more than this in non-cash support (gifts in kind, secondments etc.).

Please note that the name we give is of the parent company. You may well not know the company or its brands by this name. For example, McVities does not exist as a separate company; it is part of United Biscuits so you would make your approach to United Biscuits when you want to talk about McVities products. Dulux is part of ICI. Reebok is part of Robert Stephen Holdings.

Further information is in *A Guide to Company Giving* and *The Major Companies Guide*, both published by the Directory of Social Change.

A

Abbey National plc £450,000
Abbott Laboratories Ltd £113,000
Abbott Mead Vickers plc £105,000
Alliance & Leicester
Building Society £258,666
Allied Domecq PLC £1,601,000
Allied Dunbar Assurance plc £2,000,000
AMEC plc £139,000
Arthur Andersen £1,019,504
Anglian Water plc £125,675
Argos plc £111,938
Arjo Wiggins Appleton plc £100,000
ASDA Group plc £100,000
Associated British Foods plc £400,000
Automotive Financial Group
Holdings Ltd £215,006

B

BAA plc £646,000
Scott Bader Company Ltd £115,088
Bain Hogg Group plc £106,000
J C Bamford Excavators Ltd £131,480
Bank of England £340,000
Bank of Scotland £1,600,000
Barclays PLC £2,600,000
Bass plc £772,000
BAT Industries plc £3,000,000

Bayer plc £142,518
Beneficial Bank plc £122,157
Bestway (Holdings) Ltd £260,000
Betterware plc £140,530
BHP Petroleum Ltd £500,000
BICC plc £200,000
Biwater Ltd £172,000
Blue Circle Industries PLC £156,773
BOC Group plc £641,000
Body Shop International PLC £846,997
Booker plc £145,000
Boots Company PLC £2,060,000
C T Bowring & Company Ltd £150,000
Bridon plc £104,534
British Aerospace plc £625,000
British Airways plc £594,000
British Gas plc £2,500,000
British Nuclear Fuels plc £2,100,000
The British Petroleum
Company plc £5,000,000
British Railways Board £1,000,000
British Sky Broadcasting
Group plc £138,000
British Steel plc £504,000
British Sugar plc £100,000
British Telecommunications plc £2,700,000
Britton Group plc £108,000
BTR plc £145,157

Bunzl plc £138,000
BUPA Ltd £790,000
Burmah Castrol plc £212,000
Burton Group plc £200,526

C

C & A Stores £280,728
Cadbury Schweppes plc £760,000
Cadogan Estates Ltd £181,000
Camelot Group plc .... About £5,000,000
Canon (UK) Ltd £200,000
Caparo Group Ltd £460,000
Cargill plc £236,934
Carlton Communications plc £1,400,000
CEF Holdings Ltd £107,550
Charter plc £337,000
Chevron UK Ltd £112,000
Christies International plc £295,000
Citibank £150,150
Claremont Garment Holdings plc ... £153,000
Coats Viyella plc £193,000
Commercial Union plc £265,267
Compaq Computer Ltd £400,836
Conoco Ltd £500,000
Cookson Group plc £211,719
Cooper (Gay) Holdings Ltd £172,000
Co-operative Bank plc £597,000
Co-operative Insurance Society Ltd . £113,000
Courtaulds plc £217,236
Courtaulds Textiles plc £133,000
Coutts & Co £158,000

D

Daily Mail & General Trust plc £426,000
Dalgety plc £273,000
Danka Business Systems PLC £105,000
De La Rue plc £339,000
Diamond Trading Company £103,000
Digital Equipment Co Ltd £1,400,000
Dixons Group plc £280,000

E

Eastern Group plc £350,000
Ecclesiastical Insurance
Group plc £1,685,000
Economist Newspaper Ltd £96,000
Elf Caledonia Ltd £667,260
Elf Petroleum UK plc £322,048
English China Clays plc £300,000
Enterprise Oil plc £196,790
Esso UK plc £1,511,423
Eurotunnel plc £124,601
Express Newspapers plc £300,094

F

Favermead Ltd £143,667
Fenwick Ltd £107,772
Fine Art Developments plc £184,167
Albert Fisher Group plc £157,000
Robert Fleming Holdings Ltd £177,372
Ford Motor Company Ltd £898,000
Forte plc £369,402

G

Gallaher Ltd £346,312
General Accident plc £400,000
General Electric Company plc £1,121,000
Gestetner Holdings PLC £105,000
Gillette Industries plc £99,000
GKN plc £548,000
GlaxoWellcome plc £9,700,000
Glencore UK Ltd £202,225
Granada Group plc £500,000
Grand Metropolitan PLC £3,434,000
The Greenalls Group plc £134,712
Greggs plc £138,000
R Griggs Group Ltd £341,102
Guardian Royal Exchange plc £291,933
Guinness PLC £4,200,000

H

Halifax Building Society £1,888,945
Hambros PLC £277,000

135

Hanson plc £1,058,000
Harrisons & Crosfield plc £129,673
John Henderson Ltd £155,242
Highland Distilleries Co plc £110,000
Hillsdown Holdings plc £500,000
HSBC Holdings plc £1,242,000

I

IBM United Kingdom
Holdings Ltd £535,000
Iceland Group plc £409,000
ICL plc £230,000
IMI plc £257,000
Imperial Chemical Industries plc £800,000
Inchcape plc £401,000
Intel Corporation UK Ltd £119,783
Interpublic Ltd £223,589

J

JIB Group plc £161,000
Johnson Matthey plc £229,000
Johnson Wax Ltd £240,000

K

Kellogg Co of Great Britain Ltd £414,000
Kingfisher plc £558,413
Kleinwort Benson Group plc £294,000
Kodak Ltd £442,542
KPMG £513,000
Kwik-Fit Holdings plc £410,000

L

Ladbroke Group PLC £241,000
Land Securities PLC £135,000
LASMO plc £137,183
Lazard Brothers & Co Ltd £200,000
Legal & General plc £464,750
Levi Strauss (UK) Ltd £304,256
John Lewis Partnership plc £790,000
Lex Service PLC £232,000

Linpac Group Ltd £162,000
Littlewoods Organisation PLC £1,300,000
Lloyd's of London £253,519
Lloyds TSB Group plc £4,606,000
London Stock Exchange £113,000
LucasVarity plc £309,077
LWT £200,000

M

McCain Foods (GB) Ltd £398,256
McDonald's Restaurants Ltd £287,753
E D & F Man Plc £234,000
Manchester Airport plc £190,000
Manpower UK plc £140,269
Marks and Spencer plc £4,900,000
Marlowe Holdings Ltd £744,000
Mars GB Ltd £224,084
Matsushita Electric (UK) Ltd £200,000
Bernard Matthews plc £257,094
John Menzies plc £155,000
MEPC plc £143,000
Mercury Asset Management
Group plc £275,000
Mercury Communications Ltd £950,000
MFI Furniture Group plc £166,692
Midland Bank plc £1,060,000
Midlands Electricity plc £1,625,000
Mirror Group plc £274,000
Morgan Crucible Company plc £114,670
Morgan Grenfell Group plc £243,873
Wm Morrison Supermarkets plc £785,000

N

The National Grid Group plc £1,056,209
National Power PLC £384,000
National Westminster Bank plc £2,793,833
Nationwide Building Society £544,464
Nestlé UK Ltd £864,000
News International plc £1,005,849

Next plc £194,000
NFC plc £599,000
Nortel Ltd £174,700
Northern Electric plc £223,000
Northern Foods plc £702,000
Northern Ireland Electricity PLC £134,000
Norwich Union Life
Insurance Society £249,000
Nuclear Electric plc £325,391

O

Oakhill Group Ltd £196,257

P

P & O Steam Navigation
Company £448,000
Panasonic UK Ltd £178,241
Pannell Kerr Forster £316,500
Pearl Group plc £352,165
Pearson plc £792,000
Peoples Phone Co PLC £112,729
Pfizer Group Ltd £194,724
Pilkington plc £204,000
Polypipe plc £184,715
Post Office Group £1,973,000
PowerGen plc £1,002,670
PPP Healthcare Ltd £300,000
Price Waterhouse –
United Kingdom £150,000
Prudential Corporation plc £1,700,000

R

Racal Electronics plc £118,000
Rank Organisation plc £239,000
Reader's Digest Association Ltd £182,000
Reckitt & Colman plc £224,000
Redland PLC £733,627
Reed Executive plc £224,251

Reed International £136,000
Reuters Holdings PLC £2,500,000
Richer Sounds plc £108,393
RJB Mining plc £951,678
Rolls–Royce plc £298,800
Rothmans UK Holdings Limited £238,077
N M Rothschild & Sons Ltd £463,000
The Royal Bank of Scotland
Group plc £1,124,000
Royal & Sun Alliance Insurance
Group plc £975,600
The RTZ–CRA Group £983,000

S

Safeway plc £214,000
Saga Leisure Ltd £134,000
J Sainsbury plc £2,000,000
Salomon Brothers Europe Limited .. £176,527
Save & Prosper Group Ltd £1,347,000
Scapa Group plc £103,266
Schroders plc £536,000
Scottish Amicable Life
Assurance Society £113,872
Scottish & Newcastle plc £523,000
Scottish Power plc £327,000
Scottish Television plc £365,955
Seagram Distillers plc £4,340,000
Sears plc £504,000
Securicor Group plc £115,000
Sedgwick Group plc £177,000
SEEBOARD plc £181,838
Severn Trent plc £233,869
Shell UK Limited £1,717,978
Siebe plc £124,000
Slough Estates plc £161,600
Smith & Nephew plc £533,000
W H Smith Group plc £170,000
SmithKline Beecham plc £1,350,000
Smiths Industries plc £730,000
Somerfield Stores plc £532,000

South Western Electricity plc £148,000
Southern Electric plc £227,488
Stagecoach Holdings plc £163,000
Standard Chartered plc £250,000
Stockholm & Edinburgh
Investments Ltd £127,150
Storehouse plc £266,000
Sun Life Assurance
Society plc £400,000
J Swire & Sons Ltd £345,000

T

Tarmac plc £319,000
Tate & Lyle plc £692,680
Telegraph Group Ltd £150,000
Tesco plc £727,000
Tetra Pak Ltd £380,000
Thames Water plc £114,000
Thomson Corporation £100,000
THORN EMI plc £700,000
3i Group plc £350,000
3M UK Holdings plc £125,000
TI Group plc £216,000
Tioxide Group Ltd £325,000
TNT UK Ltd £158,750
Tomkins plc £330,276

U

Unigate plc £185,000
Unilever £3,000,000
Unisys Ltd £106,148
United Biscuits (UK) Ltd £569,000
United News & Media plc £430,000
United Utilities PLC £257,537

V

Van Leer (UK) Holdings Ltd £1,100,000
Vaux Group plc £139,000
Vauxhall Motors Ltd....................... £116,545
Vickers plc....................................... £175,000
Vodafone Group plc £261,000
VSEL PLC £143,739

W

SBC Warburg Group plc £450,000
Warburtons Ltd £100,000
Weetabix Ltd £722,000
Wessex Water plc £102,300
Whitbread plc £482,963
Wickes plc £129,000
Williams Holdings plc £209,000
Willis Corroon Group plc £230,000
George Wimpey PLC £120,000
Wogen Group Ltd........................... £150,000
Rudolf Wolff & Co Ltd £135,579
John Wood Group plc £100,499
Woolwich Building Society £208,000
WPP Group plc £300,000

Y

Yorkshire Bank plc £114,000
Yorkshire – Tyne Tees
Television Holdings plc £312,000
Yorkshire Water plc £100,000

ZENECA Group PLC £1,900,000

Useful addresses

Business in the Community

44 Baker Street, London W1M 1DH (0171-224 1260)

For advice on secondment and employee volunteering. It has regional offices throughout England.

Scottish Business in the Community

Romano House, 43 Station Road, Corstorphine, Edinburgh EH12 7AF (0131-334 9876)

Charities Aid Foundation

48 Pembury Road, Tonbridge, Kent TN9 2JD (01732-771333)
Runs the Give as You Earn payroll giving scheme.

Further reading

A Guide to Company Giving and *The Major Companies Guide*. These give details on the donations policies of all the major givers in the UK and how to contact them. A thrice-yearly journal – *Corporate Citizen* – gives information on what is going on in the company giving world. They are all available from the Directory of Social Change, 24 Stephenson Way, London NW1 2DP (0171-209 5151).

Who's Who; Yellow Pages; trade directories or magazines contain names and areas of interest of company officials.

Showing at a screen near you....
Companies are publishing increasing amounts of information on the Internet. Company annual reports contain information on community support – some of it extensive – which are often posted at company web sites.

Chapter 9

Raising money from local authorities

▪▪▪

At some point during their lifetime, most groups that work with young people look to the town hall for help. You may need equipment, help with understanding the law, buildings, running costs, training, contacts or advice. In many cases the local authority may have someone who can answer your question or know support you can apply for. The local authority remains important in a changing funding climate. It often helps with the costs of the unglamourous parts of work with young people that cannot be funded elsewhere. Even here, though, local authorities are watching budgets as never before, and your relationship with them will be made up of many parts: lobbying, profile-raising, partnership-building as well as fundraising.

Money's too tight to mention?

Local authorities are similar to other funders in the book. Increasingly, you have to build your relationship with your local authority as you would any other potential supporter. The days of widespread grant aid for anything and everything are largely over, and few local authorities now want to be cheque-writing machines. Particularly if you are a new project, you should not start by asking the local authority for money. You need to work with them, ideally in that much overused word – partnership – to develop a project and win support for the idea. All too often voluntary organisations begin their relationship with the local authority on the wrong foot, by asking for money, rather than winning support for their proposal.

A substantial part of local authority support for young people is through its youth service. In recent years youth service funding has been considerably reduced, but at the time of writing the new government was considering ways of strengthening the statutory base of the youth service, which may enable it to be more confident about its future levels of funding. It is also the case that whilst the mainstream youth service budget has been reduced, funding from other areas such as employment and training consortia, criminal justice agencies, drugs prevention bodies and health authorities has contributed significantly to expanding the overall funding available for work with young people.

What local authorities can give:

- Advice
- Equipment
- Training
- Salaries
- Running costs
- Buildings
- Transport
- Refurbishment

- Help with programme development
- Access to other funders and programmes
- Publicity
- Endorsement.

Most youth organisations will also be entitled to 80% off their rates. The local authority can chose to give you 100% rate relief if they want. Try to persuade them to do this, but in any case claim the rate relief you are entitled to.

Which local authority?

Local government in England has been transformed in recent years. At very best this chapter is a snapshot of the situation as it is now; it may be very different in two to three years. It may also be the case that as authorities change, patterns of who has responsibility for what take time to emerge.

The structure of local government will be different in each part of the country. In Scotland, Wales and Northern Ireland there is one tier of local government, although you may be working in more than one local authority area. In England you may have several levels to take into account: your county council, a district council, a borough or city council. There may be a further level still if you have a parish or town council. Or you may have just one, say a London borough, a metropolitan district such as South Yorkshire or one of the new unitary authorities such as Bristol. (At the end of the chapter is a list of the different English local authorities.)

The situation is still changing. Where you are not sure how your local authority is structured, ask around. Someone on your committee, a volunteer, a parent or a member may know. You can also ring your local councillors, and ask about the local authority and how it works. (You will need get to know him or her sooner or later, so this will be a useful introduction.) If you do not already have their number, the town hall will. Ask for the Chief Executive's department and they will inform and direct you from there.

Contacting the appropriate office in your local authority can be time-consuming and frustrating. How your local authority is set up will directly affect who you apply to, and what you ask for. So it is worth spending some time getting to know the system. Once you are inside the gates, understanding how the authority works and making progress should become easier.

If you work within a unitary authority (these include London boroughs and metropolitan districts, as well as many towns and cities), you have one authority to think about. In each of these cases, it will be a matter of making contact with the appropriate offices to talk about your proposal.

District or County?

Where you are working with a county council which also includes district, borough and possibly city councils, you need to take account of the two-tiered structure.

Here, the responsibilities and functions of the local authorities are divided between the two levels. For example:

- the county council will have responsibility for the large services and facilities which benefit the whole county. These include education and social services;
- district and borough councils on the other hand are responsible for services and resources that benefit their local areas. These include housing, environmental services and local planning.

There will be some cross-over in the responsibilities of county and district councils.

Whether you apply at the county or district level will depend upon what you are applying for. You should consider how wide the geographical area is that you cover. A regional youth association, for example, may organise activities – such as a young people's counselling and information service – that take in more than one town or district. A local youth organisation is more likely to concentrate on a smaller local area. One may apply to the county for support, the other to the district.

If you are looking for county support you may have to lobby strongly. At this level it can help to have councillors, key officials and local politicians arguing the merits of your case and persuading others of the county-wide benefits of your scheme. Council committees where decision-making powers lie are not just made up by councillors. There may also be representatives of voluntary organisations, trade unions and sometimes youth groups, all of whom need to be lobbied.

Once you have decided how your local authority is organised, you need to approach the appropriate officials. Who has responsibility for work with young people varies from authority to authority. Youth services may come under Education, and sometimes under Community Education. Some authorities will include youth provision under Leisure and Recreation; others will have a wide-ranging function called Community Services and will list youth services there. A key contact will be the Principal Youth Officer.

Parish and Town Councils

In some villages and county towns in England and Wales there can be a further tier of local government. Parish or community councils work at a very local, parochial level. Called community councils in Wales, parish or town councils in England (and neighbourhood or community councils in some urban areas), these bodies are responsible for maintaining and providing leisure and recreation facilities. In practice they look after village halls and playing fields as well as car parking, street lighting and such like. They must also be consulted in any local planning applications.

However your local authority is organised, find out:

- Who takes the lead in developing and supporting young people? Which council, county, district etc. and then, which departments?
- Who makes the policies which affect young people? (Councillors, committees)
- Who makes these policies happen? (Officers and offices).

This local council will decide on local priorities for spending and fix its own rate which will be collected by the district council. The parish council will not have vast sums of money available, but it will direct the money to very local concerns. If you are a very local club, needing or using a very local facility, and your activities contribute directly to the life of the community, you may find support from the parish council. Often, in villages, there will be a Village Plan which may include details of young people's resources, both actual and planned. Make contact with your parish council, either by attending the open meetings or by meeting parish councillors.

Council officers will be able to tell you how much is available, if anything, and how it is spent. Councillors may also be able to lobby on your behalf. Some parish council meetings are attended by local authority councillors. They may use meetings as a sounding board to find out what the local priorities are. If your name is mentioned here and wins support, there may be more note taken at a district level. Lists of local parish councillors will be posted in town and county halls, in your village hall (if you have one), or your local post office, parish church or library. The local citizen's advice bureau may also have information.

Youth Councils

In many areas, Youth Councils have been formed, largely made up of representatives of youth organisations in the area, including young people themselves. These councils may exist alongside any of the local government tiers (county, district, borough, city, parish etc.). They may have grant-giving powers or have a consultative role with other local authority committees. Here again, you need to find out who is on the council and get to know them. There may be opportunities for a representative from your own organisation to be appointed or elected onto the council.

Who does what in the local authority?

Fundraising at any level is most effective when you connect with key people who are enthusiastic about your cause. You may need to enthuse them first and then get them to enthuse others. Writing endless letters is often the least effective way of raising funds. It is more helpful to your cause to meet with people face to face. In local authorities the key people to contact are:

- local authority officers
- local councillors.

You should not leave making these contacts until it is too late. Too often groups leave meeting the people who can influence and help until the eleventh hour or even after their application has failed. It is far better to involve local authority staff, councillors, MPs and other local people at an early stage to help the process along. If you do not yet know of any local people that have influence in the community, ask around your members, parents, volunteers and staff to find someone who does. If you have someone connected with the organisation who has particular experience or knowledge of making things happen locally, use them to make introductions for you and to promote the project themselves.

Local authority officers

Your first point of contact with the authority will usually be an officer within one of the departments. These are very important to your cause and can help your project in many ways. They are paid members of staff employed to implement council policies. In local authorities there will be a Principal Youth Officer (PYO) who heads up the statutory Youth Service in the area. In some areas there will be only one Youth Officer; in others there will be several with their own projects and expertise (maybe funding or voluntary youth sector liaison), or with responsibility for particular geographical areas. You should also bear in mind that administrative officers often have detailed knowledge of what is happening, and may have the most information.

You may need to think more widely than just those officers connected with youth provision. There may be other staff working in other departments that can also help. For instance, if you are running an after-school club there may be a named officer in social services who can help and advise. You may be working closely with school non-attenders which will interest the education department. Work with those with disabilities, or young people from a particular ethnic group, may involve an officer with these specific responsibilities. In all cases you will need to keep officers informed about your organisation and ensure that your activities are promoted within their department. If you are unsure which officer you should speak to, contact the chief executive's office which will be able to give you a name as a starting point. More and more local authorities are now establishing External Funding Units to help with liaison and signposting to appropriate offices and personnel.

Officers make recommendations to councillors to act upon and you should brief them well and update them regularly. They will want to know how your proposal is to work; what resources (not just money) will be required; whether there is community support; whether there is opposition; and any possible repercussions from supporting your activity. Try to make sure that officers are well-informed and enthusiastic about your proposal. If your activity is modest, support can often be directly authorised by officers. If the proposal is more involved and needs further endorsement, officers can recommend it be supported by councillors at committee level. It may be, however, that you need to persuade councillors personally to give their support when it reaches their committee(s).

> When contacting councillors and local authority officers, follow up telephone calls and meetings with a letter, summarising the key points you wish to make. Copies are often passed on to other local authority colleagues with notes written on.

Councillors

Councillors are representatives of a ward or a county division. They are also politicians with an agenda. They serve on committees and decide policy following briefings given by local authority officers. The fact that they are local representatives gives you the greatest point of leverage as their first duty is to represent the people in their ward. If you are working with young people you are contributing to local communities and councillors should be interested in what you are doing.

Where you need help from a number of different departments within the local authority, councillors can sponsor your application, oil the local government wheels, and generally help the progress of a proposal. They may help to broker a deal between departments that can give larger funding to a project than could be given by a single department. Where you are looking for county funding (as opposed to district), councillors can also help to cross district council lines. You may need to promote the regional benefits of your proposal. Local councillors on your side will help to identify which county officers to speak to and the channels to go through. They can also make a difference on the committees they participate in.

Local councillors are listed in the local press, your town hall, the citizen's advice bureau which will also give details of their surgery hours or the Municipal Yearbook available in your local library. You can contact your ward councillor at their home address (they expect this) or through the local authority. You should write care of the local authority when contacting other councillors. Letters are always helpful. Busy councillors can attach a quick note and pass it on to the relevant officer. Be realistic in your approach and consider the scale of your activity and what you are asking help for. Whilst the chair and vice-chair of any committee are obviously important to the process, they are also the busiest people and may not be the best contacts if your proposal is modest in scale.

Remember that the balance of political power can be very different between the various tiers of local government. It is important to be able to present your case in different ways to attract the support of politicians in different parties.

Promoting your cause may seem daunting at first. However, if you are clear about why they should support you, your enthusiasm and a well-argued case will at least guarantee a hearing.

Which departments should you approach?

Local authorities organise their departments in different ways. They have various functions; for example, housing, community services, social services, education and so on. Each of these functions includes a number of different responsibilities.

Leisure services for example, (which may be a separate department or may come under education) will be responsible for parks, gardens, cemeteries, sport, arts and libraries. Where youth services comes under this department, it will be only one of a number of different responsibilities that the department has.

Following local government reorganisation, youth services may have moved to come under a different department to where it was previously. In many authorities youth, Community Services, Community identify different service areas.

The youth service and GEST funding

As outlined above funding for the youth service has been reduced and grant aid is not given as widely as it once was. Where grants are available from the youth service you should make your case in the light of current priorities and local concerns. Where the youth service has its own application form, ask for advice from youth officers as to how to complete it. Equal opportunities and inclusiveness are pre-requisites for local authority funding. Furthermore, you will need to show, even for relatively modest grants how you will measure the outcomes of your work. Can you do what you say you can and how will you show this to the local authority?

GEST funding is devolved from the DfEE to each local education authority. Money is made available to schools and others to fund training and educational support in particular areas. (In 1997-98, the major focus area will be school self-improvement with money available for schools' development.) Each year guidelines are produced to specify areas for local

> "When briefing councillors, ensure that what you say is based on facts, and argue your case on its merits. Be aware that most councillors will not know the background to the issue or have the papers to hand in the same way as officers, and will need filling in. More generally, relationships built up with councillors over time will prove the most valuable, so try and involve then in your work: invite them to address a meeting of your supporters for example. As politicians, councillors like being loved, and few will resist the temptation to say positive things about you that they know will please the audience – and that you can hold them to in the future. Early evenings are best, as most councillors will be at their own jobs during the day."
>
> *The Campaigning Handbook*, The Directory of Social Change

Making the case for your project

What features of your project make it attractive to your local authority?

How do any of the following apply to your organisation or project?

- Local benefits
- Regional benefits
- Large number of different groups benefit (which ones?)
- Community run
- Innovative approach
- Addressing special needs
- Matching funds raised
- Established track record
- Sound finances
- Fits in with local authority priorities
- Fills a gap or augments local authority service provision
- Number of different bodies/organisations involved (which ones?)
- Established and enthusiastic membership
- Large number of benefits from a small grant (what benefits?)
- Local support
- Good publicity for the local authority
- Value for money
- Other (list).

authorities to draw up spending plans. Guidelines for the 1997/98 round were published in July 1996. Grants were to support youth and community workers to develop three priority areas:

- drug education and drug prevention programmes
- crime prevention programmes that come directly from the evaluation of the Youth Action Scheme
- general youth work training which includes part-time staff and volunteer programmes.

Youth organisations should find out current priorities under GEST funding and see where their work fits in. Where your concerns and those of the local authority coincide you have already established common ground.

Depending upon what your project is, there may be a number of different parts of the local authority that you could approach. Some are obvious, others less so. In each case you will need to look into their current services, priorities and timetables for applications. You also need to look closely at who benefits from your activities, and whether there are other parts of the local authority that may be interested in your proposal. Whilst support may first come from youth services (which may be under education, leisure, community and so on), there may also be help under the following:

- sports development
- the arts
- education
- social services
- opportunities for those with disabilities
- ethnic minorities
- women
- health promotion
- increasing awareness of the local authority
- urban development and regeneration
- rural isolation
- environmental improvement
- voluntary sector liaison
- community safety.

Each local authority is different. The following are some examples of projects that may support the current priorities and concerns of particular departments. It is by no means exhaustive, and each local authority and each department within that authority will have its own approach to relationships with voluntary organisations.

The Social Services department for example, may be interested in projects such as:

- After school clubs
- Work with young mothers
- Counselling and information services

- Work with young people leaving care
- Work with young refugees
- Reducing youth crime.

On the other hand, projects which resonate with the priorities of your local Education department might include for example:

- Playground activities in schools
- Work with school non-attenders
- Training
- Playschemes
- Work with unemployed young people
- Work with young people with special needs
- Health education
- Literacy work with young people.

Local authorities and other bodies

Local authorities often work in partnership with other organisations and often apply for funding themselves (e.g. for SRB funding or European grants programmes). They generally work with other organisations such as TECs, businesses, health authorities and probation services to achieve a variety of aims and to draw up and implement locally defined strategies on a wide range of issues.

Increasingly, local authorities are gatekeepers to other forms of funding and influence. Where local authorities are working closely with other bodies on funding bids or service provision, there may be opportunities for voluntary organisations to become involved. If the youth service is not involved, the Chief Executive's office can advise you on which parties are involved. It is the case, however, that to be involved at any meaningful level you will have to be at the right meetings and in the right networks to get an invite to the table.

Local authorities have regular meetings with a host of other public agencies such as the probation service, police authorities and the local health authority. These meetings propose and advise on approaches to local issues and concerns and how services will be delivered. Where your activities reach groups targeted by these bodies or you have an approach that is innovative and professional, you can make a strong case for being included in any consultation, and then being considered as part of any service delivery.

Again, each local authority is different, but examples of projects or approaches that would interest a multi-agency initiative might include:

Probation Service and the Police

- Diversionary activities for young people at risk from crime – sports, arts
- Work with offenders
- Motor projects.

Health Authorities

- Health promotion generally (fitting in with local health strategies)
- Drugs and alcohol awareness
- HIV prevention
- Smoking
- Eating disorders.

General grant-giving by the local authority

As well as the specific functions outlined above, most councils have a discretionary grant-giving scheme for voluntary organisations. Sometimes called the Community Chest, this scheme can be applied for by any voluntary organisation within the authority's area. Grants tend to be small (up to around £500) and are often for equipment and training courses. You may be able to apply only once in any year, so plan accordingly. The scheme is often operated from the Chief Executive's office, which may also be responsible for events and activities that are not covered by other functions. Youth conferences, festivals or tournaments for example may have authority-wide benefits and may be supported more on the lines of a sponsorship, particularly if there are publicity opportunities or links with other countries, through town-twinning and the like.

All departments have budget allocations to be spent by the end of each financial year. If you apply towards the end of the budgetary period there may be too little money in the coffers, or "too much". Where there is a surplus, officers will be keen to see it spent before the next financial year, and your application may be received particularly warmly. However, if the cupboard is bare you will have to wait until the next financial year. If you get to know your council officers they may be able to tell you how much money is left under a particular budget.

Applications

By the time you fill in any application form you will know how your local authority works. You should be able to enlist the support of officers and local councillors. The application procedure will differ from authority to authority, although in almost every case there will be an application form to fill in. This may be specific to the youth service or named department or be a general form for the whole of the authority.

In general you need to know:
- the maximum and minimum grants available;
- current priorities and criteria, either for the council as a whole or the funding programme in particular;
- how you should fill in the application form;
- what information is needed and how it should be presented;
- the application timetable and deadlines for submission.

Where you are applying for a large project with other funders involved you need to allow for time lags and delays in submission and approval. Lead-in times differ according to which partners are involved, how many, and how good the relationship is. If a proposal is to go before a committee for a decision, you need to find out the timetable and to lobby for your cause well in advance.

Be clear and concise. Take advice from officers as to how the form should be filled in. Once submitted, a regular (although not too frequent) telephone call will keep you in touch with how the application is progressing. If by this time you are on good terms with the relevant officers this can be a friendly, informal chat that can help to keep the application "live".

Remember, local authorities are like other funders in what they want to know from you:
- What do you want to do?
- Why do you want to do it?
- How will you make it happen?
- Who will be accountable?
- What difference will the work make to the local area?
- What do you want from the local authority?

In other words, they will look to see if you:
- Have identified a clear need.
- Have produced a good and workable plan.
- Have costed your work.
- Will be able to measure the value and outcomes of your work.

Local authorities also appreciate credit and recognition for their contribution to a project. Show how you will publicise their grant and generally help people to view their local authority more positively.

The significance of local authorities

- May give core-funding
- Can publicise activities and events
- Access to networks
- Significant partners e.g. in SRB, European bids
- Relationships with health authorities, police authorities, TECs etc.
- Expertise on form filling
- Policy and legislation issues e.g. health and safety

In some cases the absence of a local authority from a partnership bid can cause suspicion. Some of the larger funding programmes will want to see the authority's involvement if they are to take the application seriously.

Basically, there are three ways of getting a project supported by the local authority

- Applying for a grant, but amounts are limited and available money is generally used up on commitments made in previous years.
- Through service agreements or contracts, where you are competing with a whole range of organisations – including commercial ones.
- Getting the local authority to include your project in an SRB, safer cities, ESF or other bid. Many local authorities now act as gatekeepers for external funding. But all this takes time and forward planning.

The key thing is that when you meet with your local authority, don't talk about funding; talk about collaboration. Local authorities are not cheque-writing machines. They do not see themselves as there to underwrite your core costs year in, year out. They have their own views on what service provision they want to see happen in the area. Show how you fit into and understand their priorities and concerns, rather than expect them just to support you to do whatever you like.

Local authorities and partnership funding for the National Lottery

The arts, sport, heritage and millennium boards all require some level of partnership funding from applicants. Only the Charities Board waives this condition, recognising that for charities, fundraising is tough enough already.

The National Lottery Yearbook has talked to potential applicants to the relevant distributors and to the local authority officers who must raise partnership funding themselves and who often advise their groups on how to do so. This research suggests that small organisations in disadvantaged areas, applying for relatively small lottery grants, are having the toughest time when it comes to securing partnership funding.

Local authorities are among the leading providers of partnership funding. The larger metropolitan authorities report that for projects they consider to be strategically important they have managed to raise partnership monies from their own budgets, from European Structural Funds or from the Single Regeneration Budget. Local authorities have often already budgeted for the larger developments (e.g. a new swimming pool) and the lottery is helping them complete the project earlier than expected. Smaller local authorities, however, are not as confident of their ability to provide partnership funding.

Two reports, the *London Pride Lottery Study* and *London and the Lottery – the experiences of smaller organisations*, found that the difficulty of raising partnership funding was causing applicants to postpone or abandon their bids to the lottery boards.

SOME DOS AND DON'TS

Do

- Find out how your local authority works
- Find and contact key local officers
- Build good relationships with local councillors across the party divide
- Find out about authority/function priorities
- Think creatively about your project
- Use local media to raise your profile
- Attend meetings regularly
- Be clear and to the point
- Keep well informed about changes in criteria/priorities
- Be persistent
- Budget realistically
- Find out about application procedure and deadlines.

Don't

- Give up
- Leave talking to councillors and officers until you need money
- Limit your project to one narrow departmental interest
- Forget in kind support from your local authority
- Be bashful about what you can offer
- Let information become out of date
- Plan in the short-term. Look to the future
- Waffle.

A list of local authorities in England 1997/98

London
Corporation of London
Barking & Dagenham
Barnet
Bexley
Brent
Bromley
Camden
Croydon
Ealing
Enfield
Greenwich
Hackney
Hammersmith & Fulham
Haringey
Harrow
Havering
Hillingdon
Hounslow
Islington
Kensington & Chelsea
Kingston upon Thames
Lambeth
Lewisham
Merton
Newham
Redbridge
Richmond upon Thames
Southwark
Sutton
Tower Hamlets
Waltham Forest
Wandsworth
Westminster

Metropolitan Districts
Greater Manchester
Bolton
Bury
Manchester
Oldham
Rochdale
Salford
Stockport
Tameside
Trafford
Wigan

Merseyside
Knowsley
Liverpool
St Helens
Sefton
Wirral

South Yorkshire
Barnsley
Doncaster
Rotherham
Sheffield

Tyne & Wear
Gateshead
Newcastle upon Tyne
North Tyneside
South Tyneside
Sunderland

West Midlands
Birmingham
Coventry
Dudley
Sandwell
Solihull
Walsall
Wolverhampton

West Yorkshire
Bradford
Calderdale
Kirklees
Leeds
Wakefield

Non-Metropolitan Counties & Districts

Unitary authorities

Bath & North East Somerset
Bournemouth
Brighton & Hove
Bristol
Darlington
Derby
East Riding of Yorkshire
Hartlepool
Isle of Wight
Kingston upon Hull
Leicester
Luton
Middlesbrough
Milton Keynes
North East Lincolnshire
North Lincolnshire
North Somerset
Poole
Portsmouth
Redcar & Cleveland
Rutland
Southampton
Stockton-on-Tees
Stoke-on-Trent
South Gloucestershire
Swindon
York

Two-tier areas

In each of the following areas, there is a county council (in bold***) plus the city, district and borough councils listed underneath.

Bedfordshire

Bedford
Mid Bedfordshire
South Bedfordshire

Berkshire*

Bracknell Forest
Newbury
Reading
Slough
Windsor & Maidenhead
Wokingham

* Berkshire County Council is abolished on 1st April, 1998, when the six district councils become unitary.

Buckinghamshire

Aylesbury
Chiltern
South Bucks
Wycombe

Cambridgeshire

Cambridge
East Cambridgeshire
Fenland
Huntingdonshire
Peterborough *
South Cambridgeshire

* Peterborough becomes a unitary authority on 1st April, 1998.

Cheshire

Chester
Congleton
Crewe & Nantwich
Ellesmere Port & Neston
Halton *
Macclesfield
Vale Royal
Warrington *

* Halton and Warrington become unitary authorities on 1st April, 1998.

Cornwall
Caradon
Carrick
Kerrier
North Cornwall
Penwith
Restormel

Cumbria
Allerdale
Barrow-in-Furness
Carlisle
Copeland
Eden
South Lakeland

Derbyshire
Amber Valley
Bolsover
Chesterfield
Derbyshire Dales
Erewash
High Peak
North East Derbyshire
South Derbyshire

Devon
East Devon
Exeter
Mid Devon
North Devon
Plymouth *
South Hams
Teignbridge
Torbay *
Torridge
West Devon

* Plymouth and Torbay become unitary authorities on 1st April, 1998.

Dorset
Christchurch
East Dorset
North Dorset
Purbeck
West Dorset
Weymouth & Portland

Durham
Chester-le-Street
Derwentside
Durham
Easington
Sedgefield
Teesdale
Wear Valley

East Sussex
Eastbourne
Hastings
Lewes
Rother
Wealden

Essex
Basildon
Braintree
Brentwood
Castle Point
Chelmsford
Colchester
Epping Forest
Harlow
Maldon
Rochford
Southend-on-Sea *
Tendring
Thurrock *
Uttlesford

* Southend-on-Sea and Thurrock become unitary authorities on 1st April, 1998.

Gloucestershire
Cheltenham
Cotswold
Forest of Dean
Gloucester
Stroud
Tewkesbury

Hampshire
Basingstoke & Deane
East Hampshire
Eastleigh
Fareham
Gosport
Hart
Havant
New Forest
Rushmoor
Test Valley
Winchester

Hereford & Worcester *
Bromsgrove
Hereford
Leominster
Malvern Hills
Redditch
South Herefordshire
Worcester
Wychavon
Wyre Forest

* Hereford & Worcester
County Council, Hereford
City Council, and Leominster
and South Herefordshire
District Councils are
abolished on 1st April, 1998.
They are replaced by
Worcestershire County
Council and a unitary
Herefordshire. Malvern Hills
undergoes a major boundary
change.

Hertfordshire
Broxbourne
Dacorum
East Hertfordshire
Hertsmere
North Hertfordshire
St Albans
Stevenage
Three Rivers
Watford
Welwyn Hatfield

Kent
Ashford
Canterbury
Dartford
Dover
Gillingham *
Gravesham
Maidstone
Rochester upon Medway *
Sevenoaks
Shepway
Swale
Thanet
Tonbridge & Malling
Tunbridge Wells

* Gillingham and Rochester
upon Medway are combined as
the Medway Towns unitary
authority on 1st April, 1998.

Lancashire
Blackburn with Darwen *
Blackpool *
Burnley
Chorley
Fylde
Hyndburn
Lancaster
Pendle
Preston
Ribble Valley

Rossendale
South Ribble
West Lancashire
Wyre

* Blackburn with Darwen and
Blackpool become unitary
authorities on 1st April, 1998.

Leicestershire
Blaby
Charnwood
Harborough
Hinckley & Bosworth
Melton
North West Leicestershire
Oadby & Wigston

Lincolnshire
Boston
East Lindsey
Lincoln
North Kesteven
South Holland
South Kesteven
West Lindsey

Norfolk
Breckland
Broadland
Great Yarmouth
King's Lynn & West Norfolk
North Norfolk
Norwich
South Norfolk

Northamptonshire
Corby
Daventry
East Northamptonshire
Kettering
Northampton
South Northamptonshire
Wellingborough

Northumberland
Alnwick
Berwick-upon-Tweed
Blyth Valley
Castle Morpeth
Tynedale
Wansbeck

North Yorkshire
Craven
Hambleton
Harrogate
Richmondshire
Ryedale
Scarborough
Selby

Nottinghamshire
Ashfield
Bassetlaw
Broxtowe
Gedling
Mansfield
Newark & Sherwood
Nottingham *
Rushcliffe

* Nottingham becomes a unitary
authority on 1st April, 1998.

Oxfordshire
Cherwell
Oxford
South Oxfordshire
Vale of White Horse
West Oxfordshire

Shropshire
Bridgnorth
North Shropshire
Oswestry
Shrewsbury & Atcham
South Shropshire
The Wrekin *

* The Wrekin becomes a unitary
authority on 1st April, 1998.

Somerset
Mendip
Sedgemoor
South Somerset
Taunton Deane
West Somerset

Staffordshire
Cannock Chase
East Staffordshire
Lichfield
Newcastle-under-Lyme
South Staffordshire
Stafford
Staffordshire Moorlands
Tamworth

Suffolk
Babergh
Forest Heath
Ipswich
Mid Suffolk
St Edmundsbury
Suffolk Coastal
Waveney

Surrey
Elmbridge
Epsom & Ewell
Guildford
Mole Valley
Reigate & Banstead
Runnymede
Spelthorne
Surrey Heath
Tandridge
Waverley
Woking

Warwickshire
North Warwickshire
Nuneaton & Bedworth
Rugby
Stratford-upon-Avon
Warwick

West Sussex
Adur
Arun
Chichester
Crawley
Horsham
Mid Sussex
Worthing

Wiltshire
Kennet
North Wiltshire
Salisbury
West Wiltshire

Raising money from government sources

Central or regional?

Methods of giving central government funds change over time. There is a movement away from centralised control towards giving more say to regional offices. As this pattern becomes established, so voluntary organisations will have a variety of funders to get to know. The government department with central responsibility for funding youth work is the Department for Education and Employment (DfEE). A small part of their overall budget is dedicated to supporting the statutory youth service. A further chunk of money is given to the National Youth Agency to support youth work development (see below). As well as these two sources, there are other government bodies which may be interested in supporting your work.

Each department and government body has its own set of priorities which will not necessarily include young people. You will have to be working in fields that are familiar to them and fit in with their existing policies. Where your work with young people involves main government focus areas such as crime prevention, job creation, enterprise or training for example, more funding opportunities may open up to you. However, it will be on the strength of your ability to deliver training, regeneration, new enterprise or environmental improvement that you will secure funding, rather than your commitment to the social development of young people.

Many government schemes are now regionally administered and are part of locally defined strategies and priorities. Where this is the case we have tried to say so, but a general principle applies: find out as much as possible about what is happening locally and regionally, and try to find ways to influence economic planning and local development.

The current tiers of government that voluntary organisations can target are:
- Government departments (such as Education and Employment, Environment, Health, Culture, Media and Sport, and the Welsh Office);
- Regional bodies such as Government Offices for the Regions;
- Quangos or non-departmental organisations and bodies (such as the Rural Development Commission, English Partnerships, Highland and Islands Enterprise);

- TECs (Training and Enterprise Councils) and health authorities administering funds and tenders for training and healthcare.

Some of these bodies will give money centrally; others through regional offices. Some programmes support building costs, whilst others will fund the running costs of a project. Partnership with other bodies is now a feature common to a number of the programmes. You may also find that government money can be used to match funds from other schemes such as Europe or the National Lottery.

These sources of income can provide new opportunities to finance your work; they can also bring constraints and new challenges to an organisation. Some money will only be available if there is a problem attached, such as drugs, crime or exclusion. If you cast your funding net wide to take in some of the different statutory schemes you should consider the following:

- ***We Applied Because it was There.*** Is the project you are applying for something you have planned to do in response to needs that you see, or have you conjured up a project to fit with the latest government funding programme?
- ***The Future Shock***. How will you continue the work once statutory funding has finished? Will you have had to take on extra resources to do the work, and how will these be used when the one, two or three year funding has ceased?
- ***The Compatibility Conundrum***. How do the large streams of government money fit in with the young people you work with and how they see themselves? Are there difficulties in linking these young people with crime prevention initiatives and so on?
- ***The Cuckoo in the Nest***. If you are successful in gaining support from a particular programme, will it alter the way your organisation works? How will the organisation adapt to meet any new demands that the funding will bring?

Grant programmes for youth work

Grants to National Voluntary Youth Organisations

Under its National Voluntary Youth Organisations (NVYO) Grant Scheme, the Department for Education and Employment (DfEE) gives grants to projects to further the planned personal and social education of young people. Over the three years until 1999, £9.1 million has been awarded to youth organisations .

The Youth Service Unit at the DfEE holds a central register of youth organisations eligible for a grant. To be included in the NVYO register, organisations must be both national and voluntary in nature; have large numbers of members in the 13-19 target age group, and have the planned personal and social education of young people as one of their primary aims.

There are currently 72 organisations listed. The register was revised in March 1996 and opened for new applications to join. Eight to ten new organisations joined and the list is now closed as funding has been committed up to 1999. The process of advertising the list and inviting organisations to apply to join may be the same in 1999, but youth organisations should ask nearer the time what the format will be.

Those organisations on the register were then invited to submit project proposals for funding. Around 60 organisations were supported with single projects, and

---

Organisations receiving a grant for 1996-1999:

Jewish Lads' and Girls' Brigade	£66,000
National Youth Orchestra of GB	£18,150
Ocean Youth Club	£206,200
Scout Association	£375,000
Youth Access	£149,200

Joint Projects:

Council for Environmental Education (National Federation of Young Farmers, Youth Clubs UK, RSPB and Wildlife Trust)	£257,000
YWCA (with Girls' Friendly Society)	£72,630

---

a further eight joint projects received a grant (see box above). As a general rule, the majority of the grants are awarded to cover the specific costs of project administration and only small amounts are available for capital expenditure or running costs.

During 1997/98 DfEE will review its arrangements for giving awards. Organisations which are interested in joining the register to apply for a grant in the next cycle can contact the department at any time. They will be notified nearer the time with details of any new arrangements. To approach the department about joining the register, or if you need any information about the scheme, you should contact: Tessa Thorns, Youth Service Unit, The Department for Education and Employment, Sanctuary Buildings, Great Smith Street, London SW1A 3BT (0171-925 5266; Fax: 0171-925 6954).

For groups in Scotland, contact: Debbie Swanson, The Scottish Office Education and Industry Department, Area 2A (West), Victoria Quay, Edinburgh EH6 6QQ (0131-244 0996; Fax: 0131-244 7001).

Youth Work Development Grants

These are funded by the Local Government Association and administered by the National Youth Agency. Grants are to support projects which are innovative in priority areas and give examples of good practice which can be distributed widely by the NYA for the general benefit of those working with young people.

Grants are only given to locally or regionally based voluntary organisations, which can include local or regional branches of national organisations. Projects must be new or developmental, and as with the NVYO register above, organisations should be concerned with the personal and social education of young people, particularly young people aged between 13 and 19 years.

Priority areas of work for this scheme are:

- training of staff, including volunteers
- organisational development
- development of productive partnerships with local authorities and other agencies
- work in inner-city areas.

Preference is given to projects or programmes which:

- help an organisation to develop in new and innovative ways
- show a commitment to young people participating in management and decision-making
- develop work with young people who are disabled or disadvantaged
- find or use new ways of raising and administering money.

There is around £400,000 each year (which includes the NYA's administrative costs). The grants start at £10,000 and go up to £50,000. Grants are given largely to cover revenue costs such as salaries, although spending on capital items can be up to £2,000 of each year's grant. New decisions and distributions will be made in December 1999.

Annual grants are currently given to:

Bierley Young People's Health Project – Step 2	£40,000
Community Links – Teenage health project	£45,000
Devon Youth Association – Racism in rural areas	£36,000
Hideaway Youth Project	£45,000
Hub Caribbean Youth Training Association – Ragga and Rap against racism	£13,000
Jigsaw Youth Theatre	£45,000
Lewisham Young Women's Resource Project	£15,000
London Union of Youth Clubs – Young women into safe surroundings	£40,000
Manchester Lesbian & Gay Switchboard – Young Lesbian Gay & Bisexual Peer to Peer Support Project	£40,000
Pickering Youth Forum	£4,000
Streetwise Youth	£30,000

For further information on the administration of the grants and how groups with headquarters in England can apply, contact: Terry Cane, National Youth Agency, 17-23 Albion Street, Leicester LE1 6GD (0116-247 1200).

For details of grants in Scotland, contact: Scottish Community Education Council, Roseberry House, 9 Haymarket Terrace, Edinburgh EH12 5EZ (0131-313 2488).

For details of grants in Wales, contact: Llyr Huws Gruffydd, Wales Youth Agency, Leslie Court, Lon y Llyn, Caerphilly, Mid Glamorgan CF83 1BQ (01222-880 088).

For details of grants in Northern Ireland, contact: Youth Council for Northern Ireland, Lamont House, Purdey's Lane, Belfast BT8 4TA (01232-643882; Fax: 01232-643874).

Other statutory sources of money

As well as specific youth work grants outlined above, there are other programmes which may apply to your project. You will have to think more broadly than youth work to be eligible. Much of the funding is linked to social and economic development at a local and regional level, and all of the schemes have a particular target; the environment, enterprise, rural development or urban regeneration for example.

Listed below are statutory programmes which support:
- urban regeneration and economic development
- training and enterprise
- rural development
- health
- drugs and substance abuse
- crime prevention
- environmental improvement
- sports
- arts
- volunteering.

Urban Regeneration and economic development
Single Regeneration Budget (SRB) Challenge Fund

This is the largest concentration of statutory support for local communities and is now into its fourth funding round. The total amount available for distribution is expected to gradually increase as commitments under old grant programmes are fulfilled. In 1995/96, £1.1 billion was given to support 164 proposals (with an average grant of around £300,000). The second round made £2.4 billion available for new proposals in 1996/97 and for 1997/98. The third round to run from April 1997 to March 1999 awarded around £200 million. Round four running from April 1998 to March 2000 will give around £80 million.

What it funds

The SRB Challenge Fund money is for local regeneration projects. It complements and attracts other resources which can be private, public or voluntary. The projects can last between one and seven years. So far, there have been three grant rounds to support projects which have been about good practice, value for money, and support for one or more of the following priorities:

- enhance the employment prospects, education and skills of local people, particularly the young and those at disadvantage, and promote equality of opportunity;
- encourage sustainable economic growth and wealth creation by improving the competitiveness of the local economy (including support for new and existing businesses);
- improve housing through physical improvements, better maintenance and greater choice and diversity;
- promote initiatives of benefit to ethnic minorities;
- tackle crime and improve community safety;
- protect and improve the environment and infrastructure and promote good design and landscaping;
- enhance the quality of life of local people, including their health and cultural and sports opportunities.

Examples of successful SRB bids involving work with young people

The first round of grants included the following successful bids which had a focus on young people:

Ipswich Wet Dock Area - led by Ipswich Borough Council and included a Foyer project (£85,000 in year one; £405,000 in total).

Bonus Scheme, Basildon - led by Chalvedon School and South West Essex Business Education Partnership and targeting the most vulnerable and least employable young people between 14 and 20 years (£71,000 in year one; £822,000 in total).

Tilbury Project, Essex - led by Essex County Council Education Department to improve the education and employment opportunities of young people (£77,000 in year one; £342,000 in total).

Contributing to a World Class City - led by City and Inner London North TEC to improve education and employment opportunities of young people and build new businesses (£1,042,000 in year one; £8,150,000 in total).

Education - Business Partnerships in West London - led by West London TEC to improve educational achievements of young people and thereby contribute to economic regeneration of area (£225,000 in year one; £1,280,000 in total).

Salter's City Foyer - led by Soho Housing Association (London) to improve the employment opportunities for homeless and unemployed young people (£300,000 in year one; £820,000 in total).

Unlocking the Economic Potential of Young People - led by AZTEC (London) to improve the skills and qualifications of young people and help the local economy (£540,000 in year one; £5,641,000 in total).

Motivation Programme - Enhancing the Prospects of Young People (Liverpool, Sefton and Knowsley) - new education/industry projects (£210,000 in year one; £1,800,000 in total).

Cautioning Support Programme, Cleveland - led by the voluntary sector, with support from the police, county council, probation service and others, to focus on young offenders and their families and give alternatives to re-offending. Currently the scheme works in Middlesbrough, but will also take in Lanbaurgh, Hartlepool and Stockton (£40,000 in year one; £320,000 in total).

Promoting Achievement in Education - a joint Cleveland County Council and Teesside TEC project to improve young people's numeracy and literacy and build upon existing education/business links (£230,000 in year one; £740,000 in total).

Miles Platting and Ancoats Young People Initiative - linked to city council Monsall proposals and City Pride initiatives and run by voluntary sector. The focus is on youth work, drug education, and training and employment. The project complements recent City Grant money for a major mill refurbishment in the area (£106,000 in year one; £178,000 in total).

Old Trafford - included within City Pride and closely linked to Moss Side and Hulme. The project focuses upon raising the aspirations and prospects of young people; crime and drugs prevention and linking these to local economic regeneration (£343,000 in year one; £2,591,000 in total).

St Vincent's Housing Association (Manchester) - tackling homelessness and joblessness of young people. SRB funding will attract European and Housing Corporation money (£226,000 in year one; £348,000 in total).

Regeneration in Central Brighton - led by a public and private partnership and including housing, conservation and regeneration projects. A redundant printworks is to be converted into a Foyer scheme to help disadvantaged young people and to provide workspace for media/cultural industries (£1,200,000 in year one; £2,800,000 in total).

North Yorkshire TEC - Unemployment in Rural Areas - led by the TEC and including YMCA and Education Services, to provide Foyer support in remote areas. The project is linked with North Housing Association to provide accommodation (£122,000 in year one; £355,000 in total).

Sheffield - led by a joint management group, with significant community and voluntary sector involvement. This young people and community safety programme focuses on above average youth offending in Sheffield and links with existing S11 funding and tackles high ethnic minority unemployment (£2,568,000 in year one; £38,117,000 in total).

South Yorkshire Initiative for Persistent Young Offenders - run by a partnership which includes four local authorities, the police and probation services with close consultation with magistrates. This pilot scheme aims to show that an extensive community sentence is effective and cost-effective in reducing re-offending in the 12 to 14 age range (£250,000 in total).

How the Challenge Fund works

Money and applications are channelled through the 10 Government Offices for the Regions (their addresses are given at the back of this book). They produce full guidance notes on how to organise and prepare bids, and assess applications in the light of local strategies and priorities. At every stage it is up to those bidding for funds to prepare their case and present it effectively. You must be clear about what you will do and why; how you will do it and with whom, and include other funders. You will have to show how your bid will give value for money and complement existing private and public sector activities, and how local development strategies are supported by your proposals.

Partnerships are essential

You will not win funding by going it alone. The lone youth pioneer saddling up for the Single Regeneration Budget frontier will find she is hustled out of town by the bigger TEC and local authority gunslingers. At the heart of Challenge Fund allocations is partnerships between different bodies. This is not to say that local voluntary youth organisations cannot apply or lead a bid; it is just that you will have to apply in conjunction with other bodies. The most obvious partner is your local authority or TEC, but it may be another body such as a housing association or health authority.

In the early days of the SRB it was anticipated that the voluntary sector would be a main player in constructing bids. Experience to date suggests otherwise. As the voluntary sector has had a lower profile in applications than was expected, more emphasis is to be placed upon their involvement in the future. The current guidance notes state: "Bids should harness the talents and resources of the voluntary sector and volunteers... in the preparation and implementation of bids". Youth organisations stand a strong chance of bringing expertise and good practice to bids under a number of the seven focus areas.

To participate you will have to be in touch with local decision-makers who are involved in the bidding process. SRB success for youth organisations will depend on how strong your relationships are with other local bodies. Much will also depend upon the approach favoured by your local authority or TEC. Some local authorities have a top-down approach when it comes to funding. This can mean that any money attracted to the local authority through successful bids is filtered down to local organisations, rather than them being involved in setting the agenda. Consultation where it happens can be superficial or thorough, and can vary from a "This is what your local authority will do for you in its strategic development of the community" to "How does youth work fit into to the regeneration of this community?" If your local authority has a more bottom-up approach, where organ-isations are involved at the earliest stages of policy-making, you will find it easier to influence what the authority bids for. Where the authority drives programmes and subsequent bids with less consultation you may just have to hang on for the ride (if you want to).

Strategic economic planning

There are all kinds of regional and local economic initiatives which will differ throughout the country. Some of the more generally applicable policies to take into account will be:

- Single Programming Documents (SPDs) which apply to how European Structural Funds such as RECHAR and URBAN are used in an area
- strategies prepared by local authorities and TECs
- programmes and policies decided by Urban Development Corporations (UDCs)
- initiatives such as City Pride
- housing strategies
- health strategies, including those of Drug Action Teams and Health of the Nation.

To help make your organisation part of a bid you should highlight any added value that you bring. You may have additional trust funding for instance or long-term relationships with specific funders, expertise in certain areas or be part of a European network. Personal relationships can be important. Where you know the key officers or staff within a TEC or authority, you may be in a stronger position to find out how bids are put together and who is driving the application. Within a local authority councillors can have influence and be interested if they are on the right committee or constituents in their ward will be involved in the outcome of a bid. You will have to keep up to date with policy decisions and local priorities which will change over time.

Making it Work - Successful Partnerships

SRB bidding is time-consuming and can be frustrating where bids are not approved despite your best efforts. Key factors for success are largely to do with creating successful partnerships. Where voluntary sector bids have worked there are some common features:

- good partnerships with other bodies were already in place;
- those bidding, including the voluntary organisation, kept in touch with the government regional office and worked with the advice that it offered;
- the projects were well thought out and offered real benefits that fitted in with local strategic plans;
- an early start had been made on the bid and there was a long preparation period;
- local bodies such as authorities and TECs worked together with voluntary organisations and officers supported voluntary involvement.

A possible timetable

You should consult your nearest Government Office for the Region to find out the most up to date timetable. The following will give you some idea of how long the process takes; and remember, this does not include the lead in time for creating and agreeing a partnership.

End of March 1997 ... Bidding Guidance issued.

April - May .... Bidders consult locally, and discuss their proposals with Government Offices.

By 27th June .... Outline bids (three sides of A4) submitted to Government Offices.

July - August.............. Government Offices indicate to bidders how their bids meet Challenge Fund objectives and when they can expect a response.

By 31st October .... Final bids (no more than 25 sides of A4) submitted to Government Offices.

November onwards ... Government Offices make recommendations on bids to ministers, who make the final decision.

February 1998 .... Bidders informed of decisions.

Spring 1998 .... Approved bids begin to be implemented.

English Partnerships

English Partnerships is a government sponsored body which aims to regenerate derelict, vacant and under-used land and buildings. The scope of English Partnerships is all of England, although there are the following priority areas:

- European Objective 1 and 2 areas
- Coalfield closure areas
- City Challenge and other inner city areas
- Other Assisted Areas
- Rural areas, mainly those covered by European Objective 5b
- Other areas of severe economic need identified by English Partnerships regional offices.

Again, there are big league players here and as the name suggests, you should be involved in a partnership with a local authority, TEC, private developer, or regional development body, if your bid for large scale project funding is to be successful. Support is given for schemes which create or protect jobs, offer regeneration and economic development, and improve the environment.

The project should give good value for money, be designed with local people in mind, enhance the environment, and if it is a large project, make an impact on the economy and help run-down areas become more attractive.

Community Investment Fund

If you are interested in smaller grants and work within one of the geographically defined areas, you can apply to the Community Investment Fund which is also administerd by English Partnerships. The investment fund is for capital items for small initiatives started by and working in local communities. Each year, around £3 million is made available for voluntary or community led capital projects. Grants are between £10,000 and £100,000. To be eligible groups must be looking for capital investment (buildings, renovation, new facilities for example), be part of the local community and working with and for them.

Support is given for projects which:
- will provide or significantly improve land and buildings, and therefore add to a local community's asset base;

- are proposed by voluntary groups which are based in and closely involve local communities;
- are not profit-making;
- contribute to English Partnerships and other local regeneration plans;
- give economic or social benefits at a community level;
- need support from English Partnerships of less than £100,000;
- are practical and financially sustainable.

Examples of projects funded by the scheme include: the refurbishment of a city farm, premises for a white goods recycling and job creation project, contributions towards new community centres, training and education centres, nursery and child care facilities, and a credit union and community cafe. Ashington YMCA in Northumberland received over £18,000 towards a project to transform the town's derelict telephone exchange into a community gym and motor and tool repair training workshop for local people. Three part-time posts, as well as voluntary and work placements, have been created. The gym is expected to attract over 250 users a week.

English Partnerships also look at ways to match funds with grants from the Lottery. Recently the Youth Enquiry Service (YES) in Plymouth was helped by both funders to move to new premises. YES offers counselling to young people between 13 and 25.

Small environmental schemes will not be eligible for support from the Community Investment Fund as these will be looked at within the Land Reclamation Programme. Capital projects which need more than £100,000 will be looked at by the English Partnerships Investment Fund.

Information on all forms of English Partnerships support, including the Community Investment Fund is available from six regional offices. There is a Community Development Manger in each office who will advise you on whether your project is eligible and how to prepare your application:

Midlands: Ossiers Office Park, Braunstone, Leicester LE3 2DX (0116-282 8400; Fax 0116-282 8440)

North East: St George's House, Kingsway, Team Valley, Gateshead, Tyne & Wear NE11 0NA (0191-487 8941; Fax: 0191-487 5690)

North West: Lancaster House, Mercury Court, Tithebarn Street, Liverpool L2 2QP (0151-236 3663; Fax: 0151-236 3731)

South East: Devon House, 58-60 St Katherine's Way, London E1 9LB (0171-680 2000; Fax: 0171-680 2040)

South West: North Quay House, Sutton Harbour, Plymouth PL4 0RA (01752-251071; Fax: 01752-234840)

Yorkshire & Humberside: Hall Cross House, 1 South Parade, Doncaster, South Yorkshire DN1 2NY (01302-366865; Fax: 01302-366880).

Urban Development Corporations

Within the lifetime of this handbook the English Urban Development Corporations will be wound up (their last breath will be gasped on 31st March 1998). Any existing funds will be transferred to the Government Offices for the Regions and you should enquire locally as to how regeneration projects will continue. UDCs have supported voluntary organisations generally in the past in their work for environment, training, sport, education and community facilities and projects. Information and details of future funding arrangements can be obtained from:

Birmingham Heartlands: 0121-333 3060
Black Country: 0121-511 2000
Central Manchester: 0161-236 1166
London Docklands: 0171-512 3000
Merseyside: 0151-236 6090
Plymouth: 0175-225 6132
Teesside: 0164-267 7123
Trafford Park: 0161-848 8000
Tyne and Wear: 0191-226 1234
In Wales and Northern Ireland the following areas are covered:
Cardiff Bay: Welsh Office 01222-823733
Laganside: Northern Ireland Office: 01232-328507.

Training and Enterprise

Training and Enterprise Councils - England and Wales

Training and Enterprise Councils (TECs) are local companies with responsibility for training, encouraging enterprise, and contributing to economic strategy, all in response to local needs. TECs are funded in arrears and do not receive a grant. Combined TECs contracts with the government total around £1.2 billion a year.

TECs have a key role to play in defining local economic strategies, and a number of large funding programmes will expect to see their involvement in any bid. TECs are run by a locally appointed Board of 15 members. They are employer-led organisations and are the principal private sector partner body to local authorities. As well as the two-thirds of board members who are employers, there are also other local representatives from trade unions, local government, education and training bodies, as well as the voluntary sector. There are currently 79 TECs, of which 13 have merged with Chambers of Commerce to become Chambers of Commerce Training and Enterprise (CCTEs). Contact details can be found in your local telephone directory.

Like local authorities and health authorities, each TEC will have a different way of working and involving the community. Being part of the TEC network at a local level is vital to find out how decisions are made and priorities determined. It is possible to work with a TEC to develop a project, but in the case of the Tredegar Youth Café (see box) it had to be a viable community business with commercial objectives at the forefront of the proposal. In this example, funding may have come from a discretionary fund where the TEC had made a surplus.

There can also be a direct route to funding through the TEC's commitment to training provision. In

> ## Tredegar Youth Café
>
> Tredegar Action Campaign was formed in the early 1990s as a response to the decline in the area. A partnership, Tredegar Action, was formed to include Blanenau Gwent Council, the Welsh Development Agency, Gwent Training and Enterprise Council as well as a number of other agencies. Tredegar Action's main concern was the physical regeneration of the area, although some support was also given for community development and to research community businesses.
>
> There were a large number of pressing needs, but local people felt strongly that young people should have a meeting place, and what emerged was the Tredegar Youth Café. The café was set up as a community business. The Welsh Development Agency supported the consultation phase, but direct funding has been attracted from the Welsh Office which now supports an after-school club meeting at the café, Gwent Council (under its Urban Programme) and Gwent TEC. In the case of the TEC it was both the Chief Executive's commitment to the project, and the TEC's commitment to the area that ensured the funding. Local people were key players. Their identification of a problem and a solution and their commitment to making it happen by raising over £20,000 in three months and staffing the café were strong arguments for agencies to support the project. The TEC was keen to support a local initiative and remains an important funder.

one area around £80,000 was made available by South Glamorgan TEC over two years. Support was directed through one strategic youth project to develop outreach initiatives. It was recognised that purely employer-led training programmes were not reaching groups of excluded young people, who were among those that the TEC particularly wanted to encourage into mainstream training and employment schemes. Through good contacts and local networks, the TEC was able to use the expertise of those already working with young people to develop training models that included young people who were not participating in its programmes. The youth organisations had a strong selling point for the TEC, namely that they were in contact with 'hard to reach young people'.

The South Glamorgan money for development recognises that youth organisations have contact with a target group, and that time needs to be spent in pre-training initiatives with young people who have become excluded from mainstream provision. Increasingly TECs are showing interest in local planning partnerships which include youth organisations that work with its target groups of young people. TEC staff with responsibility for education or guidance will be the best first contact to discuss the TEC's current provision and any training proposals you may have.

You will need to be involved at a strategic level though, both to be informed about the TEC's training agenda and the role youth organisations have. Local authorities often convene planning meetings to determine training and education strategy, and this will be a good forum for key youth organisations to represent young people's interests.

Scottish Local Enterprise Companies

There are 13 Local Enterprise Companies (LECs) which make up the Scottish Enterprise Network. It aims to strengthen the economy, improve the quality of life, and in south Scotland deliver youth training. In 1995/96, £89 million was allocated to youth training. Grants, loans and business advice is available from each LEC which has responsibility for a defined area. In some urban areas the scheme Local Enterprise Grants for Urban Projects (LEG-UP) may apply to help deprived communities with economic development and environmental improvement.

The Network members are:

Scottish Enterprise Network Membership, 120 Bothwell Street, Glasgow G2 7JP (0141-248 2700; Fax: 0141-221 3217)

Dumfries and Galloway Enterprise, Solway House, Dumfries Enterprise Park, Tinwald Downs Road, Dumfries DG1 3SJ (01387-245000; Fax: 01387-246224)

Dunbartonshire Enterprise, Spectrum House, Clydesbank Business Park, Clydebank G81 2DR (0141-951 2121; Fax:0141-951 1907)

Enterprise Ayrshire, 17-19 Hill Street, Kilmarnock KA3 1HA (01563-526623; Fax:01563-543636)

Fife Enterprise, Kingdom House, Saltire Centre, Glenrothes, Fife KY6 2AQ (01592-623000; Fax:01592-623149)

Forth Valley Enterprise, Laurel House, Laurelhill Business Park, Stirling FK7 9JQ (01786-451919; Fax: 01786-478123)

Glasgow Development Agency, Atrium Court, 50 Waterloo Street, Glasgow G2 6HQ (0141-204 1111; Fax: 0141-248 1600)

Grampian Enterprise Ltd, 27 Albyn Place, Aberdeen AB10 1YL (01224-211500; Fax: 01224-213417)

Lanarkshire Development Agency, New Lanarkshire House, Strathclyde Business Park, Belshill ML4 3AD (01698-745454; Fax:01698-842211)

Lothian and Edinburgh Enterprise Ltd, Apex House, 99 Haymarket Terrace, Edinburgh EH12 5HD (0131-313 4000; Fax:0131-313 4231)

Moray, Badneoch and Strathspey Enterprise, Unit 8, Elgin Business Centre, Elgin IV30 1RH (01343-550567; Fax: 01343-550678)

Renfrewshire Enterprise, 27 Causewayside Street, Paisley PA1 1UL (0141-848 0101; Fax: 0141-848 6930)

Scottish Borders Enterprise, Scottish Borders Enterprise Centre, Bridge Street, Galashiels TD1 1SW (01896-758991; Fax: 01896-758625)

Scottish Enterprise Tayside, Enterprise House, 45 North Lindsay Street, Dundee DD1 1HT (01382-223100; Fax: 01382-201319).

Highlands and Islands Enterprise Network

This is the enterprise network for communities in the north of Scotland. The Local Enterprise Companies (LECs) make up the network with Highlands and Islands Enterprise (HIE) at the centre to oversee and resource the individual LECs. Each LEC is run by a board of local people, but may call upon HIE where it needs extra resources.

LECs are primarily concerned with business start-up and support, but they also can help local voluntary organisations, especially where they make a contribution to the community. Through its Community Action programme it supports sports and arts facilities and youth training initiatives as well as a variety of other community activities.

In 1995/96, grants ranged from £15,000 towards a community playground to £100 for equipment for a local hockey club. Specific youth projects included help for a youth cafe in Ullapool and new equipment at Whitedale Youth Club.

Highland and Islands Network Members:
Highlands and Islands Enterprise Head Office, Bridge House, 20 Bridge Street, Inverness IV1 1QR (01463-234171; Fax: 01463-244469)

Argyll and the Islands Enterprise, The Enterprise Centre, Kilmory Industrial Estate, Lochgilphead PA31 8SH ((01546-602281; Fax: 01546-603964)

Caithness and Sutherland Enterprise, Scapa House, Castlegreen Road, Thurso, Caithness KW14 7LS (01847-896115; Fax: 01847-893383)

Inverness and Nairn Enterprise, Castle Wynd, Inverness IV2 3DW ((01463-713504; Fax: 01463-712002)

Lochaber Limited, St Mary's House, Gordon Square, Fort William PH33 6DY (01397-704326; Fax: 01397-705309)

Moray Badenoch and Strathspey Enterprise, Elgin Business Centre, Elgin, Moray IV30 1RH (01343-550567; Fax:01343-550678)

Orkney Enterprise, 14 Queen Street, Kirkwall, Orkney KW15 1JE (01856-874638; Fax: 01856-872915)

Ross and Cromaty Enterprise, 69-71 High Street, Invergordon IV18 0AA (01349-853666; Fax: 01349-853833)

Shetland Enterprise, Toll Clock Shopping Centre, 26 North Road, Lerwick, Shetland ZE1 0PE (01595-693177; Fax: 01595-693208)

Skye and Lochalsh Enterprise, King's House, The Green, Portree, Isle of Skye IV51 9BS (01478-612841; Fax: 01478-612164)

Western Isles Enterprise, 3 Harbour View, Cromwell Street Quay, Stornoway, Isle of Lewis PA87 2DF (01851-703703; Fax: 01851-704130).

Rural development
Rural Development Commission

The Rural Development Commission (RDC) aims to stimulate job creation and provide essential services in the English countryside. Resources are concentrated in designated Rural Development Areas (RDAs). The contacts for these are listed below.

The RDC states: "The Commission would not normally expect to fund projects which were clearly the responsibility of other bodies or agencies (e.g. local authorities). However, there may be occasions when Commission resources could be provided to enhance projects or enable adaptation to suit rural conditions and which were aimed at disadvantaged groups." These are: elderly people, sick and/or disabled people (and their carers); low income families; women, especially mothers with young children, or those seeking to join or rejoin the labour market, and children/young people with problems of isolation and limited access to services."

The Rural Development Programme (RDP)
This is the Commission's main programme for rural development. In general terms, "Enterprise, jobs and access to services are seen as the principal ingredients for successful rural economies". All projects must be located in Rural Development Areas and focus on the priorities and needs set out in the local RDA Strategy. Support is not generally available for projects located in towns with populations over 10,000 (although there are exceptions).

RDC funds are used to lever financial support from the private, voluntary and/or local authority sources. Under the Social/Community Projects heading, "Commission resources are targeted to areas and groups in greatest need and to projects which redress social disadvantage related to rurality. Projects are encouraged to:

(i) Raise the level or quality of rural services, particularly those aimed at overcoming problems of isolation and access;
(ii) Stimulate local voluntary action including self-help schemes; and
(iii) Promote community development".

Support is given to projects that are extra to mainstream provision. There is no maximum or minimum grant level and the programme supports start-up costs rather than on-going costs. Youth organisations will need to show how young people are involved in consultation and decision-making. The RDC suggests that a common weakness in applications is that projects are not sufficiently precise in setting out how the performance of the project is to be reported on.

Projects related to Community Development should gain the support of the local Rural Community Council. Applications can be made at any time and you should discuss your project with the RCC as early as possible in your planning.

Rural Challenge
Rural Challenge aims to encourage innovative partnerships to make a difference to rural areas which have a number of economic and social problems. All RDAs were invited to compete for yearly prizes of up to £1 million each to be spent in their areas. This prize is paid out over three years. In the most recent round of the competition, the judges were looking at proposals aiming to achieve at least some of the following:

- increased community involvement in service provision and the encouragement of regeneration;
- better quality of life for local people through reasonable and affordable access to services and facilities, including transport, childcare, housing and healthcare;
- diversification of the local economy, particularly extending the range of industries and occupations;
- improved performance of the local economy to make it more competitive;
- a reduction in unemployment, increased economic activity and a reduction in the outward migration of economically active young people;
- training for additional vocational and other qualifications;
- reduction in the crime rate and fear of crime;
- enhancement of the natural and built environment;
- promotion of energy conservation and in particular renewable energy projects, making use of sustainable resources.

The Rural Challenge competition is in two parts. Firstly, in each eligible RDA, any local partnerships may put forward proposals as they wish. One of these is then selected by the RDA to enter the national contest. The most recent round awarded a total of £5 million, giving £1 million to each project. Applications for the most recent round were closed in June for decisions to be made in November.

RDAs compete in alternate years, except for the four largest which compete each year. The RDAs eligible for the most recent round were:

East Anglia: Cambridgeshire, Essex, Norfolk; *East Midlands:* East Derbyshire, Lincolnshire; *North:* Durham, Lancashire, Northumberland; *South East:* East Sussex, Kent; *South West:* Cornwall and Isles of Scilly, Devon, Wiltshire; *West Midlands:* Hereford and Worcester, Midlands Uplands (covering Staffordshire and West Derbyshire); *Yorkshire and Humberside:* East Riding of Yorkshire, North Lincolnshire; South Yorkshire.

The RDC suggests: "Successful bids are likely to:

- lever in significant funding from other sources, particularly the private sector;
- demonstrate a novel approach and offer the prospect of effective action;
- respect and where possible, enhance the environment;
- involve partnerships drawn from the private, voluntary and public sectors;
- strengthen the capacity of local communities."

In a few of the eighteen successful bids so far there has been an element of community development to include facilities for young people, perhaps through a youth club, sports facilities or a meeting place. Much depends on how involved youth organisations are in local community umbrella bodies, as these tend to be consulted in helping to shape the proposals. Stainforth in Doncaster won an award in round two, and has set up a Youth Council with its own budget of £30,000 and independence to make decisions as to how this is spent. Under round three the Somerset Rural Youth Project (see p.177) won a prize that aims to improve opportunities for young people throughout the county. The RDC underlines the place of youth projects in the competition: "There have been some youth projects among the past winners, and we would actively encourage such applications in the future".

To apply, you should contact your local RDA to find out who's talking to whom and what proposals are being put forward.

General information on the RDP and Rural Challenge, together with a bidding guidance booklet are available from: Rural Development Commission, Marketing and Information Unit, 141 Castle Street, Wiltshire SP1 3TP (01722-336255; Fax: 01722-332769).

There is also a booklet giving guidelines about community involvement in Rural Challenge produced by The Community Development Foundation, 60 Highbury Grove, London N5 2AG (0171-226 5375; Fax: 0171-704 0313).

Somerset Rural Youth Project

The Somerset Rural Youth Project was successful in the 1996 third round of Rural Challenge awards. The project looked to initiate new facilities and opportunities on offer to young people in rural communities, many of whom were opting out of parish and village life and moving to the cities instead.

The project will cover half the county and take in 50 different communities. The Youth Project has developed a number of smaller projects that will tackle areas of concern to young people in the county. These include transport (more transport to activities); employment and training (a mobile information centre, coffee bar, IT trailer and rural skills workshop to be developed); ways to combat crime, drugs, vandalism and alcohol abuse (diversionary activities such as sports, coaching and arts development; mobile activities trailer; and overall involvement in the project); sports and leisure facilities, voluntary work and community involvement (research into current participation by young people in their home towns and villages).

Two of the key players in the bid are the Somerset Rural Youth Partnership (which is an umbrella body of 21 voluntary youth organisations in the county) and the Somerset County Youth Service. The partnership also includes district councils, Avon and Somerset Constabulary, the Prince's Youth Business Trust, Somerset TEC, Somerset Community Council, Somerset Health Authority, Somerset Careers, Exmoor National Park and others.

The lead in time to assemble the partnership and the bid was relatively short at less than five months. The county youth service did have existing partnerships with a number of bodies and could build upon these. When asked what advice they could give to voluntary youth organisations looking to get involved in such partnerships and funding bids, the youth service suggested: "Make sure they know what they are committing themselves to. Also, they need to ensure effective communication happens across the voluntary sector. And very simply, to allow time!"

The bid built on the experience of Somerset Youth Service and a voluntary youth organisation - Young Somerset - in developing mobile resource centres that could visit a number of rural areas. The Young Somerset Rural Activities Trailer provided activities for over 3,000 young people. The project started in 1994 with a donated Land Rover and a grant from Children in Need to equip a trailer and train volunteers. Indoors and outdoors sports activities have been offered to over 100 rural clubs, and a number of young adults have gained the Community Sports Leader Award. This innovative approach demonstrated how a flexible and mobile service could help young people in the county.

Equipped trailers will be developed as local needs require, and these will visit throughout the RDA (52% of Somerset). The Rural Challenge award will also help to support the costs of a project manager, five full-time youth workers, and a number of part-time staff to run the programme. As well as Rural Challenge money, income of £120,000 from public funders has been raised for the first year. (The funders are: Somerset County Council, Sedgemoor, Mendip, South Somerset, Taunton Deane and West Somerset District Councils, Somerset Health Authority, Avon and Somerset Police, Exmoor National Park, Somerset Careers.) Furthermore, income from private sources of £40,000 will be added to the funds in the first year. (These supporters include the Prince's Youth Business Trust, in kind support from the voluntary sector, and private companies giving equipment.)

The results of this innovative project will be closely looked at. Somerset Youth Service argues: "It is most unusual to have this level of funding for rural youth projects. Hence, the project will give an opportunity to assess the success of rural youth work."

The contact for the project is: Elizabeth Piecha, County Youth Officer, Somerset County Council, County Hall, Taunton, Somerset TA1 4DY (01823-355716) or,

Robert Sampson, Somerset Rural Youth Project Manager, Weir Lodge, Staplegrove Road, Taunton TA1 1DN (01823-351815; Fax: 01823-353056).

Local and regional enquiries should be directed to the Commission's regional offices:

East Anglia (Cambridgeshire, Essex, Norfolk, Suffolk)
Lees Smith House, 12 Looms Lane, Bury St Edmunds, Suffolk IP33 1HE (01284-701743)

East Midlands (Derbyshire, Leicestershire, Lincolnshire, Nottinghamshire)
18 Market Place, Bingham, Nottingham NG13 8AP (01949-876200)

North (Cumbria, Durham, Lancashire, Northumberland, Redcar & Cleveland)
Haweswater Road, Penrith, Cumbria CA11 7EH (01768-865752)

South East (Kent, East Sussex, Isle of Wight)
Sterling House, 7 Ashford Road, Maidstone, Kent ME14 5BJ (01622-765222)

South West (Cornwall & Isles of Scilly, Devon, Dorset, Somerset, Wiltshire)
3 Chartfield House, Castle Street, Taunton, Somerset TA1 4AS (01823-276905)

Yorkshire & Humberside (East Riding of Yorkshire, North Yorkshire, South Yorkshire, West Yorkshire, North Lincolnshire)
Spitfire House, Aviator Court, Clifton Moor, York YO3 4UZ (01904-693335)

West Midlands (Hereford & Worcester, Gloucestershire, Shropshire, Staffordshire/West Derbyshire)
Strickland House, The Lawns, Park Street, Wellington, Telford, Shropshire TF1 3BX (01952-247161).

Health

The Department of Health Section 64 Grants

Section 64 of the Health Services and Public Health Act 1968 allows grants to be given to voluntary organisations (in England) whose activities support the Department of Health's objectives relating to health and personal social services. Similar schemes run in Scotland and Wales, and further information on these is available from the Scottish and Welsh Offices.

The Department of Health gives around £20 million in Section 64 grants to voluntary organisations working in the health and personal social services fields. Many of these grants are to national organisations, or to organisations whose work is national in its scope. Included in the 1993/94 list of beneficiaries were the following young people's projects:

Health Information for Nottingham Teenagers (HINT) ... £36,000

Streetwise Youth £20,000

Young Minds £18,970

Grants are given to support innovative work and projects which contribute towards areas of current interest to the Department of Health; advisory services for young people; work to educate and inform about alcohol and substance abuse; health education would all be examples of current concerns and interests.

- Under drug, smoking and alcohol initiatives, SARG (Solvent Abuse Resource Group) was supported to provide advice and support to individuals, where a large number are young people.
- The Health of the Young Nation objective included support for Youth Clubs UK, Cities in Schools and the National Pyramid Trust in their work with young people.
- Through the Leaving Care initiative, First Key and Training for Life were supported in their work with young people making the transition from living in care and dependence to living independently.

There is no maximum or minimum grant. Grants are given under four headings: core grants; capital grants; national project grants; local project grants.

Core grants

These help with the central running costs of national voluntary organisations. Grants are awarded for up to three years and are only intended to be a small part of how the organisation is funded.

Capital costs

Grants are given for land, buildings or other assets, and are for over £5,000. (Office equipment is normally included in a core grant application.) These are a low priority under Section 64 funding, and are given only in exceptional circumstances.

National project grants

Grants are awarded for up to half the cost of a project. The work must be clearly within the department's current policy objectives and should be experimental, innovative or testing a particular service. Grants are given for up to three years, with a further year to evaluate and disseminate the results.

Local project grants

Health authorities can also make grants to local voluntary organisations, and applications should be made at a local level. However support from the department may be given in exceptional circumstances (such as very high initial costs which cannot be covered locally; where a project covers a number of different health authorities or where a project is potentially of national significance and the costs cannot be met locally). As with national projects, the award will be for up to three years with a further year to evaluate and distribute the results.

Applications

Notes of Guidance and application forms are normally available from mid-July each year and must be returned to the Department by 1st October for grants beginning the following financial year.

Further information and advice together with application forms and guidance notes are available from: Trevor Wright, Grants Administration Unit, Department of Health, Room 627, Wellington House 133-155 Waterloo Road, London SE1 8UG (0171-972 4109).

Local Health Authorities

Some health authorities may also give support to local voluntary organisations. Each area is different, and some organisations working with young people have had good working and funding relationships with health authorities, often in tandem with local authorities. In other areas, there is little or no experience of partnerships.

Banging on the door of the local health authority is unlikely to produce a successful outcome. There may seem to be large amounts of money available, but it is already committed to health service provision. Those working in health authorities that do fund voluntary organisations recognise that voluntary organisations bring flexibility, innovation and contact with areas that the authority is interested in; HIV work with young people for example. The health authority will not be interested in support for young people. It will be interested in specific health programmes, not social health or education. There will not be a programme of funding for voluntary organisations; rather your work will contribute to definite projected outcomes that are part of a public health strategy. You do need to be working at a consultative level with health agencies, including Drug Action Teams, to become part of the decision-making process.

Some guidelines when working with your local health authority:
- Each area is different, but relationships are essential in forming partnerships.
- Do not go looking for money. Be part of wider consultative and decision-making processes.
- Consider what is important for the health authority. What are the primary concerns and main health programmes that they are already running? Think about these first rather than what is important to your organisation.
- Health authorities produce public health reports which detail priorities, programmes and concerns in local health care. You need to be informed about current and projected provision before you know how you can contribute.
- Health authorities are concerned with precise outcomes. You have to be able to measure what you say you will achieve, when you will do it, and how.
- Be professional. It may seem an obvious point but turning up on time to meetings, being efficient in your accounting, and having a track record in your field are essential in a partnership with a health authority.
- Be confident of what you can contribute. You may have contact with a group of young people that are hard for the health authority to reach. You may have

built trust and firm relationships with young people over a number of years. Your approach may be innovative.

- Be well thought out and present your case clearly. One comment from one health authority was: "Back of the envelope planning won't do. We're giving over control from running our own programme to contracting a non-statutory group. We need to know what they can do and how efficient they'll be. You hear the names of the same groups time and time again. They're the ones who have established themselves with a track record of delivery and good contract management. They'll be the ones we turn to again because the experience has been positive on both sides".

Drugs and substance abuse

The Drugs Prevention Initiative

The Drugs Prevention Initiative (DPI) was set up in 1990 by the Home Office to pilot a community-based approach to drugs prevention through the work of local drugs prevention teams. The DPI works as part of a national strategy to reduce the acceptability and availability of drugs to young people.

The DPI looks at what local communities can do to reduce drugs misuse. Its second phase aims, by March 1999, to support different combinations of approaches and targets which have a positive impact upon young people's knowledge, attitudes and behaviour connected to drugs misuse. These approaches include:

- Community involvement
- Work with parents
- Activities for young people outside school
- Community support for drugs education
- Peer approaches
- Reaching and involving rural communities
- The impact of criminal justice interventions
- Effective drugs prevention training for professionals
- Local information campaigns
- Working with racially and culturally diverse groups
- Libraries and resource centres to support local drugs prevention strategies
- Effectiveness of an integrated programme of different approaches.

There are over 70 community-based projects in the programme and the focus is on learning and dissemination. This includes learning about what local people can do, working together with others in their communities to prevent young people from misusing drugs, and distributing the results where there is interest.

Most of the DPI's annual grants budget of £1.9 million is committed in advance to the published programme but a smaller amount may be available to support other work that complements the programme or otherwise meets local drugs prevention needs. Such local grants typically (although not invariably) range from between £500 to around £5,000. Current beneficiaries include:

Shepton Mallet Peer Education Group - £1,000 to support the development of this group which is now in its second year. The group uses creative activities with music and mixing equipment to develop awareness of dance drugs.

Mobile Information Shop - £3,360 towards the mobile unit's tour of five Derby schools to distribute information about drugs and alcohol concerns.

Clubs not Drugs, City Lights - £550 to produce and distribute a brochure for club goers about drugs and dance culture, health information and local organisations to be included in a club listings magazine in the Nottingham and Derby areas.

Drug Free Sport in Nottingham - £400 to make young people aware of the risks involved in using performance enhancing drugs in sport. The project uses coaching and health education and tournaments with a drug-free message.

Funding is available only in the 12 areas covered by Drug Prevention Teams:
Avon and Somerset: 0117-922 7997
Birmingham, Dudley, Sandwell, Walsall and Wolverhampton: 0121-553 5553
Bolton, Manchester, Rochdale, Salford and Stockport: 0161-736 9540
East Midlands (Nottingham, Leicester, Derby, and surrounding areas in the East Midlands): 0115 924 0648
Essex: 01245-353124
London North East (Camden, Hackney, Haringey, Islington, Newham, Tower Hamlets): 0171 837 7477
London North West: 0171-224 7229
London South (Greenwich, Lambeth, Lewisham, Southwark, Wandsworth): 0171-378 1488
Merseyside: 0151-236 4434
Northumbria: 0191-233 1972
Sussex: 01273-722221
West Yorkshire: 01274-741274.

Applications may be made by any organisation, group or individual, but you should first discuss your proposal with the local team. Further information about the work of the DPI is available from each team or centrally: 0171-217 8631.

Crime Prevention

Safer Cities Programme

The Safer Cities Programme is a crime prevention initiative running in inner city areas. It works alongside other government programmes of urban regeneration and improving the urban environment, and is now funded under the Single Regeneration Budget. Grants were awarded to over 3,600 crime prevention schemes from 1993 to 1995 and totalled £22.1 million.

By the end of 1997 the programme will come to an end, and at the time of writing it had not been decided if and how it would continue, and whose responsibility it would be. You should contact the local agents to find out more details. The objectives of the programme are:

- to reduce crime;
- to lessen the fear of crime;
- to create safer cities where economic enterprise and community life can flourish.

Projects are run by local communities with representatives from the local authority, police, probation service and voluntary bodies on the steering committee. Funding is available from the SRB to each committee to initiate and support crime prevention measures in their area. The emphasis is upon local solutions devised for local problems with community led strategies and commitment from local people. Decisions are made in the light of locally decided strategies and priorities for the area. Projects can be supported if they are offering education or alternative activities to young people who are otherwise likely to become involved in crime.

Safer Cities have funded projects in different ways. Portsmouth Safer Cities have run programmes themselves for example, whilst Brighton Safer Cities have funded individual projects (see below). You should contact your local Safer Cities programme for information on how decisions are made.

In 1995/96 and 1996/97, Brighton Safer Cities funded the following projects which involve young people.

Safety on the street for young men - workshops for young men, young gay men and men from ethnic minorities to recognise and reduce danger, and decrease the fear of crime.
What's To Do - summer break activities for young people between 11-16 from a local housing estate. Safer Cities supported the activities, worker time and some administration costs.
Brighton Outdoor Adventure Programme - Providing diversionary activities for ex-offenders (who are primarily the young but not exclusively). Those taking part in the programme are then included in existing clubs to continue their interest in an activity. Safer Cities has funded equipment.
Sussex Bangladeshi Association Sport Project - Young people in the Bangladeshi community can participate in two hours of sport a week and take part in organised

tournaments. The project aims to strengthen community participation and divert young people away from crime. Safer Cities funded the equipment costs.

Whitehawk Detached Youth Project - Young people between 11-17 years old have taken part in diversionary activities as an alternative to becoming involved in crime on a local housing estate. Staff time and some equipment costs have been supported.

Woodingdean Youth Advice & Information Mobile Unit - Safer Cities provided a new minibus to take advice and information out to young people.

Hollingdean Youth Club (St Richard's Church) - Safer Cities has supported the costs of updating the security system of the club where 60 young people meet each session.

Coalition for Youth - A grant given over two years helped towards the cost of bringing young people and agencies together to improve youth provision across Brighton and Hove. The second year's funding was towards staff costs.

Brighton and Hove Motor Project - The project offers young car crime offenders and those at risk of becoming involved in similar crime, training and diversionary activities. The project is run in conjunction with East Sussex Probation Service, and Safer Cities contributed towards the costs of safety equipment and tools.

Whitehawk Video Project - Whitehawk Youth Centre and Wide Eye Video Project have combined to teach young people video skills to make a short film to be screened at the end of the project. Safer Cities have contributed towards workers' salaries, equipment and publicity costs.

Heartbreakers Young Women's Group - Weekly activities based at a local family centre for young women aged 11-20 years (who may be single parents or school abstainers). Support has been given for outings, activities and equipment.

Young Men's Group, 11-15 Years - A weekly meeting to discuss concerns which include; truancy, violence and substance abuse. A Safer Cities grant has helped provide activities and outings and will extend the programme of the group.

The 'M' Zone - A range of activities are offered to local 11-13 year olds away from the area. The pilot project is co-ordinated by Moulsecoomb Neighbourhood Trust.

Under Phase II of the programme contracts were awarded to three organisations: Crime Concern, The National Association for the Care and Resettlement of Offenders (NACRO), and the Society of Voluntary Associates (SOVA) to run projects. Funding of up to £100,000 for three years will be available through these managing organisations. Projects will be expected to attract additional funding from other sources. Applications should be made through the local offices of the contractors (see below). You should contact the local agent for details of how Safer Cities will continue.

Phase II areas for 1995 onwards: Blackburn, Bolton, Burnley, Greenwich, Hackney, Kensington & Chelsea, Lambeth, Manchester, Merthyr Tydfil, Plymouth, Portsmouth, Southwark and Westminster are managed by Crime Concern. Contact Jon Bright 01793-514596 for local project offices.

NACRO manages: Bournemouth, Brighton, Easington, Great Grimsby, Leeds, Merseyside, Newcastle, Norwich, Oxford, Sandwell, Scunthorpe, Sheffield, Wansbeck, and York. Contact Peter Shore 0171-582 6500 for local offices.

Camden, Lincoln and Newham are managed by SOVA. Contact Gill Henson 0171-793 0404 for local offices.

Environmental Improvement

The Local Projects Fund

The LPF is a government scheme which encourages small community groups and voluntary organisations throughout England to improve their local environment. Grants are between £500 and £10,000 to schemes which are within the current priorities. In 1997/98 these were:

- to educate about the need for sustainable development;
- encourage waste minimisation, recycling, reuse of materials, and efficient energy use;
- improve the local environment and promote biodiversity by restoring waterways and derelict areas and planting and maintaining trees.

Eligible schemes will be those that can show clear environmental benefit, give value for money, raise matched funding, are run by voluntary or non-profit organisations and are of benefit to the local community. The matched funding conditions are clearly defined, and public sector contributions are not eligible. Contact the Civic Trust for further details.

Decisions are made four times a year by the Grants Panel. Applications have to be received at least six weeks before each panel meeting. The trust reports that a particular weakness in some of the applications it receives is where information on budgets or quotes on expenditure have not been included.

Examples of youth organisations supported in 1996/97:

- Burton YMCA - £600 for a recycling project
- Colden Common Youth Football Club - £2,250 towards Boyes Lane Recreation Park.

This fund is administered by the Civic Trust, an independent national charity, on behalf of the Department of the Environment. Application forms are available from The Grants Management Unit, The Civic Trust, The View, Gostins Building, 32-36 Hanover Street, Liverpool L1 4LN (0151-709 1969).

Environmental projects that need larger grants of between £10,000 and £75,000 may be supported under the Environmental Action Fund. Further information is available from: Andy Kirby, Environmental Grants Manager, Room C9/11, Department of the Environment, 2 Marsham Street London SW1P 3EB (0171-276 3919; Fax: 0171-276 4789). This office also produces a list of funders of environmental projects. Details are kept brief, and general. These funds are not specifically for youth projects; rather they support activities that are concerned with the environment.

Sports

A small number of grants are available from the Sports Council if your activities are sporting. Whilst most of the Sports Council grant-giving energy is directed into distributing National Lottery money there is a small discretionary fund for sports activities.

England Sports Council, 16 Upper Woburn Place, London WC1H 0QP (0171-273 1500)

East Midland Region, Grove House, Bridgford Road, West Bridgford, Nottingham NG2 6AP (0115-982 1887)

Eastern Region, Crescent House, 19 The Crescent, Bedford MK40 2QP (01234-345222)

London Region, PO Box 480, Crystal Palace NSC, Ledrington Road, London SE19 2BQ (0181-778 8600)

North West Region, Astley House, Quay Street, Manchester M3 4AE (0161-834 0338)

Northern Region, Aykley Heads, Durham DH1 5UU (0191-384 9595)

South East Region, PO Box 480, Crystal Palace NSC, Ledrington Road, London SE19 2BQ (0181-778 8600)

South West Region, Ashlands House, Crewkerne, Somerset TA18 7LQ (01460-73491)

Southern Region, 51a Church Street, Caversham, Reading RG4 8AX (01734-483311)

West Midlands Region, Metropolitan House, 1 Hagley Road, Five Ways, Edgbaston, Birmingham B16 8TT (0121-456 3444)

Yorkshire and Humberside, Coronet House, Queen Street, Leeds LS1 4PW (0113-243 6443)

Northern Ireland Sports Council, House of Sport, 2a Upper Malone Road, Belfast BT9 5LA (01232-381222)

Scottish Sports Council, Caledonia House, South Gyle, Edinburgh EH12 9DG (0131-317 7200)

Wales Sports Council, National Sports Centre Wales, Sophia Gardens, Cardiff CF1 9SW (01222-397571)

Arts

This is a similar case to the Sports Council above, where most support is offered through National Lottery grants. There are also some grants towards artists' work with young people available through some regional arts boards. Contact one of the following to find out what is available:

East Midlands Arts, Mountfields House, Epinal Way, Loughborough LE11 0QE (01509-218292)

Eastern Arts, Cherry Hinton Hall, Cambridge CB1 4DW (01223-215355)

London Arts Board, Elme House, 133 Long Acre, Covent Garden, London WC2E 9AF (Helpline: 0171-240 4578)

North West Arts, Manchester House, 22 Bridge Street, Manchester M3 3AB (0161-834 6644)

Northern Arts, 10 Osborn Terrace, Newcastle upon Tyne NE2 1NZ (0191-281 6334)

South East Arts, 10 Mount Ephraim, Tunbridge Wells, Kent TN4 8AS (01892-515210)

South West Arts, Bradninch Place, Gandy Street, Exeter EX4 3LS (01392-218188)

Southern Arts, 13 St Clement Street, Winchester, Hampshire SO23 9DQ (01962-855099)

West Midlands Arts, 82 Granville Street, Birmingham B1 2LH (0121-631 3121)

Yorkshire and Humberside Arts, 21 Bond Street, Dewsbury, West Yorkshire WF13 1AX (01924-455 555)

Volunteering

Make a Difference - Youth Volunteer Development Grants

The National Youth Agency administers this scheme which is funded by the Department of Culture, Media and Sport. It is open to voluntary organisations in England, and aims to encourage opportunities for 15 to 25 year olds wanting to spend time volunteering.

The programme will initially create Youth Volunteer Facilitators in fifty areas throughout England. They will work with local organisations to encourage young people to volunteer and to promote new opportunities. Each year for two years £30,000 will be available to organisations to fund these posts. Alternatively, tapered funded could be spread over three years. Grants have now been approved for April 1997 to March 1999, and there are no plans at present to repeat the programme.

Information is available from: Terry Cane, National Youth Agency, 17-23 Albion Street, Leicester LE1 6GD (0116-285 6789; Fax: 0116-247 1043).

The Department of Health - Opportunities for Volunteering

This is a general scheme funded by the Department of Health to promote volunteering opportunities for unemployed people and strengthen voluntary activity in the health and personal social services in England. Sixteen national voluntary organisations and a consortium of 12 voluntary sector umbrella bodies administer the scheme. Applications and enquiries about your project should be addressed to them rather than the Department of Health. There are separate schemes in Scotland and Wales (see addresses below).

Grants are for up to £20,000 per project. Within this, up to £10,000 can be spent on the capital costs of a vehicle, and up to £11,000 can be used to renovate buildings. You should note, however, that whilst these are permitted by the scheme, some of the organisations administering the scheme do not give capital grants. You should check with them first to find out what costs they support. Grants are given for up to three years, although some are for one or two years. Again, check with the organisation administering the grants.

The scheme is designed to increase opportunities for unemployed people to participate in voluntary work in England in the health and personal social services fields. Unemployed, for the purpose of the scheme, means someone of working age and not in full-time employment or education. It includes those who are sick or disabled, prematurely retired or on short-term working as well as unemployed people drawing Job Seeker's Allowance. The project must be designed to involve primarily unemployed volunteers, but it is not a requirement that all the volunteers concerned with the project must be unemployed.

The projects should make "a worthwhile contribution to meeting health needs or personal social service needs or both". It may, for example, be helping in a hospital, residential home, neighbourhood group, self-help group (e.g. a parent and toddler group), or a community group (e.g. adventure playground). The voluntary work should help those groups needing support from the community such as elderly people, those with disabilities, children and young people at risk, or isolated young mothers for example.

Projects will generally be supported at a local level. Grants can cover administrative, supervisory or developmental costs and can include salaries and overheads. You will have to show how these costs are linked directly to the volunteering project. Grants can also be given for training unemployed people who wish to volunteer, but do not have the necessary knowledge or skill. Short staff training courses can also be supported where these will directly assist those who are helping unemployed people to participate in voluntary work in the areas of health and/or personal services.

The following organisations administer grants on behalf of the Department of Health. You should check with them whether your project is eligible, how grants are awarded and the application timetable. Applications can be made to one organisation only. Where there is no link with any of the organisations below, you should contact the **Consortium on Opportunities for Volunteering** (address at the end of the list).

Age Concern England, Grants Unit, Astral House, 1268 London Road, London SW16 4ER (0181-679 8000). Administers applications for projects which help elderly people.

Churches Together in England, Inter-Church House, 35/41 Lower Marsh, London SE1 7RL (0171-620 4444) for community projects managed entirely or primarily by churches or other Christian organisations.

Examples of Churches Together in England projects which include youth work are: Island House Youth Project, London; a volunteer co-ordinator in Birmingham; New Opportunities in Oxfordshire; St Faith's Trust in Norwich; Grosvenor Christian Response in Devon; Young Volunteers Development Project in Hereford; and a YMCA Volunteer Project in Hove.

CRISIS, 7 Whitechapel Road, London E1 1DU (0171-377 0489) for volunteers helping single homeless people. Priority is given to emergency accommodation schemes.

Royal National Institute for the Blind, Voluntary Agencies Link Unit, 224 Great Portland Street, London W1N 6AA (0171-388 1266) for applications from local societies and other local organisations of and for blind and partially sighted people.

SCOPE (formerly the Spastics Society), Pamwell House, 160 Pennywell Road, Easton, Bristol BS5 0TX (0117-941 4424) for projects supporting disabled people, especially projects involving disabled volunteers.

United Kingdom Council on Deafness, OFV Grants, PO Box 13, Abbots Langley, Herts WD5 0RG (01923-264584) for projects helping deaf, deaf/blind or hard of hearing people.

As well as the above agencies the following administer applications from their own projects only: Barnardo's; British Association of Settlements and Social Action Centres; Children's Society; Community Service Volunteers; MENCAP; MIND; NACRO; National Association of Leagues of Hospital Friends; Pre-school Playgroups Association; RADAR.

The Consortium on Opportunities for Volunteering, Carriage Row, 183 Eversholt Street, London NW1 1BU (0171-383 0441) administers applications that do not come under any of the above agencies.

Scotland: Unemployed Voluntary Action Fund, Comely Park House, 80 New Road, Dunfermline, Fife KY12 7EJ.

Wales: Wales Council for Voluntary Action, Crescent Road, Caerphilly, Mid-Glamorgan CF8 1XL.

Scotland

The Scottish Office produces a guide to its grant-giving programmes for the voluntary sector. Young people's projects might be supported by cultural grants, ethnic minority programmes or rural challenge money for example. For a copy of the guide, contact: The Scottish Office, Voluntary Issues Co-ordinating Unit, Room 52b, James Craig Walk, Edinburgh EH1 3BA (0131-244 5464; Fax: 0131-244 5315).

Urban Programme in Scotland

Grants are directed towards the most deprived urban areas in Scotland to contribute to their regeneration and development. From 1996/97 the Programme for Partnership has been introduced. The Scottish Office will now not approve individual project applications but will make block grant allocations to programmes and proposals submitted by local councils. Voluntary organisations should therefore contact their local authority to contribute to and participate in this new arrangement.

Wales

The Welsh Office produces guidelines for grants programmes available in Wales. Contact: Welsh Office, Cathays Park, Cardiff CF1 3NQ (01222-825111; Fax: 01222-825823).

Chapter 11

Raising money from Europe

Mission Impossible?

The good news for those looking towards Europe for youth funding is that young people are close to the Community's heart. Many funding programmes include a youth element. The bad news is that, as ever, raising money is not easy. Whilst the European budget is large (around £170 billion) much is tied to general priority areas such as agriculture, poor countries or regions, research and so on. A large part of the EU cake is also taken up with large infrastructure projects. Even when you are successful, you often have to find around half the money for the project from non-EU sources.

Raising money from Europe requires expertise and a large investment of time. You will have to learn new rules for playing the game. You should think carefully about what your organisation does, how it does it and who benefits from what you do. You should note the impact your activities have on your local area and region, and also be aware of any Europe-wide dimension there is to your work.

But if European funding seems too daunting, think again. Whilst it may involve a new language, literally, it can also pay dividends. European money can be one way to unlock matched funding in the UK (including National Lottery and central and local government funds). Furthermore, transnational partnerships (that is, projects involving people from more than one European country), which are at the heart of a number of funding programmes, can give valuable experience to your young people and leaders, as well as bringing resources to your organisation.

The following is a brief guide to the different pots of European money that may be appropriate for your group. Most is tied to economic development, vocational training and job creation. However, if you are prepared to think widely and creatively about your organisation you can apply under any one of a number of headings. You should also bear in mind that in 1999 all funding programmes will be reviewed and objective areas will change, largely to take into account the expansion of the community with former eastern European countries. Money will therefore be spread more thinly, and competition will become more intense.

Preliminary research

There are plenty of European funding sources. You have to decide which ones, if any, are appropriate to you. This may be straightforward and based on advice and expertise within your organisation or that given by a consultant. Increasingly, matching your project to the right fund needs specialised knowledge. You should do some preliminary research first. Take soundings from any groups you know that have been successful or who have failed in their bid. This will be invaluable in giving an insider's view of the process. There are a number of documents and general handbooks that give information on procedure, policies and programmes (see page 215. European documentation centres throughout the country will have all you ever wanted to know about Europe, and a large amount that you did not. See page 214 for contact details.

Remember, a large part of European money has already been ear-marked for particular countries and regions. This money is then distributed through existing networks based on published policies. You need to explore what is already out there and work within that. You should find out what the local economic strategies are in your area and how any bid you make would fit in. This will strengthen any application. If for example, you can show how your work with young people is part of local employment training initiatives, you will increase your chances of success with certain EU programmes.

The local authority (economic development department), TEC or regional government office (European officer) may have experience and knowledge and can give advice. You should also talk to Commission officials, MEPs and technical staff to get as much information as possible. There are a number of consultants working in and out of Brussels who will be able to help put a bid together and iron out some of the wrinkles. Whether you favour the custom built consultant-crafted model, or the Do-It-Yourself flat pack assembly approach, get as much advice as you can.

The following can help with preliminary advice before you start brushing up your French in Brussels:

NCVO European Funding Team for all voluntary organisations (0171-713 6161; Fax: 0171-713 6300)

Wales Council for Voluntary Action European Office (01938-552379; Fax: 01938-442092)

Scottish Council for Voluntary Organisations (0141-332 5660; Fax: 0141-332 4225)

National Youth Agency for youth organisations, Keith Raynor, Youth Work Development Adviser (0116-285 6789; Fax 0116-247 1305).

> Prior systematic investigation works much better than "rushing in" – fewer and fewer EU funds are available through personal contacts, or because you happen to be in the right place at the right time.
> *A Guide to European Union Funding for NGOs, ECAS*

There are over 100 different funding programmes, however many of these will soon finish and be replaced by new schemes. The European funding scene is constantly shifting, although the fondness for abbreviations and naming programmes after philosophers is likely to continue. Once a particular programme's objectives are met, it is appropriate that the programme finishes and money is directed elsewhere. Much will change in the light of former eastern European countries coming into the Community. However, this makes for an uncomfortable life for the Euro-fundraiser. You have to keep in touch with developments at a local, regional, national and European level.

Budget Lines, DGs and Programmes

> European officials and all Commission switchboard staff speak good English. Commission offices are as approachable as central government departments, and are often easier to get clear information from.

European funding is divided into two streams. There is money attached to named funding programmes (ESF, ERDF, Eurathlon and so on), but there is also money given under certain budget lines. As with central and local government money in the United Kingdom, European funds are administered by different departments. Each department or Directorate General (DG) has responsibility for an area of European policy and its own budget line. Youth policy for instance, comes under DGXXII which covers human resources and education as well as youth. It may be the case that you can apply under a budget line rather than a programme. If for example you are working with young refugees, you may contact DGV direct which has responsibility for refugees within the Community, rather than apply under the refugee programme. As with central and local government departments, if money has not been allocated your application will receive particular attention.

Dedicated Youth Programmes

Youth for Europe III

The EU sets great store by its aim to break down barriers between the Member States. The Youth for Europe programme which runs until 1999 promotes exchanges of young people within Europe, especially those who are disadvantaged. These exchanges will help young people to learn from each other, to share experiences and to build bridges between Member States. You will need to show how your project will help this process of understanding and co-operation.

The following types of projects are supported:
- exchanges between projects in two or more Member States, with groups of young people aged 15 to 25 and where the exchange lasts at least a week;
- projects where young people are involved in innovative or creative initiatives, especially those that combat all forms of exclusion, as well as projects which foster the cultural and artistic interest of young people;
- the development of networks and partnerships involving different Member States;
- projects which encourage young people to participate in voluntary service which benefits the Community;
- youth worker exchanges which increase awareness of practice and experience in other Member States;
- study visits, seminars which increase awareness of other countries' practice and experience;
- projects which help Member States generally to cooperate on youth programmes;
- building links with non-Member States.

Grants are available, generally for 50% of eligible travel or hosting costs. Examples of recent grants include:
- Havering Youth Service, where members worked with local authorities in Seville towards environmental protection, including encouraging cycling. Following campaigning in Seville, the group also went Spanish hill-walking.
- Homeless North, Newcastle joined with a group in Paris to draw attention to a wide range of social concerns. The Newcastle group were on income support or paid low wages and were homeless or threatened with homelessness. "It was a ground-breaking experience, not only for the young people, but for the community workers, who realised how much co-operation is needed between the organisers on both sides to ensure an effective exchange."
- St Neots Twinning Association organised a multilateral event involving groups of around ten young people from France, Italy, Germany and Greece. There was a planning meeting in Italy. The self-funding twinning association with support from volunteers, the youth service and the local MEP, organised a two-week programme of workshops on unemployment, drugs and family violence, together with sports and music activities.

The above projects received grants which covered over half the cost of their outward travel and around 40% of the costs of hosting the visit from their partners. The St Neots project also received a grant towards half of the costs of partners' travel costs to England.

For further details contact: Joane Anthony, Information Officer, Youth Exchange Centre, The British Council, 10 Spring Gardens, London SW1A 2BN (0171-389 4030; Fax: 0171-389 4033).

European Voluntary Service

Also based at the Youth Exchange Centre is the European Voluntary Service. This relatively new scheme encourages young people between 18 and 25 to offer six to twelve months as volunteers for a project in another part of the Community. There are three parties in any placement: the host project, the sending project and the volunteer. Sending projects receive 50% of the total costs of each placement (between £2,000 and £4,000) which is to be shared with the host project, as well as covering the management costs of setting up the placement.

The Youth Exchange Centre is responsible for the decentralised schemes and will receive around £750,000 to organise about 200 volunteers. The aim is to make the process as easy and unbureaucratic as possible, and the application process is as informal as they can make it. For more information contact: Dorothy Saunders, Youth Exchange Centre, The British Council, 10 Spring Gardens, London SW1A 2BN (0171-389 4080).

Vocational training for young people

LEONARDO da Vinci

The strong drive within the EC to encourage young people to learn more about other Member States is at the centre of LEONARDO. This programme was launched in January 1995 to run until December 1999, and supports training and cultural exchange programmes for young people. LEONARDO concentrates on sustaining quality and supporting innovation in Member States' vocational training through transnational exchanges, placements and partnerships. Projects may include:

- pilot projects involving more than one Member State;
- exchange programmes of trainees and trainers between Member States;
- work experience placements for young trainees, young workers or job seekers;
- development of language skills and innovative practice;
- surveys, analyses and data exchange.

Some of the activities that will be covered by grants will be transnational projects that, for example, develop common training modules; provide training for trainers and those who manage training; and encourage lifelong learning and the promotion of lifelong learning.

Young people under LEONARDO are defined as people less than 28 years of age, who are undergoing training, or who are searching for work.

Transnational exchanges and placements are for:
- short work placements for young people in initial vocational training (3 to 12 weeks);
- long work placements for young people in initial vocational training (13 weeks to 9 months). Applications for these traineeships are particularly encouraged;
- work placements for young workers or young job seekers (3 to 12 months);
- exchanges of trainers (2 to 8 weeks), concentrating on the exchange of good practice. Note that in this case exchanges do not have to be reciprocal, as exchange here can mean the transfer of expertise.

Projects must be transnational by involving a minimum of three participating countries, that is the 15 Member States as well as Iceland, Liechtenstein and Norway. Competition between bids is intense. If successful, the grant represents a contribution by the Community towards the project costs. Organisations are expected to make a significant commitment with their own resources. As in all Community programmes you will need to show how your bid brings "added value". There have been three Calls for Proposals so far in 1995, 1996 and 1997. The successful applications to date best answer the following questions:

- Why – do the activity? How does it meet a defined need, or offer a solution? How does it fit into a wider training or academic strategy?
- Who – are the partners? What types of organisation will be involved and what will they bring to the project?
- How – will the project be managed? What is the timetable, and who will be responsible for the project? How will the partners' roles be defined and how will you communicate with one another and the Commission? How has the project been costed?
- What – are the intended outcomes? What difference will the completed project make in this country and in Europe? How will you measure the outcome and the results? How will it help a target group or solve a training problem?

You should also have clear ideas and strategies for spreading the word about your project and its outcomes and results.

The budget for the LEONARDO programme is ECU 620 million (about £440 million). Up to 75% of the costs of pilot projects can be supported by the EC, up to a maximum of ECU 100,000 (£71,000) per year. Projects can last up to three years, although some will be up to two years. Transnational exchanges and placements can be helped with up to ECU 5,000 (£3,550) for each participant. Any organisation that is involved with vocational training will be eligible for funding.

The closing date for the 1997 round of applications will be 30th September, with selection being confirmed in the autumn. For further information and clear and full guidance notes, contact: Ms Subha Ray, Central Bureau for Educational Visits and Exchanges, Seymour Mews House, Seymour Mews, London W1H 9PE (0171-486 5101; Fax: 0171-935 1017).

Money for Deprived Areas and for Training The European Structural Funds

Whilst the above are dedicated schemes for young people, anyone looking to Europe should remember that the lion's share of European money for general projects is routed through a number of programmes called structural funds. The two main funds are:

> The European Community is largely an economic entity. Many of its activities centre on the economic development of the Community with job creation encouraging economic competitiveness. Europe will be more welcoming if your organisation can help to further these ends.

- The European Social Fund (ESF) for training schemes.
- The European Regional Development Fund (ERDF) for capital investment in deprived areas.

There are also two smaller structural funds which will not apply to youth activities: the European Agricultural Guidance and Guarantee Fund (EAGGF) for agricultural and forestry regions; and the Financial Instrument of Fisheries Guidance (FIFG) to cover fishing.

Structural funds may be relevant to youth organisations if your activities include training opportunities and/or are part of the economic development of certain tightly defined geographical areas. If you secure funding from these schemes it will be because your proposal has real economic or training benefits rather than because you are a youth project. In other words, you will have to be helping to create jobs, providing training or initiating enterprise, to be considered.

The European Community is largely an economic entity. Many of its activities centre on the economic development of the Community with job creation encouraging economic competitiveness. Europe will be more welcoming if your organisation can help to further these ends.

The structural funds focus on economic decline in urban and rural areas in the European Community. For many in the EC the main challenges in the 21st century will be to halt industrial decline and revitalise deprived urban and rural communities. This can be done through job creation, the protection of declining

Which UK regions receive ESF and ERDF money?

Objective 1: Highland & Islands; Merseyside; Northern Ireland (see below)

Objective 2 (industrial): West Midlands (including Birmingham); East England (Yorkshire & Humberside and East Midlands); North West England; West Cumbria; North East England; Industrial South Wales; East Scotland (administered by the Scottish Office Industry Department); West Scotland (administered through the Scottish Office Industry Department); East London and the Lea Valley; Thanet; Stoke-on-Trent; Burton-on-Trent; Plymouth; Barrow; Gibraltar

Objective 3: Throughout the UK for projects under the European Social Fund only.

Objective 5b (rural): Devon, Cornwall and West Somerset; Dumfries and Galloway (administered through the Scottish Office Industry Department); Rural Wales; the Northern Uplands; East Anglia; English Marches; Lincolnshire; Derbyshire; Staffordshire; Borders; Rural Stirling; Grampian; Tayside (each of the last four is administered through the Scottish Office Industry Department)

Objective 1 areas
Large streams of European money have been earmarked for regions throughout Europe where development has lagged significantly behind other parts of the Community. Around £600 million for each of the following areas is available and administered separately. You should approach the following regional contacts with any proposals:
Highlands and Islands: The Scottish Office, New St Andrews House, St James's Centre, Edinburgh EH1 3TG (0131-556 8400; Fax 0131-244 4785).
Merseyside: Objective One Secretariat, Government Office for Merseyside, Graeme House, Derby Square, Liverpool L2 7UP (0151-224 6300).
Northern Ireland: The Industrial Development Board for Northern Ireland, IDB House, 64 Chichester Street, Belfast BT1 4JX (0232-233233).

sectors as well as encouraging new industries. Those areas hardest hit by economic change or isolation are given priority through EC programmes for "least favoured" or underdeveloped regions.

The European Social Fund (ESF)

This fund deals with employment not welfare as the name might suggest. It gives money for vocational training so that people are more likely to gain or retain a job. The Fund pays for the running costs of vocational training schemes (for employed or unemployed people), not capital expenditure as the ERDF does. There has to be an expectation that a reasonable number will go on to find employment or on to further training at the end of the course. The minimum age for participants is usually 16.

The training opportunities being offered clearly have to make people more employable. Trainees should gain recognised qualifications or credits towards them, or be able to go on to further training, keep employment or become self-employed. Training should lead to vocational qualifications, be suited to the needs of the labour market, and provide good value for the money spent.

The Objective 3 Single Programming Document (SPD) for 1997-1999 sets out a number of priorities for funding.

Support is available throughout Great Britain (ESF comes under Objective 3) for the following groups or "Pathways":

- Pathways to employment (also known as Priority 1) – those aged 25 or over who have been out of work for over six months. Attention is given to groups which are particularly disadvantaged.
- Pathways to a good start in working life (also known as Priority 2) – young people between 16 and 24 who are without work. Attention is given to groups which are particularly disadvantaged.
- Pathways for equal opportunities (also known as Priority 3) – to promote equal opportunities between men and women in the labour market.
- Enhancing capacity for community development (also known as Priority 4) – supports the development of local organisations and structures which helps the most disadvantaged under the above three priorities. This is a new development under the ESF. At the time of writing it had only just been introduced, and it was too early to see how it would work for voluntary organisations.

Any legally constituted organisation such as a TEC, college, local authority or voluntary organisation can apply for ESF support as long as it can secure matched funding for a given project. ESF will usually provide up to 45% of the cost of the project (although this may be higher in Objective 1 areas, covering some projects by up to 50% in Merseyside and 55% in the Highland and Islands). Matched funding must include contributions from a recognised public match funder which can include one or more of the following:

- a central government body;
- a local government body;
- a registered charitable trust;
- any organisation which directly or indirectly receives over 50% of its money from central government, local government or levies raised for training purposes.

Most items, apart from capital expenditure and interest charges, can be funded. Eligible costs include staff costs for trainers and others, childcare or the care of dependants, subsistence, travel, rent and leasing, rates, heat, light, telephone, stationery and training materials, depreciation of equipment, advertising and publicity, project evaluation, distribution of project results, costs of transnational working. Individuals may not apply for ESF money.

ESF applications are generally made annually and where successful, approval is issued for the calendar year in question. In 1997, for instance, the call for applications was issued in January, the deadline for completed applications was the end of March, and the successful projects published in July 1997.

Competition for all ESF awards is fierce. However, if you are successful you can expect the award to be paid in three stages. There can be time lags between approval and payment and this should be taken into account when budgeting.

How to apply: Application forms and extensive guidance notes are available from the Department for Education and Employment or the Scottish Office Development Department at the addresses below. It is strongly advised that applications should be made after consultations with sector managers and regional government offices who are the first point of contact for ESF applicants. A list of contacts is included in the guidance notes from the DfEE.

European Social Fund Unit, Department for Education and Employment, Level 1 Caxton House, Tothill Street, London SW1H 9HF (0171-273 3000; Fax: 0171-273 5540).

YOUTHSTART

ESF resources are also used to support the Community Initiative on Employment and Development of Human Resources (1994-1999). The funding is divided into four strands: YOUTHSTART which covers those projects concerned with young people; HORIZON which funds schemes for disabled people; NOW which promotes equal opportunities between men and women; and INTEGRA for work with vulnerable and disadvantaged groups such as lone parents, ethnic minorities, refugees and migrants, homeless people, ex-offenders, alcohol and drug dependants and people in disadvantaged areas.

The programme is a transnational initiative, and projects in Great Britain must be working in partnership with organisations in at least two other European Member States.

Projects involving young people aged 16-20 were covered primarily by YOUTHSTART. This programme supported 45% of project costs in non-objective 1 areas. The application round closed in April 1997 for projects to run until 1999. Although this initiative is now closed there may be future youth themes under ESF which may be relevant to work with young people. You can be added to the EMPLOYMENT Support Unit mailing list to keep in touch with developments. Information on all four strands is available from: The EMPLOYMENT Support Unit, ECOTEC, Priestly House, 28-34 Albert Street, Birmingham B4 7UD (0121-616 3661; Fax: 0121 616 3680).

Youth Projects supported under YOUTHSTART 1995-1997

Manchester Youth Service Targeted Resources for Youth – Manchester Youth Service

Moving On – Suffolk County Council

Youthstart Prevent – VT Southern Careers Limited

Translink – Wakefield Metropolitan District Council Youth Service

Youthtrain 2000 – Wakefield Metropolitan District Council Youth Service

Young Women's Access to Opportunities – Young Women's Christian Association of Great Britain

Young People's Social and Economic Development – Croxteth and Gillmoss Community Federation

Note: Nearly 70 projects are funded under YOUTHSTART in Great Britain (1995-1997). A full list of projects with contacts and telephone numbers is available from the EMPLOYMENT Support Unit.

YOUTHSTART case study

Croxteth & Gillmoss Community Federation YOUTHSTART Project

Productive Learning in Europe II – INEPS – Economic and Social Development in Europe by Young People

Croxteth and Gillmoss Community Federation in Liverpool has a track record of community led initiatives. One of the first steps in setting up this project was to contact and work with small groups of local young people to find out what they wanted and needed and how they could be involved in developing new ways of training.

The result has been a project where young people are offered informal training opportunities and direct work experience which can lead to basic qualifications in Youth and Community work accredited by the YMCA George Williams College. So far, fourteen young people been involved in the training and in a range of youth and community work activities.

The project was successfully incorporated into a partnership between organisations in Sweden, Germany and Spain. This was the Community Federation's second attempt following an initial partnership between Italy, Portugal and Spain which broke down when Croxteth was successful in its application, while the other members were not. ECOTEC then circulated information on projects looking for partners and a match was made with the Germany, Spain, Sweden network which had similar aims and ways of working. The main negotiating and consultation language has been English, but language skills in French and German have been important in the running of the project. The project has been supported by YOUTHSTART with funding of £119,000 over a period of two and a half years.

The Croxteth experience of European partnerships has been very positive. Links with the existing partners and in turn with other connected networks have made the project truly transnational. Fifty young people from throughout Europe have been able to take part in European youth forum meetings and been given the opportunity to exchange experiences and learn new ways of working. Mobility and participation, which is seen as essential for young people to take part in society and in the wider Europe, has been encouraged and the project has developed a new way of training and applied this at a European level.

Some of the benefits of the project have been:
- Developing international links.
- Involvement in the partnership and other resulting networks has been exactly in line with what the project aims to promote – the development and participation of young people.
- Participation in innovative social and economic development at a European level.
- The opportunity to develop other European funding bids.
- Becoming a hosting and sending organisation for the European Volunteer Scheme.
- Young people participating at a significant level in European youth networks.

There are also some lessons to be learned and warnings to be applied:
- There can be significant cash flow problems which require clear accounting, financial planning and understanding management.
- The administrative requirements of European funding need good systems to handle information (the reporting requirements for example, changed from a form in the first year to a full annual report in the second).
- Matched funding is needed under YOUTHSTART and this can cause headaches.
- You do have to live with your budget, and if the project is a pilot some of this is bound to be guesswork.
- There is a steep learning curve, and the administration is considerable. The form-filling alone is a large undertaking, and puts a greater strain on small organisations than on the larger players such as local authorities and colleges.
- Good domestic links are important. Croxteth had relationships with ECOTEC and the Merseyside Objective 1 office, which both gave advice and support.

The Croxteth experience of Europe has been a genuinely productive one. Rather than funding a general need, it works with the spirit of the programme to fund the project directly. The youth and community worker Lyn Boyd stresses: "YOUTHSTART was suitable for what we wanted. What was crucial was that we were looking to fund what we were doing anyway, not coming up with something to fit the guidelines. Our Youth Information Project is new and innovative; it is about forming international links between young people; it fits in with social and economic development in a needy area; and it has employment and education training at its heart. It is a truly transnational project and that is one of the keys to its success."
For more information on the project, contact: Lyn Boyd, Youth and Community Worker, Croxteth and Gillmoss Community Federation, 35 Mossway, Croxteth, Liverpool L11 0BL.

The European Regional Development Fund (ERDF)

The second structural fund is The European Regional Development Fund. It aims to reduce regional economic differences between the poorest and most affluent parts of Europe. Much of the money is directed towards large capital projects (such as buildings, items of equipment) and infrastructure development.

The Fund concentrates on the least favoured regions of the Community. These include areas of acute industrial decline and remote rural areas. These are defined by the Objective 1 (areas lagging behind); Objective 2 (industrial) and Objective 5b (rural) areas listed in the box above.

Support is given to job creation projects; the development of small and medium-sized enterprises; infrastructure projects; initiatives which improve the attractiveness and image of the region; tourism, and research and development.

ERDF includes a number of different initiatives aimed at solving problems which have an impact across the Community. Some are targeted at those areas which have been affected by the decline of particular industries. These include RESIDER for declining steel areas and RECHAR for declining coal-mining areas; KONVER for defence areas; RETEX for areas dependent upon textile manufacturing and PESCA for fishing ports. Money is available for diversification and introducing new industries to these areas. The total budget for the structural funds is about £20 billion, of which around 47% is ERDF. In 1995, £673 million was allocated to the UK from the ERDF.

The maximum grant for Objective 1 areas is 75% of the total project cost. For Objective 2 areas it is 50%. However, the precise level of grant varies according to the type of project being funded. The minimum grant available is 50% of public expenditure for Objective 1, and 25% of public expenditure for Objective 2. ERDF grants must be matched and can include a combination of any of the following:

- Public money (e.g. national bodies, central or local government, City Challenge, development corporations)
- Charitable trusts and the National Lottery
- Private sector finance
- The organisation's own resources including mortgages, loans and earned income.

This matched money must be spent in the same ratios as the ERDF grant throughout the period of the project. Eligible expenditure can only be claimed once full approval has been granted for the scheme and against invoiced bills that have been paid.

Applications must identify the specific economic benefits their scheme will achieve and identify the local benefits of the project. They will also be expected to show

how the benefits were estimated and how they will be monitored to guarantee success.

A large number of ERDF applications are submitted by local authorities in partnership with regional bodies. You will need to consult with them to strengthen your application. Some areas that have been funded which may apply to young people's organisations are: business start-up initiatives; area image improvement programmes; tourism and economic regeneration.

How to apply: The current Objectives 1 and 5b are eligible for support up to 1999. Objective 2 areas will be reviewed before the end of 1996. Applications may be submitted to the regional authority (usually the Government Offices for the Regions) at any point during the lifetime of the programme. Your first contact point will invariably be your local authority, TEC or Government Office. Centrally, the DTI or the Scottish Office will also give you the nearest regional contact to discuss your proposal.

For England and Wales, contact: Ian Facer, Department of Trade and Industry, Regional Policy Division (0171-215 5698; Fax: 0171-215 2520).

For Scotland, contact J Walker, The Scottish Office Industry Department, European Funding and co-ordination Division, Room 5/89, New St Andrew's House, St James' Centre, Edinburgh EH1 3TG (0131-556 8400; Fax 0131-244 4785).

For Northern Ireland contact: Industrial Development Board for Northern Ireland, IDB House, 64 Chichester Street, Belfast BT1 45X.

Other EC programmes that may support your project

A large part of EC money is directed to large priority areas such as regionalism, economic development and agriculture for example. The Commission is largely an economic unit, and while supporting voluntary organisations is not its main priority your activities may reach one of its target audiences. There are smaller funds attached to some of the main interest areas which can apply to what you are trying to do. The following are small programmes of money which may be appropriate for your project.

Development
Rural development – Leader II supports innovative, often transnational projects which help in the development of rural communities. Projects include encouraging small firms and craft trades, promoting rural tourism, and improving the environment, living conditions and local services. This programme has helped voluntary organisations in remote rural areas which otherwise would not have received funding. England and Scotland Objective 5b and Highland and Islands Objective 1 areas are eligible.

England: Cyril Rice, Department of the Environment, South West Regional Office, Tollgate House, Houlton Street, Bristol BS2 9DJ (0117-987 8000 ext 8172)

Northern Ireland: Jack Layberry, Department of Finance and Personnel – NI, 213 Parliament Buildings, Stormont, Belfast (01232-521092)

Scotland: Lynn Henni, Scottish Office Development Department, Victoria Quay, Edinburgh EH6 6QQ (0131-244 0694)

Wales: Alan Lansdown, Welsh Office, Section ERP2A, New Crown Building, Cathays Park, Cardiff CF1 3NQ (01222-823127).

Urban regeneration – URBAN Initiative supports projects which help to improve depressed urban areas with a population of more than 100,000 people and with high unemployment, poor housing and few facilities. The areas proposed are: Belfast (Greater Shankhill) Merseyside, London (Hackney/Tower Hamlets, Park Royal), Manchester, Birmingham (Sparkbrook), Nottingham, Sheffield, Swansea (Townhill), Glasgow and Paisley.

A small number of projects can be supported such as new economic activities, employment schemes, environmental improvement and improving public health facilities such as anti-drug centres and improving cultural, recreational and sporting facilities. The projects should be completed by 1999. The Greater Shankhill project for example has received 390,000 ECU from ERDF and 740,000 ECU under ESF for a community training initiative with young adults and parents with young children.

Contact: Gary White, Department of the Environment, P2 148B, 2 Marsham Street, London SW1 3EB (0171-276 3815).

Disability
People with disabilities: HELIOS II is the EC's main fund for integration of people with disabilities. Support is given to projects which for example promote closer co-operation between Member States and improve the flow of information. Around 250 voluntary sector activities are funded each year.

Contact: European Commission, Bernard Wehrens, DGV – Employment, Industrial Relations & Social Affairs, Rue Joseph II, 27, B-1040 Brussels (00 32 2 295 05 61; Fax: 00 32 2 295 10 12)

England: Edward Webb, Department of Health (0171-272 4125)

Scotland: Bruce Powell (0131-244 2458)

Wales: Jenny McKinlay (01222-823357)

Northern Ireland: Brian Gryzmek (01232-524242).

Education

SOCRATES is the EU training and education programme running from 1995-1999 with a total budget of 850 million ECU. Areas which may apply to those working with young people are the measures to cover open and distance learning, intercultural education and the education of migrant workers and travellers.

Open and distance learning: England, Wales and Northern Ireland: DfEE, Sanctuary Buildings, Great Smith Street, London SW1P 3BT (0171-925 6053; Fax: 0171-925 6971)

Scotland: Hope Johnston, SOEID, International Relations Branch, Victoria Quay, Edinburgh EH6 6QQ (0131-244 4649; Fax: 0131-244 5581)

Young travellers and intercultural education: England, Wales and Northern Ireland: Robert Mace, DFEE, Room 1.59, Sanctuary Buildings, Great Smith Street, London SW1P 3BT (0171-925 5559; Fax: 0171-925 6971)

Environment

Environment: LIFE II which includes measures to encourage environmental education, improve the environment of urban areas and promote sustainable development.

Contact: European Commission, DG XI, 200 Rue de la Loi, B-1049 Brussels, Belgium (Fax: 00 322 296 9556).

Health

Drugs, Alcohol and HIV Prevention: projects promoting the exchange of information and to encourage co-operation between Member States. Health workers' training can also be supported, together with information and awareness campaigns including those aimed at young people.

Contact: European Commission, DG V, 200 Rue de la Loi, B-1049 Brussels, Belgium (00 322 235 1111).

Public health which includes health promotion, information on health, health education and public health training, projects which develop training programmes for those in public health and health promotion, producing teaching materials and developing EU-wide networks. Applications for projects in the second half of the year should be received by 15 March of the current year, or by 15 September for projects to be begun in the first half of the following year.

Contact: European Commission, Georgios Gouvras, DG V – Employment, Industrial Relations & Social Affairs, Bâtiment Jean Monnet, Rue Alcide de Gasperi, L-2920 Luxembourg (00 352 4301 334 65; Fax: 00 352 4301 345 11).

Public awareness of the European Union

Events that increase awareness of the EC: The EC has a small budget to support events that strengthen its citizens' feelings of belonging to the community. The organisers must have expertise and experience, and there must be good media coverage. The EC funding is there to add a European dimension to the event and substantial media coverage is expected.

Applications should in the first instance be made through the Eurathlon programme (see below). The appeal of the project, however, will be its contribution to increasing awareness of, and giving publicity to, the European Community.

Contact: Niels Thogersen, DGX, Audio-Visual, Information, Communication and Culture, Rue de la Loi 200, 1049 Brussels, Belgium (00 32 2 296 92 58; Fax: 00 32 2 295 77 47).

Racism

Combating racism, xenophobia and anti-semitism: projects to fight against discrimination on the grounds of race, colour, religion and national, social or ethnic origin. Money is given towards research, training materials and other innovative measures to combat prejudice. Decisions are taken three to four months after receiving applications.

Contact: European Commission, Annette Bosscher, DGV – Employment, Industrial Relations & Social Affairs, Rue Joseph II, 37, B-1040 Brussels (00 32 2 295 10 52; Fax: 00 32 2 295 18 99).

Sports and the arts

Artistic activities and culture: Kaleidoscope 2000 is a relatively new programme to encourage the arts within the Community. Cultural events such as festivals must involve at least three different Member States. All areas of the arts are eligible. Applications will be assessed for innovation, quality, any wider impact and the potential for enduring partnerships and co-operation.

Contact: European Commission, 8 Storey's Gate, London SW1P 3AT (0171-937 1992).

Sports events – Eurathlon: Sports events with a particular emphasis on those involving young people. The event should be non-elitist and involve at least three Member States.

Grants are up to a maximum of 50% of the project budget, ranging from 5,000 ECU (£3,550) up to 50,000 ECU (£35,550). In 1995, the first year of the programme, 700,000 ECU was given to 82 projects. Application forms are available from the Commission Offices at the following addresses:

England: Jean Monnet House, 8 Storey's Gate, London SW1P 3AT (0171-973 1992; Fax: 0171-973 1900).

Northern Ireland: Windsor House, 9-15 Bedford Street, Belfast BT2 7EG (01232-240708; Fax: 01232-248241).

Scotland: 9 Alva Street, Edinburgh EH2 4PH (0131-225 2058; Fax: 0131-226 4105).

Wales: 4 Cathedral Road, Cardiff CF1 9SG (01222-371631; Fax: 01222-395489).

Completed application forms should be returned to: The European Commission, DG X-B-5/Sports Sector, Eurathlon Programme, 200 Rue de la Loi, B68-4/40, B-1049 Brussels, Belgium (00 32 2 296 92 58; Fax: 00 32 2 295 77 47).

Sports events for people with disabilities: Events must have a European dimension, should involve disabled participants from at least four Member States and should raise awareness of their sporting abilities. It should also promote the EC and should show sport as an activity for people with disabilities.

Applications can be made at any time up to 1 September in the year before the event. They are made through DGX – 5/Sports Sector offices in Brussels (see Eurathlon address above).

Contact: The British Paralympic Association, Delta Point, Room G13A, 35 Wellesley Road, Croydon, Surrey CR9 2YZ (0181-666 4556; Fax: 0181-666 4617).

Town Twinning

Town Twinning: There are small amounts of money available to help exchanges and joint events. Priority is given to isolated communities, where the language is "obscure" (e.g. links with Danish or Portuguese communities); where the population of a town is less than 5,000 people; partnerships which are more than 1,000 km apart; new twinning links and links with countries which have recently joined the EC. (This will also include partnerships with countries from Central Eastern Europe.) The grants are small (between 500 ECU and 5,000 ECU) but there may be help for hosting and travel costs for those attending an event such as that given towards the cost of hosting delegates from a new twin attending the annual Lancaster youth games. Grants are for a minimum of 10 people and up to 100 participants.

Contact: Your local authority town twinning officer, and the Twinning Officer, Local Government International Bureau, 35 Great Smith Street, London SW1P 3BJ (0171-222 1636; Fax: 0171-233 2179).

Young people and the European Union

Citizenship: Citizens First – Projects which distribute information on the rights and opportunities available to people under the single market, information on living or studying abroad and travel and health concerns for people working in the European Union. Up to half of the project costs, up to 200,000 ECU can be supported.

Contact: DG XV A/1, Internal Market and Financial Services, 200 Rue de la Loi, B-1049, Brussels, Belgium (00 32 2 299 11 11; Fax: 00 32 2 295 43 51).

Informing Young People about the European Union: Support for up to 50% of the project costs up to a maximum of 40,000 ECU.

Contact: European Commission, DG X/A/5, 200 Rue de la Loi, B-1049, Brussels, Belgium (Fax: 00 32 2 299 92 02).

International Non-Governmental Youth Organisations: Yearly programmes of events that increase awareness of the EU can be supported. Support for up to 50% of the project costs can be given. Projects must be submitted at least four months before it is intended to start. Decisions will be made after considering the value of the programme for the whole EU, the quality of the programme and its organisation (number of activities, countries, languages, participants etc.), as well as how representative the organisation is within the EU.

> **Contacts for programmes change regularly. Keep in touch with your local authority, TEC and Government Offices for the Regions for up to date information and advice.**

Contact: M Tsolakis, European Commission, DG XXII/C/2, B-7, 7/24 200 Rue de la Loi, B-1049 Brussels, Belgium (Fax: 00 32 2 299 92 02).

Young people and violence
Violence against young people - DAPHNE: grants for voluntary organisations for projects which distribute information and help co-operation between groups across the EU which are working in the violence and sexual exploitation fields. Funding is generous, up to 80% of project costs, between 10,000 and 100,000 ECU.

Contact: Anthony Simpson, EC Justice and Home Affairs Task Force 9-6/19 Avenue de Nerviens, B-1049 Brussels (Fax: 00 32 2 295 01 74).

More Addresses for European Programmes
Co-operation with Eastern Europe – Article 10: Local Government International Bureau, 35 Great Smith Street, London SW1P 3BJ (0171-222 1636)

Educational Multimedia: Multimedia Educational Task Force, 29 Avenue De Beaulieu (Office 6/05) B-1160 Brussels, Belgium (Fax: 00 32 2 299 3738)

Equal Opportunities Projects: Diana Cunliffe, Sex and Race Equality Division 4 DfEE, Caxton House, Tothill Street, London SW1H 9HF (Fax: 0171-273 5476)

European Young Consumer Competition: Community Protection Department, South Ayrshire Council, 5-7 River Terrace, Ayr KA8 0JB

European Youth Foundation (for visits, publications, information campaigns for example. Projects need a minimum of four Council of Europe countries): Council of Europe, F-67075 Strasbourg, Cedex, France (0033 8841 2019; Fax: 0033 8841 2778)

Eastern Europe Partnership – PHARE: Susan Brooks, Charities Aid Foundation, 114-218 Southampton Road, London WC14 3HB (0171-831 7798)

Raphael and European Heritage Day Awards (5,000 ECU prizes for public awareness, campaigns, twinning events, roadshows etc.): Kate Anderton, Co-ordinator, Civic Trust, 17 Carlton House Terrace, London SW1Y 5AW (Fax: 0171-321 0180)

Information Technology – TELEMATICS: European Commission, DG XIII/c – Telematics (Education & Training), 200 Rue de la Loi, Bu29, 4/05, B-1049 Brussels, Belgium (Fax: 00 32 2 295 23 54)

Women in Rural Areas: European Commission, DGVI.F.I – Rural Development, 130 Rue de la Loi, B-1049 Brussels, Belgium (00 32 2 295 8834; Fax: 00 32 2 295 1034)

Developing links with other Member States

Some of the European funding programmes detailed above (e.g. YOUTHSTART, LEONARDO) will only give money to projects which involve a number of different Member States. Projects which have more than one country participating give additional benefits or "added value" to the Community.

Developing partnerships across the Community is not just about unlocking European money. When viewed positively, it can lead to the exchange of information and ideas which is often innovative and pioneering. Participants can learn more about their own organisation as well as others, and see different ways of doing things. There are also opportunities to raise the profile of the organisation both in the home country and within the community, which will help to open up new funding opportunities.

You will only be eligible for some of the schemes outlined above if you have, or are developing, significant links with organisations in other Member States. These are known as transnational relationships. You will need to evaluate your long-term strategy as an

The 15 Member States of the European Union	
Austria	The Netherlands
Belgium	Portugal
Denmark	Spain
Finland	Sweden
France	United Kingdom
Germany	The European Economic Area (EEA) also includes:
Greece	
Ireland	Iceland
Italy	Liechtenstein
Luxembourg	Norway

The National Youth Agency European Funding Calendar 1997-98

The National Youth Agency produces regular European updates. The following is a list of deadlines for applications to European funding sources for young people's organisations. There may be changes throughout the year, so you need to keep informed (contact Keith Raynor at the National Youth Agency).

Applications under some programmes can be made at any time – e.g. Youth for Europe, Town Twinning – so these are not included on the calendar. Where the precise date is not known, the date for the preceding year is given with the year shown in brackets.

Calendar

September 1997
Mon 15th Health awareness e.g. drugs, alcohol, AIDS (1996)
Tues 30th LEONARDO Strand I.1.2
November 1997
Sat 15th Ethnic Minority Languages and Culture (1996)
December 1997
Fri 26th Young Women's Networks in Rural Areas (1996)
Tues 30th EURATHLON (1996)
January 1998
Tues 6th Europe Heritage Awards (1997)
Tues 6th KALEIDOSCOPE
Sat 10th LIFE
Fri 30th Launch of Subject for European Year (1997)
Sat 31st Young Consumer Competition (1997)
Sat 31st Europe Heritage Day Awards (1997)

February 1998
Sun 1 SOCRATES (Intercultural education and open and distance learning) (1997)
Fri 20th Rural Young Women's Networks (1997)
Sat 28th International Non-Governmental Youth Organisations (1997)
Sat 28th European Social Fund Objective 3 for young unemployed (1997)
March 1998
Sun 1st Raphael Cultural Heritage Awards (1997)
Tues 3rd TELEMATICS – information in non-profit making organisations (1997)
Sat 14th Educational Multimedia (1997)
April 1998
Thurs 30th PHARE – Eastern Europe Partnership (1997)
June 1998
Tues 30th Citizens First – rights and opportunities under the single market
Tues 30th DAPHNE: Violence Against

The Mating Game

Transnational projects stand or fall by the quality of the relationships between organisations. If your organisation is not yet linked with partners across the Channel, you may be able find organisational buddies through:

- Past contacts through individuals, exchanges, conferences, international events etc.
- European newsletters, journals and periodicals with case studies
- National bodies and networks such as ECOTEC or the European Youth Forum
- Local town twinning associations, local authority twinning officers, Chambers of Commerce
- Contacts through TECs, colleges, training organisations or youth associations
- National "dating agencies" such as the partner finding service run by the Central Bureau for Educational Visits and Exchanges (particularly for LEONARDO)
- The Internet has information posted on funding programmes and organisations. LEONARDO for instance has details of potential partners, and you can also give details of your organisation. (Look at: http//www.leonardo centre.fi/psd/)

organisation and consider the investment of time and resources, particularly of staff, that will be needed if you are to make the most of transnational opportunities.

Transnational project funding will be of particular interest to organisations wishing to promote exchanges of young people and staff; establishing networks throughout the community for like-minded organisations; exchanging information, and raising awareness through activities such as conferences and training events. For example, you may be planning an international youth arts festival or organising a training conference on good practice for youth workers. In each case you will need to connect with similar bodies in other countries.

There is no fail-safe way of matchmaking, and there may be some trial and error involved. You should also be wary of over-egging the pudding. Too many partners can cause as many problems as too few. Projects can become difficult to manage where there are a number of players involved. Make sure you have answered all the whys, wheres, and hows within your own organisation before you join discussions with other partners.

Key questions and answers

Question: What are we applying for: building work, running costs or to try an innovative piece of work?

Response: Look at the programme criteria carefully. If it says pilot project, that is what it means, and your work should be genuinely new. If you are looking for capital investment you will need to fit in with existing economic and infrastructure development plans in your area. Running costs, as ever, are not widely funded, although programmes supporting training should allow for some core costs.

Question: Do we need a consultant?

Response: Look at your budget first. This may decide the question anyway. If your expertise is minimal you may need some initial help. Ask other organisations for their experiences and for their recommendations.

Question: Do we have the resources to manage a transnational project?

Response: Look at your existing expertise and what gaps in resources there are. Draw up a resources inventory that shows what you have available within the organisation and what will have to be developed. Be realistic. It can be more costly to develop links with organisations in other Member States than any income you may eventually secure.

Question: Do we have clear objectives and measurable outcomes?

Response: European applications are rigorously scrutinised to make sure they have specific expected results, and that these can be measured. If these are not in place, how can the organisation and the Commission assess whether the project has been successful? You should write and present the intended outcomes clearly and test-drive them for good road-holding first before approaching potential European partners.

Question: Do we know how local and regional European applications are prepared?

Response: Find out. Talk to local authorities and TECs/LECs and local government offices before you prepare your bid. They are likely to have some expertise and can tell you where your activities fit into existing plans.

Question: Can we divide our project into smaller, independent units if necessary?

Response: Look carefully at each element of your project. Where it is possible, break it down into smaller parts. If one part has to go then the whole project need not necessarily be abandoned. This is particularly important when negotiating with partners in other countries so that the aims, methods and expectations are agreed.

Question: Does our project have regional, national and international impact?

Response: Assess your project for any applications it may have beyond your local area. It will strengthen your proposal greatly if the results and good practice arising from your project can be tried in other parts of the Community.

Useful contact points

Members of the European Parliament (MEPs): If you do not yet know who your MEP is, a full list can be obtained from the London Office of the Parliament, 2 Queens Anne's Gate, London SW1H 9AA (0171-222 0411; Fax: 0171-222 2713).

UK Offices of the Commission: These provide information on policy and all things European, although it can take time to get through on the telephone:

England: Jean Monnet House, 8 Storey's Gate, London SW1P 3AT (0171-973 1992; Fax: 0171-973 1900)

Northern Ireland: Windsor House, 9-15 Bedford Street, Belfast BT2 7EG (01232-240708; Fax: 01232-248241)

Scotland: 9 Alva Street, Edinburgh EH2 4PH (0131-225 2058; Fax: 0131-226 4105)

Wales: 4 Cathedral Road, Cardiff CF1 9SG (01222-371631; Fax: 01222-395489).

European Documentation Centres (EDCs): There are a number of European Documentation Centres throughout the UK, often in universities and libraries, where European information can be easily accessed. Your nearest EDC address can be found in the telephone book or by ringing:

Belfast: 01232-491 031
Birmingham: 0121-455 0268
Bradford: 01274-754 262
Bristol: 0117-973 7373 x311
Cardiff: 01222-229 525
Exeter: 01392-214 085
Glasgow: 0141-221 0999
Hull: 01482-464 935
Hove: 01273-326 282
Inverness: 01463-702 560
Leeds: 0113-283 3126
Leicester: 0116-255 9944
Liverpool: 0151-298 1928
London: 0171-489 1992
Maidstone: 10622-694 109
Manchester: 0161-237 4000
Newcastle: 0191-261 0026
Norwich: 01603-625 977
Nottingham: 0115-962 4624
Sheffield: 0114-953 2126
Slough: 01753-577 877
Southampton: 01703-832 866
Stafford: 01785-277 380
Telford: 01952-208 213

There are also six Rural Development Information and Promotion Centres (CARREFOURS):
Ayr: 01292-520 331
Carmarthen: 01267-224 859
Cirencester: 01285-653 477
County Tyrone: 016625-488 72
Garstang: 01995-601 207
Inverness: 01463-715 400

Internet sites: The EC is committed to distributing as much information as possible through the Internet. A number of programmes will have their own site, and most will be interlinked. These include:
European Union site: http://europa.eu.int
LEONARDO da Vinci site: http://www.leonardo centre.fi/psd/

Further Reading

A Guide to European Union Funding for NGOs 1996 ECAS
Sources of European Funding and *Finance from Europe, A Guide to Grants and Loans* from the European Union – both published by the European Commission and available free from their offices or from some European Documentation Centres.

Chapter 12

Youth organisations and charitable status

Many youth organisations are eligible for charitable status, as long as their objects, structure and activities meet certain requirements. There are many benefits to being a charity, but it can also bring restrictions. This chapter looks at the pros and cons of being a charity, who can register as a charity and how you do this.

What are the benefits of being a charity?

There are a number of advantages to being a charity. Most of them are financial. Here are some of the main ones:-

- Charities are exempt from paying most direct taxes (e.g. Income Tax, Corporation Tax, Capital Gains Tax), although there is no general exemption from VAT.

- Investment income is exempt from tax so bank and building society interest can be paid gross.

- Charities receive a mandatory 80% relief from the Uniform Business Rate. This can be increased to 100% relief at the discretion of the local authority.

- Members of the public are generally sympathetic to charities and people are often more prepared to give time and money to a charity.

- Some funders, such as grant-making trusts (see separate chapter) will only give grants to registered charities.

- Tax-payers, whether they are members of the public or commercial companies can make certain payments such as gift aid and covenants to the charity tax-effectively. This adds almost an extra one third to the value of the donation (at current 23% tax rates).

What are the disadvantages of being a charity?

The disadvantages of being a charity are some bureaucracy and more importantly greater regulation and restrictions on the actions and activities of the organisation.

These include:

- Charities have to prepare annual reports, accounts and those with an annual income of £10,000 have to send them to the Charity Commission. They also have to send them to members of the public on request, although you can charge a reasonable administration fee for this. Charities with an annual income of £10,000 must also state the fact that they are a registered charity on most published materials including cheques, receipts and invoices.
- Charities also have to make an annual return to the Charity Commission although this is not very onerous (particularly for smaller charities).
- If charities are also companies they have to report to Companies House each year and fulfil company law requirements as well as those of charity law.
- Charities are run by trustees (these may also be called management committee, members or directors). These people cannot usually receive any benefit from their trusteeship although in some circumstances it is now possible to make provision for some payments to trustees in a new constitution.
- Charity trustees have greater legal responsibilities and potential liabilities.
- Matters such as the disposal of land and buildings are subject to special rules and procedures.
- Charity law imposes restrictions on several types of activity such as political activities and trading.
- Some amendments to the constitution will require Charity Commission consent.
- If a charity is wound up, the assets and funds must all be transferred to another similar charity or for some similar charitable objects.

What is a charity

A charity is a body which is established exclusively for charitable purposes. This means that *all* its activities must be charitable in law. It is not enough to be partly charitable. Purely social activities for example are not charitable. If an organisation has exclusively charitable objects then it is automatically a charity. It must register with the Charity Commission if it has a gross annual income of over £10,000.

There is no statutory definition of what is a charity. Charity law is based on a statute of 1601 which has been clarified and developed by case law through the centuries. Charities must come under one or more of the following 'heads' of charity.

- The relief of poverty, sickness and distress
- The advancement of education
- The advancement of religion
- Other purposes beneficial to the community in a way recognised as charitable.

To be a charity, it is not enough simply to be established for good causes or to be non-profit making. The objects clause of your constitution must contain exclusively charitable purposes and this must reflect the actual activities. Charities must also exist for the public benefit. A youth club limited to a small number of selected members run as a private members' club would not satisfy the public benefit test and would not be charitable.

The education and setting up in life of young people has been charitable since the original 1601 statute. Youth organisations today may come under several different categories or 'heads' of charity.

Educational Charities

Many youth organisations have educational objects. These are some of the areas they may cover:

- Formal education in schools and colleges.
- Scholarship funds.
- Vocational training and work experience.
- Sports organisations for young people, provided there is open access and training for all members.
- Arts organisations for young people such as youth theatre groups or musical bands.

To be an educational charity there must be some element of training and the subject must be of some educational worth. A young people's chess club has been held to be charitable, but a tiddlywinks club would probably not qualify. Many youth clubs have been registered with objects to educate young people to develop their skills so as to develop their full potential as members of society.

Recreational Charities

The Recreational Charities Act of 1958 specifically included the provision of facilities for recreation – or any other leisure time occupation in the interest of social welfare – as being charitable if the organisation is established for the public at large or for any disadvantaged group, which includes young people.

Many youth clubs and organisations involved in outdoor activities will come within the Act.

Other Heads of Charity

Youth organisations may also come within several other heads of charity. Church groups or religious youth organisations for example will be charitable under the advancement of religion. Organisations for young people with some type of disability would come within the relief of poverty, sickness and distress. Organisations coming under the head of poverty would include those giving direct financial assistance or legal advice or the provision of housing to disadvantaged young people.

Organisations concerned with finding employment for young people may often be charitable and these would also come under the head of the relief of poverty.

Different legal structures

Charity registration depends on the objects of the organisation, not its legal form. Several legal structures are acceptable. The most common are:

(a) an unincorporated association which has its own constitution
(b) a trust which is governed by a Trust Deed
(c) a company limited by guarantee which has a Memorandum and Articles of Association.

(a) and (b) are less complicated to set up and run than (c). However, they also bring a greater risk of personal liability for their trustees and the property must be held in the names of individuals. The particular circumstances of the organisation will determine the most appropriate legal structure and advice should normally be taken on this point.

How do you register as a charity?

In order to be registered with the Charity Commission they must be satisfied both that your constitution is charitable in law and that you intend to operate within the stated objects. The procedure is as follows.

1. Write to or telephone the Charity Commission for a copy of their charity registration pack (see address below). This includes information on setting up a charity and some of their guidance booklets as well as an application form. Tell them if you intend to use an agreed model constitution as a special application form will be available for these cases.
2. Establish your organisation either by executing and stamping the Trust Deed, adopting the constitution at a members' meeting or incorporating the company.
3. Send a certified copy of the governing document to the Charity Commission, together with completed application forms, a copy of the latest accounts and a declaration by trustees.
4. If all the documentation is acceptable, the charity will be registered and you will receive written confirmation and your charity registration number. If not, the Charity Commission may call for additional information or require amendments to the governing documents. In straightforward cases, particularly those using a model constitution, registration will only take about three weeks. More complex cases may take considerably longer.

Model constitutions

As stated above, it is essential that the constitution and particularly the objects clause complies with charity law. In many cases, it may well be advisable to use a model constitution.

- If you are a branch or a local group of a national organisation you should first approach your national body which will usually have a model constitution that has been agreed with the Charity Commission.
- For a sports charity for young people (up to university age) contact the Central Council for Physical Recreation, Francis House, Francis Street, London SW1P 1DE (0171-828 3163).
- For a youth club contact: NABC Clubs for Young People, 369 Kennington Lane, London SE11 5QY (0171-793 0787) which provides a model constitution for affiliated clubs; Youth Clubs UK, 2nd Floor, Kirby House, 20/24 Kirby Street, London EC1N 8TS (0171-242 4045) provides a model constitution (see p223).
- For a general charitable trust, constitution or Memorandum and Articles of Association contact the Charity Commission (see address below). These models do not include objects clauses.

Sources of advice

The Charity Commission has three offices:

London: St Albans House, 57-60 Haymarket, London SW1Y 4AX (0171-210 4477).

Liverpool: 2nd Floor, 20 Kings Parade, Queens Dock, Liverpool L3 7SB (0151-703 1500).

Taunton: Woodfield House, Tangier, Taunton, Somerset TA1 4BL (018123-345000).

You may need to get legal advice, especially if you are not using one of the model constitutions. If you need legal advice, make sure you find a solicitor who specialises in charity law.

Scotland and Northern Ireland
The Charity Commission only has jurisdiction in England and Wales.

Organisations in Scotland should contact: The Director, The Scottish Charities Office, Crown Office, 25 Chambers Street, Edinburgh EH1 1LA (0131-226 2626).

Organisations in Northern Ireland should contact: The Department of Health and Social Services, Charities Branch, Annexe 2, Castle Buildings, Stormont Estate, Belfast BT4 (01232-522780).

Other addresses:

The Directory of Social Change also has information on charitable status. They can be contacted at: 24 Stephenson Way, London NW1 2DP (0171-209 5151).

The National Council for Voluntary Organisations (NCVO) has a Legal Advice Team for Charities. They can be contacted at: Regent's Wharf, 8 All Saints Street, London N1 9RL (0171-713 6161).

This chapter has been written by Lindsay Driscoll, Partner, Sinclair Taylor & Martin, Solicitors, 9 Thorpe Close, Portobello Road, London W10 5XL (0181-969 3667).

Model Constitution for a Youth Club
Youth Clubs UK has produced the following constitution for clubs.

NAME

1. The name of the club shall be...........

OBJECT

2. The object of the club is to help young people, especially but not exclusively through leisure time activities, so to develop their physical, mental and spiritual capacities that they may grow to full maturity as individuals and members of society.

MEMBERSHIP

3. Membership of the club shall be open to young people between the ages of..... and..... residing in.......................

Committees

MEMBERS' COMMITTEE (*SEE NOTE 1*)

4.1 The conduct of the day to day running of the general affairs of the club shall, in conjunction with the leader, be controlled by a members' committee consisting of not less than.... members elected annually by ballot. The members' committee shall appoint such officers as they deem necessary. Only those members with membership of at least..... weeks shall be allowed voting rights or to hold any office.

4.2 The members' committee shall in addition to the responsibilities stated in 4.1 be responsible also for such matters of policy and finance as are appropriate, subject to the ultimate oversight and responsibility of the elected Management Committee.

MANAGEMENT COMMITTEE (*SEE NOTE 1*)

4.3 The club shall be managed by a committee of not less than..... persons elected annually by ballot at the annual general meeting.

The club shall be managed by a committee which consists of not less than..... elected persons and of not more than..... co-opted persons.

...... of the elected members of the committee shall retire annually by seniority but shall be eligible for re-election after an interval of..... year(s).

4.4 The committee shall appoint a Chairman, Secretary and Treasurer and such other officers as they deem necessary.

4.5 The committee shall meet at least four times a year.

4.6 The committee shall have power to co-opt as additional members such persons as, in their opinion, are able to render special service.

4.7 The duties of the committee shall be to safeguard the interest of members by providing the premises, leadership and finance and by encouraging members to take a full and active part in the running of their club, by devising methods of achieving the object of the club exercising with the members a general oversight and assisting in the development and extension of activities.

4.8 Nominations for election to the management committee shall be submitted in writing, countersigned by the person nominated, not less than seven days before the annual general meeting.

Model Constitution for a Youth Club (Cont.)

ACCOUNTS

5. The Management Committee shall cause to be kept proper accounts of all the monies belonging to the club and presented to the annual general meeting of the club.

ANNUAL GENERAL MEETING

6.1 A general meeting shall be held within fifteen months of the previous meeting. Not less than twenty-one days notice of the meeting shall be given. Any person desirous of submitting any matter for discussion shall give not less than seven days notice to the member of the management committee nominated for this task. Those entitled to vote shall be those present at the meeting who are members defined in clause 3.

6.2 General meetings may be convened at any time by the management committee and shall be convened by them on receipt of a requisition signed by..... members.

CONSTITUTION (*SEE NOTE 2*)

7. The above constitution shall only be altered by resolution passed by a two-thirds majority of the members in general meeting. Notice of proposed amendments to the constitution must be given in writing not less than twenty-one days before the general meeting. No alteration shall be made to the constitution which shall cause the club to cease to be a charity by law.

DISSOLUTION

8. In the event of the club being dissolved any property remaining after satisfaction of all its debts shall be put at the disposal of.............

NOTES

1. The Management Committee should be a joint adult and club members' committee in which case members, both adult and club members, are elected at the Annual General meeting.

2. Clubs are recommended to apply for charitable status if they own any property or are liable for payment of rates without remission.

Charitable status confers several privileges, including exemption from income duty and a reduction in the payment of rates. The OBJECT clause given above has been approved by the Charity Commission and the Board of Inland Revenue and should therefore not be altered in any way, including the punctuation.

Other clauses in the above are recommendations only and can be varied in detail to suit circumstances. It is recommended, however, that none of the clauses should be entirely omitted.

Drafted by Youth Clubs UK and reproduced with their permission. Contact: John Bateman at Youth Clubs UK, 2nd Floor, Kirby House, 20/24 Kirby Street, London EC1N 8TS (0171-242 4045).

Chapter 13

Tax and VAT

Tax and VAT can seem a daunting subject, especially when all you want to do is work with young people and keep your club afloat. Giving general advice on tax and VAT is equally difficult because the situation is so complex. It is complicated because (a) not all income is taxable; (b) there are different types of organisations; (c) there are different types of taxes to consider, and (d) because for every rule there seem to be 10 exceptions.

We have a duty to pay tax, whether or not we are asked to by the Inland Revenue or Customs and Excise. If we get it wrong the penalties can be severe. Not knowing the law is no excuse.

Youth clubs enjoy no special tax exemptions or advantages. If you are not careful, unexpected liabilities arise and income is lost. The same rules generally apply if you are a company or an unincorporated association, although registering as a charity can bring savings (for example you should not pay Corporation Tax) and you can easily reclaim tax made on tax-effective donations (Gift Aid and covenants).

As far as fundraising is concerned, the two main areas to worry about are direct tax and indirect tax (ie. Value Added Tax - VAT). This chapter gives a quick outline on each and how they apply to your fundraising. It also has a brief look at how to get the most from your donations through covenants and Gift Aid.

You may well need to take specialist advice, especially at an early stage. For example, if you are planning a major fundraising campaign, you may go over the VAT threshold for the first time. That will affect not just that appeal but all your other activities as well. Or if you organise an event which generates a surplus, the profit may be taxed (usually to Corporation Tax) and there is the chance that either VAT will need to be levied on the price charged or, just as bad, VAT incurred in mounting an event will not be recoverable.

In general, direct taxation is kinder to the voluntary sector than indirect taxation. The sad fact is that the change of taxation policy over the last 20 years or so has resulted in a shift away from direct taxation to indirect taxation, so that many groups in the voluntary sector are paying taxes which they were not paying some years ago. Further, those taxes are "hidden" in that they are invariably a tax on the cost of mounting an event.

Direct taxation

If you are an individual, you pay tax on all your income over a certain amount. If you are a company, you only pay tax on your profits (through Corporation Tax). However, not all income may be liable to Corporation Tax. For example, if you get your income only from members (eg. through subscriptions) and you plough any surpluses back for the benefit of those members, this income should not be taxed.

There are three basic areas to worry about and these are described below:

Profits from the sale of capital assets

Capital Gains Tax is payable on the profit element of the disposal of certain capital items (eg. land and buildings). If you are selling off such capital items and think that you may be caught by this tax, consult a professional adviser before making the sale.

Investment income

Typically, this will be bank or building society interest, rent received and the like. This is normally assessable to tax on the full amount. Youth projects which are charities will not have to pay tax on these sources of income.

Trading income

Trading is a difficult subject. Voluntary organisations frequently trade and just as frequently do not recognise that the activity which they are undertaking can be classed as trading by the Inland Revenue. The definition of what constitutes a trade in the Taxes Acts is very loose: "trade" includes every trade, manufacture, adventure or concern in the nature of trade.

There is nothing more precise than this, but over time a set of pointers has emerged to decide whether or not the activity classes as a trade. So when assessing tax, the authorities will ask the following kinds of questions. If the answer to one or more of them is "yes", then you may be looking at a tax bill.

Is the activity carried on with a view to profit?

All traders carry on their activity with a view to making a profit; retailers mark up their stock against the price paid at the wholesalers, and, after marking up again for other expenses of sale, ensure that there is a surplus after all costs have been paid. In business, this is referred to as the profit; voluntary organisations euphemistically refer to it as a surplus. Either way, it may still be a trading profit, and assessable to tax.

EXAMPLE: The Scout Group requires an extension to its headquarters. The leaders decide that they will build a surplus into the costs of the summer camp so that a fund can be started for the building, and the surplus over the costs of the camp is £200. The camp is a trading activity and the £200 will be liable to tax.

Is the activity organised in the same way as a professional event?

Traders cannot survive without setting out their stall. They advertise their wares, set up a system for the storing and delivery of stock, perhaps employ staff, organise bank finance, arrange for the use of machinery, insure against loss, and undertake a host of other activities to ensure that a profit results. These activities embrace many of the pointers to a trade. Their chief value is that they reinforce the view that an activity is carried on for profit, and that the surplus generated by the activity is assessable to tax.

EXAMPLE: Voluntary Sector Spice is an old girl of St Hilda's school. The head asks her to devote the proceeds of one of her concerts at Wembley Stadium to the Building Fund. When she agrees, the Parents' Committee sets about booking the stadium, hiring a backing group, selling franchises to ice cream and hot dog vendors, preparing a programme for sale, souvenir mugs, T shirts, hiring a security firm and engaging a ticket agency. The net proceeds of this concert would be assessable to tax.

How frequently is the activity carried on?

Occasional sales do not generally mean that the person who is making the sales is seriously in business. For instance, a person might buy a picture, enjoy it for a number of years, grow tired of it and then sell it in order for it to be replaced. The motive for buying the picture was to enjoy it; the period between acquisition and sale is likely to be some years, and the motive for sale was to dispose of something no longer required. The only tax likely to arise is capital gains tax, which means that the prospects of a trading venture are remote.

EXAMPLE: The youth club decides to raise funds by way of operating a cafe one day a week, to coincide with the day on which the premises are used as a drop-in centre by the elderly. Because this event is run so regularly, it is likely to be classed as a trading venture.

Is the asset sold one which has been worked on to make it saleable?

What is behind this pointer is the fact that a trader might well buy stock in its raw state and convert it into a product for sale. A tax case held that the restoration of a fishing boat for sale amounted to a trading activity even though there was only one transaction.

The above list is not exhaustive. There are other questions which might need to be answered (such as does the person carrying out the activity already have an existing business, similar or different from the one sought to be taxed). However, note the following:

- a single transaction can amount to a trade;
- a grant can become a trading receipt if there is an existing trade, or if it is to start up a trade (provided that the grant is not made for the purchase of capital equipment);
- how the profits are applied is not generally a factor in deciding whether the profits of a trade are taxable. So, just because the funds are raised for a good cause doesn't mean to say that it will not be deemed to be a trade.

How are the profits of a trade calculated?

Again, this is complicated. The basic rule is a negative one in that it tells you what is not deductible rather than what is. There is a catch-all phrase as to what is not deductible, namely "any disbursements or expenses, not being money wholly and exclusively laid out or expended for the purposes of the trade, profession or vocation". In other words, only expenditure which is incurred specifically as part of that trade is tax-deductible.

EXAMPLE: A Guide company pays rent for the use of a hall to meet weekly. Say the Guide company also carries on a trade from those premises. In such cases only the part of the rental which relates to the use of the building for the trade will be allowed as a deduction.

The situation is further complicated by what classes as capital expenditure. The court has spent a lot of time in deciding what is a capital item as against what is a revenue item. The test is, put simply, consumables are revenue; enduring expenditure made once and for all is capital.

These points are relevant because a simple account can show that an organisation can enter into a trading venture, have nothing in the bank, and still be faced with a tax bill. For example, St Hilda's PTA decide they want to sell Christmas cards to raise funds. The Chair of the PTA has a friend in the stationery trade who she takes out for a meal so the PTA can have a consignment of Christmas cards at half price. These are then sold door to door using a van. The accounts are kept on computer. The final account on your trading activities may look like the example below.

The only item spent exclusively on your trading was the stock bought for it. The van and the computer are enduring assets (capital) and will be used for other activities, so they are not deductible. The Inspector will disallow these items so that, for tax purposes, you have made a profit of £500 even though you have no money left in the bank.

Total takings	£1,000
Less	
Stock	£500
Entertaining	£50
Van	£400
Computer	£50
Balance	**NIL**

Can a youth project avoid paying tax on trading profits?

The answer to this question is that it all depends on the tax status of the project which is actually conducting the trade, and the nature of the trade being carried on.

A local authority project

Where the project is a local authority project, then the project is an activity of the local authority which has a statutory duty to provide youth services. The income of the project will be wholly exempt from tax under the provisions in s.519 Taxes Act 1988, which exempt local authorities from Income Tax and Corporation Tax. For a project to qualify, its accounts are likely ultimately to be incorporated into the accounts of the local authority, and that the local authority will direct policy and provide the majority of the funding for the project.

An organisation without charitable status

The ordinary rules of taxation apply, so if you have any income which the Taxes Acts say should be taxed, then you will be taxed, subject to the rules regarding deductions as explained above.

An organisation with charitable status

There are certain tax benefits in being a charity. However, the line you sometimes hear that "because we are a charity we never pay any tax" is simply not true. To work out what tax you may need to pay you must:

- identify all sources of income;
- work out for each source whether it falls within the provisions of the Taxes Acts as assessable income;
- apply the reliefs afforded to charities by the Taxes Acts.

What tax reliefs are available to charities?

If you are a charity you can qualify for various tax reliefs. These include:

- exemption from Income Tax, Corporation Tax and Capital Gains Tax;
- investment income is exempt from tax so bank and building society interest can be paid gross;
- charities receive a mandatory 80% relief from the Business Rate (contact you local authority about this). This can be increased to 100% at the discretion of the local authority;
- charities can reclaim tax on some donations paid by tax-payers (see below).

However, the two most complicated areas are those dealing with trading profits accruing to a charity and the profits of a lottery conducted by a charity.

The Trading Exemption

The law states that there is an "Exemption from tax under Schedule D in respect of the profits of any trade carried on by a charity, if the profits are applied solely to the purposes of the charity and either:

- the trade is exercised in the course of the actual carrying out of a primary purpose of the charity; or

- the work in connection with the trade is mainly carried out by the beneficiaries of the charity."

> **A word of warning; fundraising is not itself a charitable purpose, and can never therefore be a primary purpose trade of a charity.**

Primary purpose trading

What are the primary purposes of a charity? Well, each charity is different. In order to discover what are the primary purposes of your charity, look at the objects clause in the constitution or governing instrument of your charity. In the event of a school for instance, the objects are the advancement of education, so that the trade carried out by a charitable school would be the delivery of education in return for school fees. In a research charity, the primary purpose trade would be the sale of the results of research undertaken by the charity.

Where youth projects are concerned, it is difficult to see how a primary purpose trade can be carried on, except for membership fees or something like the running of courses designed to improve the conditions of young people and to assist in their spiritual, moral and physical development. The mounting of such courses for a fee, and the levying of membership fees for a youth club, would both count as primary purpose trading in these circumstances and would thus be exempt.

Basically, if you are thinking of trading (ie. charging for any service) get professional advice before you start, rather than just hope that the trade will qualify.

A trade carried on by the beneficiaries

The other exemption covers things like workshops for disabled people in which goods are produced for therapeutic or training purposes and are then sold to the public in order to continue the training or therapy. In the case of youth projects, young people may be trained in a skill and then carry out that skill by way of a trading venture as part of the actual training. People on college courses often have to serve some time in the real live situation (eg. catering students will be required to prepare and serve food for the public as a part of their course). In this instance, the trade is not part of the primary purpose of the charity, but because the work is mainly carried out by the beneficiaries of the charity it will be exempt.

However, be very careful to work out exactly who are the beneficiaries of the charity. For example, a charity may be established to relieve the elderly and carry out that purpose by providing gardening services to them. The work may be carried out by young people but the fees charged will not be exempt in this situation simply because the work is carried out by young people - they are not the beneficiaries of that charity. Again, an excursion to the governing instrument of your charity is the starting point.

Occasional fundraising

Because active fundraising events (as opposed to street collections and similar events) are undertaken to make a profit, there is always a risk that the event might be classed as the conduct of a trade (remember that mere fundraising is not a charitable purpose). However, to help charities, the Inland Revenue has published an Extra Statutory Concession - C4, which is intended to remove the uncertainty in respect of these events, and to exempt the profits arising from tax.

Basically, the concession exempts small local events which are not regularly carried on, and which the public know are charity events. So how do you know whether you will be exempted? Basically, there are four key issues:

- the degree of commercial organisation involved;
- the level of input by professional organisers and celebrities (including those who give their services free of charge);
- the numbers of people attending;
- the level of turnover and profits.

Applying these guidelines it becomes clear that major national events, even if they are one-off, will not be exempt. Nor would the event organised by Voluntary Sector Spice mentioned earlier, even though she agreed to provide her services free for the good of her old school.

Once the event is held to fall within the concession, then all profits generated by that event are covered (so long as the activity is a necessary part of the event). So, admission charges, the sale of refreshments, raffle tickets, programme sales and advertising revenues will all be exempt - the key is, as with these examples, that the sales do not constitute a separate profit-making activity, since they cannot stand alone.

Income from Lotteries

There are two kinds of lotteries which are exempt from taxation:

Small lotteries incidental to exempt entertainments

Exempt entertainments are bazaars, sales of work, fetes, dinners, dances and similar events which are limited to one day or extend over two or more days. These are exactly the kinds of events which are exempted from tax on their profits as small local fundraising events (see above). Key features of such a lottery are that there is a cap on the amount of money which might go to private gain, and none of the prizes in the lottery shall be money prizes. In addition, the tickets can only be sold at the entertainment, and the result must be declared during the entertainment.

Societies' lotteries

Societies' lotteries are lotteries which are promoted, among other things, for charitable purposes, for support of athletic sports or games, or for activities of a cultural nature. They must be registered with the local authority (or the Gaming Board if the total proceeds are to exceed limits as set down from time to time), and the net proceeds – after deducting proper prize money and proper expenses – are applied to the purposes of the society. The Gaming Board sets out the maximum proportion of the gross proceeds of the lottery which can be distributed as prizes, and the maximum proportion of the gross proceeds which can be spent on administration.

The profits in both cases must, of course, be applied for charitable purposes for the tax relief to be available.

The chief issue in qualifying for the exemption is to ensure that the lottery to be conducted falls within the conditions set out for it under the terms of the Lotteries and Amusements Act 1976. This is frequently amended as the National Lottery develops, so that it is always necessary to check that your information is current. This is another occasion when a professional adviser should be consulted before the lottery is advertised and the tickets printed.

Indirect taxation (VAT)

Value Added Tax (VAT) is a tax on goods and services (or supplies). These can range from petrol to computers to membership fees. VAT is possibly even more complicated than direct tax and if you get it wrong there are strict penalties.

There are four categories of VAT:

- **standard rated** supplies are taxable and attract VAT at the standard rate (currently 17.5%);
- **zero rated** supplies are also taxable and liable to VAT but at 0%. This means that although this income is considered to be taxable no VAT has to be accounted for;
- **exempt supplies** are specifically exempt from VAT and do not attract a VAT charge. Exempt income is not taken into account when deciding whether you have to register for VAT;
- certain forms of income are entirely **outside the scope** of VAT so VAT is not chargeable. Again such income is not taken into account when deciding on registration.

The basic position is that you must register for VAT if the annual value of your VATable supplies (ie. those which are standard rated or zero rated) exceeds or is likely to exceed the registration threshold (£48,000 in 1996/97). Please note, this does not include exempt supplies or supplies outside the scope of VAT. Therefore, if your only income is from subscriptions and joining fees (which are exempt from VAT) then you will not have to register for VAT. However, if you land a company sponsorship worth £50,000 a year, then you must register as sponsorship is a full-rated supply. Alternatively, if you have five different areas of full-rated or zero-rated income and they total over £48,000 (even though individually they are less than £48,000), you will have to register. In other words, you need to bear two things in mind:

- VAT registration is only calculated on your standard-rated and/or zero-rated supplies (ignore exempt supplies and those outside the scope of VAT for this calculation).
- VAT registration only becomes necessary if VATable supplies total more than £48,000 in one year. Therefore, if they total under £48,000 a year, you don't need to register.

The next question is: "How do I know which supply falls into which category?" The following is a general list, although do not treat it as fail-safe. There are, unfortunately, lots of exceptions to lots of rules so each case needs to be approached differently.

Standard rated

- Sponsorship
- Hire of equipment and facilities to non-members (but see under 'exempt')
- Catering
- Sales of goods (but see under 'zero rated')
- Vending machine income
- Bar sales
- Telephones
- Gaming machine income
- Profit making competitions (but see under 'exempt')
- Fundraising events (but see under 'exempt')
- Sales of assets/equipment

Zero rated

- Books, magazines and handbooks
- Programmes and fixture cards
- Overseas tours
- Cold take-away food
- Donated goods
- Some advertising for fundraising purposes

Exempt

- Continuous hire of facilities
- Lotteries and raffles
- Other lettings
- Competition fees (where all proceeds are returned as prizes or when provided by non-profit distributing bodies)
- Interest and insurance commission
- One-off fundraising events

Outside the scope

- Donations
- Grants
- Insurance settlements
- Compensation payments

In practice, much of your grant income will be outside the scope of VAT. Occasional fundraising should be exempt from VAT. However, if fundraising becomes more regular and starts to contribute a substantial proportion of your revenue, it will probably become VATable.

The consequences of registering

Once you register, you will have to charge VAT on all full-rated supplies at the standard rate (eg. on catering) and do a quarterly VAT return to Customs & Excise. The good news is that you can "offset" some VAT you have to pay against the VAT you charge. But the other point to note is that you may well have a range of activities some of which may be exempt from VAT, some full-rated and some outside the scope. In any case, you will probably need a VAT specialist to help you, at least in the early stages.

When planning your fundraising, it is worth thinking about the VAT situation. If you are planning major building alterations, is there a way of recovering some or all of the VAT? Will your fundraising mean you go over the VAT threshold anyway? Is there a way around this (eg. organising payments so that you do not receive more than £48,000 VATable income in any one financial year)?

Tax-effective giving

In one sense all donations to charities and voluntary organisations are tax-effective in that the organisation in receipt of them is unlikely to have to pay income or corporation tax on them. But some donations to charities are even more tax-effective

---

The value of tax-effective giving

Assume someone covenants £100 a year to a charity. To have given this amount, on current basic tax rates (23%) the person would have needed to earn £129.87, of which £29.87 would have been paid over in tax. The charity can then reclaim the £29.87. In other words, tax-effective giving increases the amount available to the charity by nearly a third at no extra cost either to the donor or to the charity.

because the charity in receipt of the donation can recover the income tax on the donation thereby increasing its value by around 30%. There are procedures to follow, but they are not that complicated.

Deeds of Covenant

A deed of covenant is a promise in the form of a legally binding document to donate a stated amount to charity. This then allows the charity to reclaim the basic rate tax paid by the covenantor. A valid deed must:

- be for an annual amount (although you can actually pay in instalments - weekly, monthly, quarterly or whatever);
- be for more than three calendar years (ie. in practice a minimum of four years). Covenants can be made for an indefinite period (these are called lifetime or perpetual covenants);
- not be able to be cancelled by the donor before the four years are up (although if the donor is unable to make the payments during that time the charity can release the donor from his/her commitments).

There are certain key words and phrases which a deed of covenant must contain if it is to be legally valid. And they must be signed in the presence of a witness. However, so long as they conform to these requirements you can make your own documents and personalise them to your club. The requirements and model deeds are set out in an Inland Revenue Charities Series Leaflet entitled *Deeds of Covenant; Guidance for Charities*. These are available from the Inland Revenue FICO (Trusts and Charities) office - see useful addresses at the end of the chapter.

The situation for basic rate taxpayers is pretty straightforward. The charity reclaims all the tax paid by the donor. For higher rate tax payers, it is more complex and there are tax benefits to the donor. Further details are available from the Inland Revenue FICO (Trusts and Charities) office.

You need to keep good, comprehensive records of the various covenants made out to you. These records should include:

CAF and other vouchers

If someone gives you a donation using a Charities Aid Foundation (CAF) voucher – or another charity voucher – you cannot reclaim any tax on these. This is because the donor has already made out a covenant to CAF and CAF have then reclaimed the tax on the covenant. Tax cannot be reclaimed twice (unfortunately!).

Other issues in tax-effective giving

This chapter cannot deal with all aspects of tax-effective giving. You may wish to check:

- The rules for loan or deposited covenants. This is where a single gift is made which does not qualify under the Gift Aid scheme. Under a loan covenant (sometimes called a deposited covenant) the tax can be reclaimed over a four-year period.
- There are limits on the benefits which donors can receive in respect of their gift. Be careful what you offer in return for a gift.
- There are slightly different rules for companies when they give to charity, although some can use Gift Aid.

These and other issues are covered in the various Inland Revenue booklets or in chapter 45 of *The Voluntary Sector Legal Handbook*, published by the Directory of Social Change.

- a register of covenants showing the donor's name and address, the date of their deed, method of payment, date the covenant expires, the amount the donor actually paid in each year, the consecutive number of payments and the amount of tax reclaimed;
- copies of forms R185(AP) and R185(Covenant) which need to be completed and returned to the Inland Revenue;
- the original deeds of covenant;
- accounts records showing that each donation has been received and the tax has been recovered;
- bank statements, if payments have been made directly to the bank.

All records should be kept for at least six years.

Gift Aid

Gift Aid is a scheme which allows you to reclaim tax on one-off donations. It is easier to administer than a covenant because:

- no forms have to be completed before the donation is made;
- the relevant form – R190(SD) for individuals – can be sent to the donors for them to fill in after the donation has been received and even after it has been paid into the bank;
- the form does not have to be witnessed;
- the donation is a one-off so the donor does not need to make any long-term commitment.

The main problem with Gift Aid is that each donation made under the scheme must be at least £250 (in 1996/97). Any joint gifts can only be made if each donor gives at least £250 personally and has earned enough money to have paid tax on this amount. Therefore, you cannot use Gift Aid if a group of people have collected some money which then totals over £250, because the individual donors will have given less than £250 each. Another restriction is that the donor must live in the UK.

However, Gift Aid is a really good scheme for charities. If you receive a donation of £250 or more, it is always worth checking whether the donor can sign a Gift Aid form because this would increase the value of the gift by about £75 at no extra cost to the donor or to the charity.

You recover the tax in a similar way to covenants and you also need to keep proper records.

Conclusion

You need to make sure that you get paying taxes right. The Inland Revenue or Customs & Excise won't be swayed by the fact that the committee are volunteers and did not know the law. If tax is due then tax is due and you will have to pay it. This chapter should have alerted you to the main areas of possible concern. The message is that if you are not sure get specialist advice and get it early.

This chapter has been written by Allan Hargreaves, an independent charity consultant, formerly of Inland Revenue Charity Division and Binder Hamlyn. He can be contacted at 37 Burnedge Lane, Grasscroft, Oldham, Lancashire OL4 4DZ (01457-873854).

Useful contacts

Inland Revenue - for Corporation Tax
Look under "Inland Revenue" in your local telephone directory and contact your local office

Inland Revenue FICO (Trusts and Charities) - for tax-effective giving
St John's House, Merton Road, Bootle, Merseyside L69 9BB (0151-472 6000; Covenant helpline: 0151-472 6037; Gift Aid helpline: 0151-472 6038)

Customs and Excise (for VAT)
Look under "Customs and Excise" in your local telephone directory and contact your local office

Index of funding sources

The following is a list of the main funding sources in this book.

Arts Councils	71, 186
Department for Education and Employment (DfEE)	160
Department of Health Section 64 Grants	178
Drugs Prevention Initiative	181
English Partnerships	168
Eurathlon	207
European Regional Development Fund	203
European Social Fund	198
European Voluntary Service	195
HELIOS II	205
The Heritage Lottery Fund	72
Kaleidoscope 2000	207
Leader II	204
Leonardo	195
Local Projects Fund	185
Make A Difference	187
Millennium Commission	73
National Lottery Charities Board	69
The Rank Foundation	106
Rural Challenge	175
Rural Development Commission	174
Safer Cities Programme	183
Scottish Local Enterprise Companies	172
Single Regeneration Budget (SRB)	163
Sports Councils	72, 186
Training and Enterprise Councils (TECs)	170
Urban Development Corporations	170
URBAN Initiative	205
Youth for Europe III	194
Youth Service and GEST	147
Youth Volunteer Development Grants	187
Youth Work Development Grants	161
YOUTHSTART	200

Useful addresses
and contacts

■■

Here are some general sources of information and advice. Several chapters in the book also contain addresses of useful contacts for that particular subject, but the following should get you started.

General information

The National Youth Agency
17-23 Albion Street, Leicester LE1 6GD
Tel: 0116-285 6789; Fax: 0116-247 1043

Scottish Community Education Council
Roseberry House, 9 Haymarket Terrace, Edinburgh EH12 5EZ
Tel: 0131-313 2488; Fax: 0131-313 6800

Scottish Youth Agency
Scottish Community Education Council
Scotland European Centre
Square de Meeus 35
B – 1000
Brussels
Tel: 00 322-512 6155

Wales Youth Agency
Leslie Court, Lon-y-Llyn, Caerphilly CF8 1BQ
Tel: 01222-880088; Fax: 01222-880824

Youth Council for Northern Ireland
Lamont House, Purdey's Lane, Belfast BT8 4TA
Tel: 01232-643882; Fax: 01232-643874

Irish Youth Work Centre
20 Lower Dominick Street, Dublin 1
Tel: 00 35318 729933; Fax: 00 35318 724183

Visits & exchanges

Central Bureau for Educational Visits and Exchanges
Seymour Mews House, Seymour Mews, London W1H 9PE
Tel: 0171-486 5101

Youth Exchange Centre
The British Council, 10 Spring Gardens, London SW1A 2BN
Tel: 0171-389 4030; Fax: 0171-389 4033

Law & Finance

The Charity Commission
London: St Albans House, 57-60 Haymarket, London SW1Y 4AX
Tel: 0171-210 4477
Liverpool: 2nd Floor, 20 Kings Parade, Queens Dock, Liverpool L3 7SB
Tel: 0151-703 1500
Taunton: Woodfield House, Tangier, Taunton, Somerset TA1 4BL
Tel: 018123-345000
Web site: http://www.open.gov.uk/charity cc.intro htm

Scotland and Northern Ireland

The Charity Commission only has jurisdiction in England and Wales.
Organisations in Scotland should contact:
The Director, The Scottish Charities Office, Crown Office, 25 Chambers Street, Edinburgh EH1 1LA
Tel: 0131-226 2626

Organisations in Northern Ireland should contact:
The Department of Health and Social Services, Charities Branch, Annexe 2, Castle Buildings, Stormont Estate, Belfast BT4
Tel: 01232-522780

Inland Revenue

England, Wales and Northern Ireland
FICO Trusts & Charities, St Johns House, Merton Road, Bootle, Merseyside L69 9BB
Tel: 0151-472 6036

Scotland

FICO (Scotland), Trinity Park House, South Trinity Road, Edinburgh EH5 3SD
Tel: 0131-552 6255

Customs & Excise

Look in your phone book under "Customs and Excise".

The Government Offices for the Regions

East Midlands Region

Government Office for the East Midlands, The Belgrave Centre, Stanley Place, Talbot Street, Nottingham NG1 5GG
Tel: 0115-971 2444; Fax: 0115-971 2558

Eastern Region

Government Office for the Eastern Region, Room 115, Heron House, 49-53 Goldington Road, Bedford MK40 3LL
Tel: 01234-796135; Fax: 01234-796110

London Region

Government Office for London, 7th Floor, Riverwalk House, 157-161 Millbank, London SW1P 4RT
Tel: 0171-217 3086; Fax: 0171-217 3461

Merseyside Region

Government Office for Merseyside, Cunard Building, Pier Head, Liverpool L3 1QB
Tel: 0151-224 6467; Fax: 0151-224 6339

North West Region

Government Office for the North West, Room 1225, Sunley Tower, Piccadilly Plaza, Manchester M1 4BE
Tel: 0161-952 4351; Fax: 0161-952 4365

Northern Region

Government Office for the North East, 12th Floor, Wellbar House, Gallowgate, Newcastle Upon Tyne NE1 4TD
Tel: 0191-202 3649; Fax: 0191-202 3768

South East Region

Government Office for the South East, Bridge House, 1 Walnut Tree Close, Guildford, Surrey GU1 4GA
Tel: 01483-882322; Fax: 01483-882309

South West Region

Government Office for the South West, The Pithay, Bristol BS1 2PB
Tel: 0117-900 1820; Fax: 0117-900 1917

West Midlands Region

Government Office for the West Midlands, 2nd Floor, 77 Paradise Circus, Queensway, Birmingham B1 2DT
Tel: 0121-212 5171; Fax: 0121-212 5301

Yorks & Humberside Region

Government Office for Yorks/Humberside, Room 1206, City House, New Station Street, Leeds LS1 4JD
Tel: 0113-283 6402; Fax: 0113-283 6653

Other useful addresses

British Youth Council (for representing young people)
57 Charlton Street, London NW1 1HU
Tel: 0171-387 7559

Business in the Community (for information about companies)
44 Baker Street, London W1M 1DH
Tel: 0171-224 1260

Council for Environmental Education (for environmental action)
Youth Unit, University of Reading, London Road, Reading RG1 5AQ
Tel: 0118-975 6061

Directory of Social Change (for publications & training)
24 Stephenson Way, London NW1 2DP
Tel: 0171-209 5151 (publications); 0171-209 4949 (training); Fax: 0171-209 5049

National Council for Voluntary Youth Services
Peel Centre, Percy Circus, London WC1X 9EY
Tel: 0171-833 3003

Youth Clubs UK
2nd Floor, Kirby House, 20/24 Kirby Street, London EC1N 8TS
Tel: 0171-242 4045

Youthnet
http://www.youthnet.org.uk/youthnet

Also available from DSC Books

The Sports Funding Guide

Nicola Eastwood

The first ever comprehensive guide to raising money for sporting activity. A must for sports clubs, societies or individuals wanting to raise money for sporting activity. Covers the Sports Council, National Lottery, sports aid foundations, sporting governing bodies, company sponsorship and Sportmatch. Also grant-making trusts, Europe, tax and VAT issues and guidance on how to plan a fundraising strategy. 246x189mm, 272 pages, 1st edition, 1995.
ISBN 1 873860 48 X **£15.95**

The Complete Fundraising Handbook

Sam Clarke & Michael Norton
Published in association with ICFM

The book no fundraiser can afford to be without, The Complete Fundraising Handbook offers down-to-earth advice on every aspect of raising money for charity. It includes sections on: the different sources of funding, fundraising strategies, local fundraising, direct mail, sponsorship, events, membership, TV and radio appeals, working with volunteers, working with celebrities, marketing and public relations. 246x189mm, 432 pages, 3rd edition, 1997.
ISBN 1 900360 09 8 **£14.95**

Writing Better Fundraising Applications

Michael Norton & Mike Eastwood
Published in association with ICFM

This practical guide will help you produce the sort of applications that get results. It will show you the ingredients of a good application, how to cost a project, how to improve your communication skills, and how to write punchy, effective applications. With worked examples, exercises, and ideas for worksheets.
A4, 144 pages, 2nd edition, 1997.
ISBN 1 900360 20 9 **£12.95**

The Directory of Social Change aims to help voluntary and community organisations become more effective. In addition to the above titles, we publish a wide range of guides and handbooks on all aspects of fundraising, charity finance and law, management, and communications. For a full publications list, or for details of the training we provide, please contact:
Directory of Social Change, Publications, 24 Stephenson Way, London NW1 2DP.
Telephone: 0171-209 5151, Fax: 0171 209 5049, e-mail: info@d-s-c.demon.co.uk